NICHOLAS BERDYAEV

Aleksei Stepanovich Khomyakov

(1912)

(Kl. № 6)

Translated by Fr. S. Janos

frsj Publications

Aleksei Stepanovich Khomyakov

Copyright © 2017 by translator Fr. Stephen Janos

ISBN: 978-0-9963992-5-8 *Hardcover*
ISBN: 978-0-9991979-1-2 *Paperback*

Library of Congress Control Number: 2017906012

No part of this book may be reproduced or transmitted in any form or by any means, graphic, electronic, or mechanical, including photocopying, recording, taping, or by any information storage retrieval system, without the written permission of the copyright holder.

In the event of the eventual demise of the present copyright holder, in accord with United States copyright law, copyright of this work devolves to Andrew M. Janos, son/heir of Fr. Stephen Janos.

Printed in the United States of America

Printed on acid-free paper.

For information address:

frsj Publications
Fr. Stephen J. Janos
P.O. Box 210
Mohrsville, PA 19541

Contents

ALEKSEI STEPANOVICH KHOMYAKOV

Preface 1

Chapter I. The Origins of Slavophilism 3

Chapter II. Aleksei Stepanovich Khomyakov as a Person 23

Chapter III. Khomyakov as Theologian, His Teachings
    about the Church 59

Chapter IV. Khomyakov as Philosopher.
    His Gnosseology and Metaphysics. 83

Chapter V. Khomyakov's Philosophy of History 103

Chapter VI. The Teaching of Khomyakov Concerning Society
    and the State 131

Chapter VII. The Teaching of Khomyakov On Nationalness
    and the National Vocation 147

Chapter VIII. The Significance of Khomyakov. The Fate
    of Slavophilism 163

ADDENDA

The Slavophilism of the Ruling Powers 179

Translator Comments 191

Preface

My monograph on Aleksei Stepanovich Khomyakov is not an historical investigation and makes no pretense to be exhaustingly complete. This is a work -- not so much historical, as rather philosophico-systematic, psychological and critical. I seek to provide an integrally whole image of Khomyakov, of what is central and chief in his world-concept and world-feeling. And together with this I am pursuing the aims of a critical appraisal of the Slavophilism of Khomyakov. Alongside the theme of *Khomyakov* there is another theme that is of interest to me -- that of *Khomyakov and us*. Since, in my opinion, Khomyakov stands forth as a central figure within Slavophilism, the *Khomyakov* theme is, together along with this, a theme concerning Slavophilism in general, whereas the theme *Khomyakov and us* is a theme about the fate of Slavophilism. It is time long since already that there should have commenced a serious investigation of Slavophilism and an evaluation of its significance in the history of our self-consciousness. A non-religious and de-nationalistic consciousness lacks the ability to do this, -- Slavophilism has fallen outside of its field of view. Only a religious and national renewal has the ability to understand Slavophilism and evaluate it. I believe, that it has thus started.

My monograph about Khomyakov belongs to the series of monographs by the publisher "Put'", concerning Russian thinkers of religious a spirit. As regards these monographs, they are not intended to be the undertaking of scientific investigations, nor historical works, with any pretense to completeness and detail, -- rather, they are intended instead to provide composite images and integral an appraisal from the point of view of a delimited world-outlook. Earlier on I anticipated, that my work about Khomyakov would be considered subjective, since it was written from the point of view of a definitive religio-philosophic perspective. But I believe, that there is in this world-view -- is truth and right, and in the name of the truth and right the image of Khomyakov is not distorted.

I include here the most important elements of a bibliography on Khomyakov, without any pretense to completeness. The basic source for works on Khomyakov is served by the *eight* tomes of his collected works. In Tome VIII are collected the most important letters of Khomyakov.

Nicholas Berdyaev

I have made use of *the third*, the *supplemented 1900 edition* and it is from this edition that my citations are made. After the actual collected works of Khomyakov per se, a prime source is the extensive, and as yet unfinished investigation of the Kiev Spiritual Academy professor *V. Z. Zavitnevich*, "*Aleksei Stepanovich Khomyakov*". There have appeared -- the first tome, *Book I: "The Youthful Years, the Social and Scientifico-Historical Activity of Khomyakov"*, and also *Book II: "Works of Khomyakov in the field of Theology"*, 1902. This work, rather on the apologetic side, is the most valuable of anything written up to the present about Khomyakov, and I am much indebted to it. I suggest likewise the work of *V. Lyaskovsky, "Aleksei Stepanovich Khomyakov, his Biography and Teachings"* -- from Russian Archives 1896, as 11th book and also separately a book. The book of professor *L. E. Vladimirov, "A. S. Khomyakov and his Ethical Social Teachings"*, 1904, was of no especial interest. Much important materials and the Slavophils can be found in the three-volume work of *N. Koliupanov, "Biography of Aleksandr Ivanovich Koshelev"*; in the appendix is printed a valuable list of the Slavophils, which sheds light on the central role of Khomyakov and gets into the religious questionings of the Slavophils. Of significance is *D. F. Samarin's "Biographic Data on Yu. F. Samarin for Years 1840-1845"* in Tome V of the collected works of Yu. Samarin; also the *"Biographical Materials on I. V. Kireevsky"* located in Tome I of the collected works of I. Kireevsky. From the general works on Slavophilism I suggest as valuable the work of *M. Gershenzon, "Historical Notes"*, and his article, "*P. V. Kireevsky*", in the preface to a collection of Russian articles of P. V. Kireevsky. The well-known book of *Pynin, "Characteristics of Literary Opinions"*, holds little of significance and distorts the Slavophil teaching. For a critique of Slavophilism, important is *Vl. Solov'ev's "The National Question in Russia"*, and his preface to the "*History and Future of Theocracy*". One of the materials that can serve towards a characterising of the Slavophil era and also of individual Slavophils is *Hertsen's "My Past and Thoughts"* and his "*Diary*". But the characterisations by Hertsen must be used with caution. For the expression of the world-view of Khomyakov, significant are the collected works of other Slavophils, especially those of I. Kireevsky and Yu. Samarin. A detailed bibliography can be found in V. Z. Zavitnevich.

15 September 1911

Chapter I

The Origins of Slavophilism

The history of the XIX Century Russian self-consciousness was filled by the dispute between Slavophilism and Westernism. In this dispute amidst torment was begotten our national self-consciousness. Yet ultimately our national self-consciousness will become mature and manly only then, when this everlasting dispute ceases, when there is surmounted the split between Slavophilism and Westernism, having assumed such varied forms, at a point when the eternal truth of Slavophilism together with the eternal truth of Westernism organically enter into our national existence. We are, evidently, entering into suchlike an epoch, and at its portals we thus ought to recall to mind our fathers and grandfathers, and thence fondly investigate the history of our spirit. Ignoble it would be to forget one's paternal heritage and not know its origins. The time is already past, when could disdain and ignore Slavophilism, seeing only its transitory aspects, and with nothing of a residue for eternity. Slavophilism has become antiquated, it passed away into the field of history, and some sides of Slavophilism have deteriorated to the point of becoming unrecognisable. We cannot return still back to Slavophilism, we have lived through too much, and the teachings of the Slavophils and their psychology in quite much is foreign to us. But in Slavophilism also there is the eternal, which has carried over into us, and we ought to remember the classical Slavophils as though fathers and grandfathers for us. The naive and old-fashioned quaintness of the Slavophils does not diminish their significance even in the modern time.

Slavophilism -- is a first attempt at our self-consciousness, our first ideology to stand upon its own. The Russian way of life dragged on for a thousand years, but Russian self-consciousness takes its start only from that point of time, when Ivan Kireevsky and Aleksei Khomyakov with audacity proposed the question, concerning what indeed is Russia, in what is its essence, its vocation and place in the world. Alongside this deed of theirs in engendering the self-consciousness, there can be placed only Chaadayev, since in the genius of his anguish over Russia there was a tormented birthing of Russian self-consciousness, and his Westernism was as much indeed a national event, as was also the Slavophilism of Kireevsky and Khomyakov. Before the Slavophils, before Chaadayev, in Russia there was only a superficial, an affected and artificial Westernism of the Russian gentry and the half-barbaric Enlightenment period, indeed a government cabinet nationalism, -- moreso the practice of power, than of any ideology. Yet prior to the Slavophil self-consciousness there came Pushkin, -- a Russian national genius. But Pushkin was a great manifestation of the national existence, and not of a national self-consciousness. Through Pushkin, and only after Pushkin could there begin an ideological self-consciousness. Dostoevsky well understood this. The Slavophils also were the first Russian Europeans, European in more deep a sense of the word, than were Russian people of the XVIII Century, who took on only the costumes, only the externals of the European Enlightenment. The Slavophils were those Russian people, who began to think independently for themself, who proved themself to be at the summit of European culture, who not only adopted for themself the European world culture, but also creatively attempted to take part in it. The only genuine European is one, who creatively participates in world culture and world consciousness. One remains a barbarian still, who only but merely imitates European culture, who only apes and mimics, adopts for oneself the superficial aspects. And it is time to recognise, that the Slavophils were fine Europeans, people moreso cultured, than many, many of our Westernisers. The Slavophils creatively brought into focus within our national spirit that which had occurred on the heights of European and world culture. Better than the Westernisers, the Slavophils immersed themself in European philosophy, they passed through Schelling and Hegel, -- these being at the apex of the European thought of this period. The chief and original merit of the Slavophils was not in this, that they were non-dependent upon the influences of the Western world whilst recoursing in everything only to the East, but rather in this, that they were the first to relate creatively and independently to ideas of the Western world, i.e. they had the boldness to enter into the sphere of world cultural life. The significance of the Slavophils mustneeds be sought not in this, that they somehow did not want to know Hegel and Schelling nor acknowledge the influence of these upon themself, but rather in this, that they creatively attempted to rework Hegel and Schelling, they related to them independently and by this they had their own say within the developement of philosophic thought.

ALEKSEI STEPANOVICH KHOMYAKOV

The Slavophils defined Russian thought as something predominantly religious. In this is their undying merit, and herein it necessitates a true searching out and uncovering of the nature of our national spirit. The Slavophils were the first to clearly formulate, that the centre of the life of the Russian spirit -- is religious, that the Russian agitation and the Russian searchings are, at their core, religious. And up through our own day everything, that has been and is original, creative, everything remarkable in our culture, in our literature and our philosophy, in our self-consciousness, all this -- is religious in theme, in its striving, in its sweep. Our non-religious thought has always been lacking in originality, stale, borrowed, unconnected to our brilliant talents, and without need to look for any sort of Russian genius. Not all the Slavophils were geniuses and talented, and there were among them also the antagonists of Slavophilism, but all of them, all were religious and by this they defined the Slavophil consciousness. Chaadayev, Kireevsky, Khomyakov, Gogol, Tyutchev, Dostoevsky, L. Tolstoy, Vl. Solov'ev -- herein was the blossoming forth of Russian culture, herein is what we have given to world culture, with what our genius is connected. All these people lived and created in a religious pathos. How drab, how unoriginal and lacking in genius in connection with this spirit has been the Westernising current, -- rationalistic, and hostile to religious awareness. And even here, when there has occurred something remarkable, always it was connected with a religious agitation, even though it be in the form of a passionate and peculiarly religious atheism. Yes indeed, Slavophil thought has become out-moded, their inner disposition seems foreign to us and their descendants decrepit, yet not out-moded and eternally resilient is that Slavophil awareness, that the Russian spirit is religious and that Russian thought has a religious vocation. Herein Slavophilism has seized upon something forever enduring, important and needful to one, for whom the antiquated Slavophil attire is not needful and even repugnant. And hence the Slavophils remain as the founders of our national self-consciousness, the first to become aware and to formulate the direction of Russian culture. The Russian Westernisers, those for whom the religious principle has stood at the centre, are those who recognise the religious vocation of Russia, and attest to the basic truth of the Slavophil awareness. Vl. Solov'ev was suchlike a Westerniser, and his Westernism was an unique affirmation of the truth of Slavophilism, of the eternal within Slavophilism. The eternal truth of Slavophilism is not the truth of some current of thought, it is not the truth of some sort of school or party, this is rather -- a truth in common to all the people, to all the nation. Slavophilism as a current of thought, a school or party has degenerated and become moribund, but its truth as common to all the nation lives on and resides in quite distinct currents of thought, schools and parties. The truth of Slavophilism is attested to by both Lev Tolstoy, and by Vladimir Solov'ev, and by the newest works in Russian literature and art.

The remarkable epoch of Alexander I preceded the birth of the Slavophil consciousness. This epoch was noteworthy for its strong mystical stirrings; but this mysticism was almost fruitless within the history of our self-consciousness, it left no tradition after it and its traces are difficult to seek out within Russian literature and philosophy. The mysticism of the Alexandrine period was something artificial, borrowed, brought over, something not connected organically with our national spirit, and was therefore superficial. Khomyakov from the very beginning had a negative attitude towards this type of mysticism. It is difficult to note barely any sort of connection with Labzin and his "Herald of Zion" or with the then popular Western mystics Jung-Stilling and Eckhartshausen. This mysticism on the Russian soil was just as superficially Western, as was the Voltaireanism of the XVIII Century. Within this mysticism there was born no national self-consciousness, there was created no original ideology. This was only a mere episode, interesting, a fad, but not deep, not creative. There was however another fact from the Alexandrine epoch, in general very noteworthy and significant, which proved a defining influence upon the whole history of our self-consciousness of the XIX Century, which deepened the Russian soul, forced it to become thoughtful, and shook off the superficial Westernism of our gentry. I speak about the 12 year Fatherland War, the significance of which is immeasurable. Within it was born a national self-consciousness, in it was provided an experience for all the people, in common for all the nation, -- a felicitous effort, after which Russia was reborn to a new life. The Fatherland War prepared the soil, upon which sprouted forth the Slavophil self-consciousness, and this is one of the vital wellsprings of Slavophilism. After the tribulations of the Fatherland War there was born a generation more profound, with a strengthened feel for Russia. The question concerning the national self-determination and the national vocation was put afront the Russian people. There began a reappraisal of the Peterburg period of Russian history. The perception of Russia was detached from the bureaucratic mechanism and connected with the life of the people. The glittering, in its own way peculiarly cultural and stylish century of Catherine receded into the past. There appeared the need to define the spirit of Russia and the national visage of Russia not by a glittering imperial court, nor by an outwardly civilised gentry unable to speak Russian, but by the organic life of the people, in accord with what is sacred to the people. The entirety of the people passes through a moment of acute awareness of its national calling. In such a self-consciousness there is as yet nothing specifically Russian nor Slavic. But the merit of the Slavophils consists in this, that they took the first steps in this great deed for all the nation. Slavophilism first consciously expressed the thousand year old mode of Russian life, of the Russian soul, of Russian history.

It would be ludicrous to deny the Western influences upon the Slavophils. Certainly, the Slavophils had imbibed Western thought also, and certainly, they transformed within themself the Western culture. It would be a pity, if the Slavophils had no sort of connection with the spiritual and intellectual history of Western Europe, if they had learned nothing from it. Slavophilism enters into the common stream of world history, and therefore Russia also enters into it and occupies its own place within it. It is impossible to deny the influence of Schelling and Hegel upon the Slavophils, and it is impossible to deny also, that Slavophilism enters as well into the worldwide "romantic" reaction of the beginning XIX Century against the rationalism of the XVIII Century. But this romanticist reaction, which was not only romantic, but also realistic, and not only a reaction, but also progress, in each land assumed a form uniquely national. French romanticism bears very little semblance to German romanticism. But in all the lands of the romantic movement it conformed to the history and the spirit of the people, it was not open to any sort of rationalisation, it presented acutely the problem of national self-consciousness, of a national calling. The German nation became conscious of itself within the romantic movement. The same also in Poland, in its messianic stirrings, akin to the worldwide romanticism. And it mustneeds be said, that this side of romanticism, -- the turning towards nationality, towards history, was deeply realistic, and this healthy realism comprised a revolt against the rationalistic lack of flesh and blood. That which is wont to be called the reaction of the beginning XIX Century was, certainly, a creative movement forward, a bringing of new values. The romantic reaction was a reaction only in the psychological sense of this word. It brought fertility to the new century with a creative historicism and a liberating recognition of the irrational fullness of life. Our Slavophilism belongs to this worldwide current, which drew all the nations towards a national self-consciousness, towards organicity, towards an historicism. Herein was the great merit of the Slavophils, that in this worldwide current they were able to occupy an unique place and to express with originality the spirit of Russia and the vocation of Russia. They -- were flesh from flesh and blood from blood of the Russian land, of Russian history, the Russian soul, and they sprouted forth from a different spiritual soil, than did the French and German romantics. Schelling, Hegel, and the romantics directly or either indirectly influenced the Slavophils, tying them in with European culture; but in this, the vital source of their national and religious self-consciousness was the Russian land and Eastern Orthodoxy, nowise known to Schelling, nowise known to Western peoples. *Slavophilism brought about a conscious, an ideological expression of the eternal truth of the Orthodox East and the historical mode of existence of the Russian land, uniting both the one and the other organically. For the Slavophils, the Russian land was first of all the bearer of Christian truth, but this Christian truth was in the Orthodox Church. Slavophilism regarded the appearance of Orthodox Christianity as an unique type of culture, as unique a religious experience, distinct from the Western Catholic and therefore creative of different a life.* Slavophilism therefore played a tremendous role not only in the history of our national self-consciousness, but also in the history of the Orthodox self-consciousness.

Vl. Solov'ev was not fond of Khomyakov, nor was he always just towards him and with the exception of the first period of his literary activity he related towards Slavophilism very critically. But he acknowledged the tremendous merit of Khomyakov and Samarin in uncovering the core content in the concept of the Church. Khomyakov and the Slavophils, in essence, make a first attempt at an ecclesial self-consciousness of the Orthodox East. Before them in Russian the religious thought, or more precisely, the theological thought, swayed now to Protestantism, and now then towards Catholicism. The Orthodox churchly self-consciousness in philosophical-theological a mode simply did not exist. "The concept of the Church, -- says Vl. Solov'ev, -- as an actual being was not an absolutely new discovery by our Slavophils. A firm foundation for this thought is situated within Holy Scripture, especially the Apostle Paul. It was weakly developed in the works of the Patristic fathers, then forgotten by both the Catholic and the Protestant scholastics, and this idea in the present century has been restored and finely expounded upon by certain German theologians (Möhler).[1] But for the ultimate working out and vital realisation of this idea as a principle of universal unity it would be very important, that it appear from the two sides, not only in the Western, but also in the Eastern trappings. Its introduction into our religious consciousness is a chief and undeniable service of Slavophilism".[2] "To the question, about where the Church is, the Slavophils answered: "The Church is there, where the people are, united by a mutual brotherly love and free oneness of mind, they are rendered a worthy receptacle by the singular grace of God, which also is the true essence and vital principle of the Church, forming it into a single spiritual organism".[3] In my chapter concerning the ecclesiastical and theological ideas of Khomyakov I have endeavoured to show, that Khomyakov was a genius of a theologian. In him, the Orthodox East became conscious of itself, and expressed its own unique religious path. Khomyakov wanted to formulate the consciousness of the Universal Church and he attempted to express what was most essential in the Church universal. But indeed all this religious awareness of his was a consciousness Orthodox Eastern, and not of the oecumenically universal, for his consciousness was directed against the Catholic West. Khomyakov denied that the Catholic world belonged to the Church of Christ. Upon this basis sprouted up all the defects of Slavophilism, in this was rooted its limitation. It is remarkable, that during the XIX Century the greatest theologian of the Orthodox East was the secular writer Khomyakov, just as the greatest theologian of the Catholic West was the secular writer Joseph de Maistre. Both Khomyakov and Joseph de Maistre had nothing in common with the academic sort school theologising, with the traditional theological scholastics. They both were first of all living people, people of a living religious experience. In both Khomyakov and

---

[1] Vl. Solov'ev unjustly disparages the originality of Khomyakov's theology in the citation in Möhler. In any case, the Slavophil theological ideas were not borrowed from Möhler.

[2] Vide: The Collected Works of Vl. Solov'ev, SPg., n.d. Tome IV, p. 223.

[3] Ibid., p. 223.

Nicholas Berdyaev

Joseph de Maistre the Orthodox East and the Catholic West became conscious of themselves in their exclusiveness and one-sidedness. And this was an important moment in the movement towards religious unity, towards oecumenical a consciousness. In any case it mustneeds be acknowledged, that the Slavophils were the first self-sufficiently independent Russian theologians, the first original Orthodox thinkers. In them, and not in the school theologising of our clergy world, one could discern the essential within Orthodoxy, in them was moreso the life of Orthodox Russia, than in the greater part of the bishops or professors of the Spiritual Theological Academies, who theologise by profession, and not by vocation. Yurii Samarin proposed calling Khomyakov a "teacher of the Church". In this, certainly, there was a friend's embellishment, but there was also a grain of truth. From the times of the old teachers of the Church the Orthodox East knows no theologian so powerful, as Khomyakov. The theologising of Khomyakov shows clearly, in what was the chief source of Slavophilism, its vital nourishment.

I think, that at the basis of every profound self-awareness, of every remarkable idea, there resides an experience that is religious, not only individual, but also a collective, a national religious experience. Slavophilism, certainly, grew out of a religious experience, and not from bookish influences, not from philosophic and literary ideas. In all this is its significance. What however is behind this experience, finding its intellectual expression within Slavophilism? This was the religious experience of the entire Russian people over a thousand year span of its history, the religious experience of Eastern Orthodoxy, transformed within the Russian soul. At the basis of Slavophilism lies namely an Orthodoxy that is Russian, and not Byzantine, which had its own nationally-psychic type of faith. The whole uniqueness of this type of faith, the Russian national physiognomy of the faith can be learned in the Slavophils. Russia received Eastern Orthodoxy from Byzantium, and there was much of the Byzantine that entered into the local Russian Church. But the Russian soul is immeasurably distinct from the Byzantine: in it there is no Byzantine treachery, nor the Byzantine cringing afront the powerful, the cult of statecraft, the scholasticism, the Byzantine sombreness, cruelty and gloominess. In the element of the Russian people the seed of the Church of Christ, thrown over to us from Byzantium, sprouted forth with unique shoots. The ideal sproutings of Christianity within the Russian soul can be learned through Slavophilism. Herein is an unique democratism, and the thirst for Sobornost'-communality, the prevailing of the oneness of love over the oneness of authority, the dislike for statecraft, for formalism, for outward guarantees, the prevailing of inward freedom over the externally official, a patriarchal populism, etc. With Sts. Sergei of Radonezh and Nil Sorsky, the Russian startsi-elders, the Russian holy fools, everything of the unique Christian experience upon the Russian soil, all this left its imprint upon Slavophilism. If from Slavophilism, -- as a literary current of the XIX Century, -- we come searching out over deep centuries its mystical subsoil, we then arrive at the mysticism of the Eastern Orthodox, situated at the foundation of all the Christian culture of the East, at the Dobrotoliubie (Philokalia), at mental action and mental prayer. This Eastern Christian mysticism is uniquely focused in the Russian soul, in the Russian element, in the Russian primitive paganism. There is an innate uniqueness to the Slavs in general, and to the Russians in particular. This uniqueness comes from back in the pagan times, it constitutes our national flesh and blood, our paternal legacy by nature, and not by spirit. This youthful, in cultural regards, virginal flesh and blood had nothing in common with the decrepit and decaying flesh and blood of Byzantium. The sap of life was no longer there in Byzantium, it was too old in its constitution, and its flesh had become too withered. But these life-juices were there in the young Russia. The Slavophils loved to say, that the seed of the truth of Christ fell in Russia upon a virgin soil, unspoilt by anything, and in this they saw the chief justification to their conviction, that Russia is preeminently a Christian land. In this conviction there was a grain of truth, but there was also an element of embellishment, confuted by historical science. In the Slavophil consciousness we meet with not only the Russian national Christianity, but also with the Russian national paganism. And herein we tend to confront another vital, a non-bookish source of Slavophilism, in the Russian national mode of life.

    Slavophilism vitally imbibed not only the Eastern Orthodox Christianity, but it also drew upon the Russian mode of life, that of the Russian countryside, upon historical remembrances, all the thousand year accumulations of Russian life. At the initial basis of this source lies the age-old Russian paganism, a paganism enlightened by Christian truth, but an enlightenment not complete. The Russian nation in the mannerism of its history, as with any nation, is a nation both pagan and Christian, and not purely Christian. It is difficult to acknowledge as Christian either the pre-Petrine mode of Russian life or the post-Petrine mode. The assertion of many of the Slavophils, that in ancient, pre-Petrine Rus', Christianity was realised almost completely, sounds monstrously false. Khomyakov himself protested against this assertion of Kireevsky. The truth of Christ has not yet been realised in any sort of national mode of life: Christians have not yet their City, they seek for the Adventive City to Come. The Slavophils however lived and thought thus, that they had precisely their own City, that they had lived in it for a thousand years, that they had set down taproots into it so strongly, that no sort of forces could uproot them from it. But the city, to which the Slavophils in their flesh and blood belonged, was a city pagan, and not Christian. This searching for the City of God in ancient Rus', this regarding the Russian national mode of life as almost a chiliastic epoch, reveals a twofold aspect within Slavophilism, -- that of their pagan and their Christian nature. They confused the pagan city with the thousand year reign of Christ. M. Gershenzon to good effect says: "They all -- whether Ivan Kireevsky, or Khomyakov, or Koshelev, or Samarin -- were in their thought like canals, through which into the Russian social consciousness was rushing heaped-up centuries worth, like underground waters, of the world-view of the Russian nation".[1] The world-view of the Russian nation however was not only Christian, but also pagan: the Russian people had accepted the truth of Christ, the spirit of Christ, but in its flesh and blood it belonged still to the pagan city, to the pagan mode of life. In the same work, however, Gershenzon says: "They emerged from long established and stable, warmly settled nests. Upon the fertile soil of the rights of the serf-owning gentry, contentedly and with this comfortably, like an oak, there grew up these kindred sorts, with roots invisibly rooted into the people's life and nourished off their sap, attaining the heights of European enlightenment, at the utmost in the best families -- and suchlike particularly were the families of the Kireevskys, the Koshelevs, the Samarins. This is a most important fact in the biography of the Slavophils. It defined much of their personal character, and the direction of their thought... For us, at present, it is difficult to understand Slavophilism, since we have grown upon something totally otherwise -- catastrophically".[2]

---

[1] Vide M. Gershenzon, "P. V. Kireevsky", biography//"Songs of the Russian People", collected by P. V. Kireevsky. M(oscow), 1911. Tome 1, p. xxix.

[2] Ibid., p. i.

ALEKSEI STEPANOVICH KHOMYAKOV

The Slavophils were people of a structured familial lifestyle, typical Russian land-owners, solid in their soil. From their mother's milk they imbibed their convictions in life. The bonding with their fathers as regards flesh and blood was strong in them. And from the years of childhood there lived in the Slavophils the vision of a Russian Christianity, an Orthodox way of life, the vision about Christianity -- about the peasant commune, about the Christian family, about the Christian patriarchal state, un which all the relationships are arranged on the model of fathers and children. There was much of the idyllic in this conservative romantic idealisation of the past, in this naiveté and geniality of the old classic Slavophils. But in the ultimate course of Russian life there was transmitted from this pagan-life source something not still good, something not idyllic and not romantic. All our obscurantist, contorted, reactionary nationalism, filled with self-smugness and exclusiveness, is bound up with our age old pagan mode of life, but it is a paganism already in decay, already rotted. With the Slavophils there was still a paganism in the good sense of the word, but with the nationalists that have followed after them there has remained nothing good. Vladimir Solov'ev recoiled in horror at the fruits of the Russian pagan nationalism, and this horror made him not always fair towards the old Slavophils. All the Slavophils, however, were universalists, they did not ultimately deny the West, they sought within the Russian nation for the universal truth of Christ, they sought for the City of God. And if their chiliasm was yet half pagan, this was because its time and hour was not yet come. Since the time of the Slavophils we have lived through many an experience, many a catastrophe: we have experienced Dostoevsky and Tolstoy, nihilism and anarchism, socialism and revolution, Nietzsche and decadence. It is easier for us now to fling off from ourself the burden of the pagan mode of life, we are more free, more up in the air, more directed towards the Adventive City to Come. We live in an era of the disintegration of established modes of life and we know already no settled existence.

    I have spoken about the religious and national sources of Slavophilism, derived from life. Slavophilism -- is of the soil, grown of the land, gotten of experience. But Slavophilism -- is likewise a cultural thing, standing at the heights of the European culture of its time. Slavophilism in its own way reworked Western intellectual currents. It is impossible from any perspective to deny the influence of Hegel and Schelling. Hegel and Schelling helped the Slavophils to become conscious of their experience on the land. The Slavophils, and after them all the original Russian thinkers, have always begun to philosophise beginning with Hegel, with the need to surmount him, to pass over from his abstractness into the concrete, and always they come nigh the strivings of Schelling. Hegel -- represents the dizzying apex of rationalistic philosophy, in Hegel there is a titanism and demonism. It is impossible to ignore Hegel, and perhaps, the chief defect of contemporary philosophy consists in this, that it has insufficiently come to grips with Hegel, this summit, limit, end-point. The Slavophils with genius perceived, that it was necessary to come to grips with Hegel, to surmount him, that in him is a probative touchstone. They underwent the experience of Hegel, they surmounted Hegel and passed through from abstract idealism to an idealism of the concrete, -- to an original fruition of Russian thought. In this philosophic endeavour of Kireevsky and Khomyakov comprised their eternal service to Russian culture. The West with its abstract Hegelianism, from which the living being had vanished, passed over to Feuerbach and materialism: it was in matter and in economics that they began to search for the substrate, the existent. In Russia there was followed a different creative path, a path of coming upon the existent, the substrate, the living being within a mystical apperception, within a religious experience. And herein the organ of cognition for the existent is considered not the abstract reason, the abstract intellect, but rather the integrally whole spirit. Indeed, in Germany Schelling had had striven towards this, but had stopped midway; at the end with him thus it was unclear, what stood at the head, whether religion over philosophy or philosophy over religion. Upon the path of an integral and mystical cognition stood Franz Baader, but the Slavophils evidently did not know of him and thus were not influenced by him. The Slavophils on their own realised Schelling's task of surmounting the Hegelian abstract rationalism. In this matter they stood at the apex of European thought, they sensed, what was transpiring at the heights of culture, and they had presentiments of where both the world and the Russian consciousness was heading in the years of the 1860's-70's in our era. European rationalism roamed the wilds of an abstract materialism, positivism, criticism, only to arrive at an impasse and become aware of the inevitability of mystical experience, to reunite itself with religion. The Slavophils long since already had become aware of the inevitability of this transition, they had foretold that upheaval of thought, which begins with the collapse of Hegelianism and winds up at dialectical materialism. Yes indeed, Kireevsky and Khomyakov did undergo the influence of Hegel and Schelling, but they transformed these influences into an original philosophy, setting in place the foundation of the Russian philosophic tradition. This was a concrete philosophy of the integrally whole spirit, and not the abstract philosophy of a decapitated reason. The Slavophils discerned to an utmost degree a creative relationship to that Western thought, which they imbibed, and they were not passive receptors of Western influences.

Finally, as I have already pointed out, the Slavophils participated in that world movement of the beginning XIX Century, which bears the conventional and inaccurate name of the Romantic Reaction. With this movement is connected historicism, organicity, a respect for the past and a fond empathy for it, an acknowledging of the irrational in life, and the engendering of national self-consciousness. The irrational nature of the human individuality and the individuality of the national principle was set free from the grip of the rationalism of the XVIII Century. In this era was born the idea of developement as an organic principle and it came to fruition with all the thought of the XIX Century. This is a merit of the "reactionary romanticism", which ought not to be forgotten by the successive "progressive realism". The Slavophils belonged to this worldwide torrent, they plied their way in its current and occupied in it their own unique place. It is possible to find also in the Slavophils -- teachings about organic developement, and a respect for the irrationality of history, and a national messianism. But the very character of this worldwide movement was such, as to preclude any mere borrowings or transfer. This movement summoned forth originality and irrationality from all the peoples, it called for a national creativity. Therefore, to assert that upon the Slavophils there was the influence of romanticism, in the broad sense of this word, does not mean to deny their originality. In Germany, in France, in England, in Poland, in Russia the romantic movement, having awakened in connection with it the national self-consciousness, assumed forms quite original, individual, and very different. In Slavophilism the "romantic reaction" assumed a form distinctly Orthodox, in Polish messianism -- a form distinctly Catholic. And it is especially important to note, on the Russian soil, on the basis of our religious and spiritual experience, this movement received incomparably more realistic and less visionary an hue. Romanticism in general tends to be foreign to the spirit of Eastern Orthodoxy, in it there was not insatiableness, there was not that passionate thirst, which begat romanticism in the loin of Catholicism.

Slavophilism therefore can be listed into the worldwide "romantic" movement only in conditional a sense. The Slavophils -- were not romantics in their emotional type, they were too regular, too much people of the land, too healthy. In them was moreso a religious satiety, than a religious thirst. And this especially has to be said concerning Khomyakov, a man organically of the land, strong and sober, a realist. In him there are no traces of the romantic dreaminess and emotion. He had moreso a sense of himself organically grown of a Russian city, rather than dreaming and thirsting for the city to come, in him was not the romantic torment. Even the quiet despondency and dreaminess of Ivan Kireevsky was not the passionate yearning, thirst, anguish. The world romantic movement was transmuted into the spiritual satiety of Orthodoxy, a satiety not in the pejorative sense, but in the sense of a deep fullness of churchly life; it was transmuted also into the realist aggregate of the Russian people.

It is impossible to deny the great merits of M. Gershenzon in the expressing of the significance of Slavophilism within the history of the XIX Century thought. In the historical works of Gershenzon is felt a fresh breeze. His attitude towards Slavophilism is distinct both from the Western school and from the Slavophil school, he attempts to peel through to the valuable core kernel of the Slavophil current. But this operation is effected by him by way of a dissection of the Slavophils. Gershenzon considers the precious and eternal core kernel of Slavophilism to be the teaching about the integral life of the spirit, about person as a cosmic primal-foundation. This teaching of the Slavophils is indisputably important, but it cannot be separated from their Christian faith. For the Slavophils, the integral life of spirit is realised only in the Church of Christ and therein only hath person received plenitude and freedom. Integral wholeness is attained only religiously, but the Slavophils did not acknowledge just any sort of religion in general, an abstract religion, -- they acknowledged only the Christian religion and in this furthermore, only Orthodoxy. The truth about the integral life of spirit was also for them the truth of Christ, attainable only through Christ and His Church. Outside of Christ and His Church, the integral life of spirit is hewn asunder and rationalism triumphs. The mystical integral wholeness of spirit is given only by the Christian experience, only by mental action. It is necessary to distinguish that which is eternally valuable within Slavophilism from the antiquated garb of the Slavophils, and also from the pitiful fate of the Slavophil school. But Gershenzon himself is situated upon that rung of religious consciousness, with which is not visible the Christian depths of Slavophilism. Amidst his consciousness it would be impossible to formulate the eternally valuable within Slavophilism, otherwise than he has done. But all things considered, Gershenzon has provided a psychological interpretation of Slavophilism, contrary to certain indisputable historical facts. A. I. Koshelev said: "Without Orthodoxy our populism -- is rubbish. With Orthodoxy our national populism possesses worldwide a significance". And then too Ivan Kireevsky said: "The singularity of Russia consists in the fullness and purity of that expression, which the Christian teaching has been bestown in it, -- in all the extent of its societal and private mode of life". Khomyakov however was first of all an Orthodox theologian, a Christian thinker, a knight chivalrant of the Orthodox Church. In the same measure that Gershenzon clearly dislikes and ignores Khomyakov, he is passionately fond of Kireevsky. Such an attitude towards Khomyakov hinders Gershenzon from evaluating Slavophilism in full, it distorts the historical perspective. The central role of Khomyakov in the Slavophil camp is witnessed to by all the Slavophils, and by all their references to him. And this role ought to become all the more apparent through the considerations within this my present book. The strength of Khomyakov was in his extraordinary assuredness, the rock solidness of his consciousness of the Church and his feel for the Church. The other Slavophils were not so assured, they wavered, they doubted, and Khomyakov surfaced as their teacher. I quite esteem the work of Gershenzon, I regard it of great merit in his struggle with the tradition of Pypin and other historians of our thought, I consider him very sensitive to the religious motif of the Slavophils and to their psychological features. He was perhaps the first to have seen in Slavophilism a venturing forth of the Russian national self-consciousness, and not merely one current in a series of others. But his religious estimate of Slavophilism bears the evident imprint of the limitations of his own religious consciousness and experience, and his ignoring of Khomyakov reveals a bias.

It is considered to be a disputable question, who was the founder and spiritual father of Slavophilism: Khomyakov or I. Kireevsky? And who moreso influenced the other. I do not see in this the need to choose, and I think, that both were the founders of Slavophilism and that each of them influenced the other. If to I. Kireevsky belongs the honour of the first formulation of the basic positions of the Slavophil philosophy, which later were developed by Khomyakov, then to Khomyakov belongs the still greater honour of the first formulations of the religious mindset of the Slavophils, the teaching about the Church, i.e. the most profound basis to Slavophilism. Khomyakov wrote quite moreso than did Kireevsky, and he was moreso multifaceted and the more active. Khomyakov was not only the greatest theologian of the Slavophil school, he was likewise one of the greatest theologians of the Orthodox East. Slavophilism essentially was not and could not be an individual affair. Within it there was a sobornost'-communality of consciousness and a sobornost'-communality of creativity. Slavophilism was created by collective efforts. But in this collective, this supra-individual matter it is to Khomyakov that there belongs the central place: he was the most powerful, the most many-sided, the most active, and dialectically the most equipped man of the school. In Khomyakov one can find be it a Slavophil theology, a Slavophil philosophy, a Slavophil history, and a Slavophil philology, and a Slavophil journalist and Slavophil poet. I. Kireevsky was the romantic of the Slavophil school, by nature a contemplative, quiet and mystical, not militant, not given to bring things to fruition. Khomyakov -- was the nature most realistic in Slavophilism, and together with this, one that was militant, martial, with powerful dialectic, with the talent of a polemicist. They complemented each the other. But if one sees Christianity to be at the heart of Slavophilism, then the foremost place mustneeds be ceded to Khomyakov. Throughout all his life Khomyakov had a firm churchly sense, a Christian faith solid like a rock, it was tempted by nothing, it was shaken by nothing, and he experienced no crisis of faith. I. Kireevsky became an active Christian comparatively later, already in the 1840's, religiously and churchly, Kireevsky followed the lead of Khomyakov and was under his influence. Khomyakov -- was the foundation stone of Slavophilism, a granite type rock. He also wrote verses, but he was less the poet, than was Kireevsky. I. Kireevsky is more attractive than Khomyakov, closer to our era. But Khomyakov for us is the more necessary. Throughout all this present book I shall speak about the mutual interaction of I. Kireevsky and Khomyakov, particularly in the chapter concerning the gnosseology and metaphysics of Khomyakov. But now I shall first offer several quotes from Kireevsky, important for one to glean the characteristics of Slavophilism and the Slavophil attitude towards the West, which usually is inaccurately presented.

Prophetically there resound these words of Ivan Kireevsky: "Namely from this, that Life is *refined* by poetry, ought we to conclude, that the aspiration for Life and Poetry *has come to pass*, and that, consequently, the hour for the poet of Life hath ensued". Herein is formulated the problem of theurgy, of theurgic creativity, the problem of our day. The old, the classical Slavophils did not regard the West, such as the pretensions of their successors and legacy claim them to regard it. Khomyakov called the West "the land of holy miracles". And I. Kireevsky said: "Yes, to speak frankly, I also still now love the West, I am connected with it by many inseparable common bonds. I belong to it by my upbringing, by my habits in life, by my tastes, by my disputing proclivity of mind, even by my heartfelt connections".[1] "The orientation towards nationality is for us truly as an highest step of cultural refinement, and not as merely an emotional provincialism. Therefore, guided by this thought, one could look upon European enlightenment as upon something incomplete, rather more one-sided, not pervaded by true meaning and therefore false; but to deny it, as though it did not exist, means to stunt one's own. If the European is in actual fact false, it actually it contradicts the principle of true cultural refinement, then this principle, as true, ought not to give up on this contradiction in the mind of man, but on the contrary, to receive it into itself, to evaluate and posit limits in it, and in such manner while subjected to its arbitrariness, to impart to it its true meaning. The surmounting of the falsity of this enlightenment not at all contradicts the possibility of its subordination to truth. For everything false has at its basis something that is true, only that it is posited in the wrong place: the essence of a false principle is as a principle of existence in falsehood".[2] And further on: "And in actual fact, what good does it do us to spurn and despise that, which was and is good in the life of the West? Is it not, on the contrary, an expression however of our own principle, if it be a true principle for us? The consequence of its dominance over us, in that everything beautiful, beneficent, everything Christian is needful for us as our own, even though it should be European, even though it be African".[3]

---

[1] Vide "Complete Collected Works of I. Kireevsky" under the editorship of M. Gershenzon, publisher "Put'", Moscow, 1911, Tome 1, p. 112.

[2] Ibid., Tome 1, p. 156.

[3] Ibid., p. 157.

Nicholas Berdyaev

And how well Kireevsky speaks about the necessity for philosophy in Russia: "Philosophy *is necessary* for us: the total developement of our mind demands it. By it alone lives and breathes our poetry; it alone can provide a soul and wholeness to our as yet infant sciences, and our very life, perhaps, depends upon its refinement of construct. But from whence cometh it? Where to search for it? Certainly, our first step towards it ought to be the appropriation of the mental riches of that land, which in its speculation has defined every nation. But foreign thoughts are useful only for the developement of one's own. German philosophy cannot take root with us. *Our* philosophy has to develope from out of *our* life, to be created from the prevailing questions, from the governing interests of *our* national and private mode of life". In what does Kireevsky see the uniqueness of Russia? To this question he answers with the famous words, already alluded to by me: "The uniqueness of Russia consists but in the very fullness and purity of that expression, with which the Christian teaching has been bestown in it, -- in all the extent of its societal and private mode of life".

The Slavophils not only defined our national self-consciousness as religious in its spirit and purpose, they likewise posited our consciousness a basic theme, -- the theme of East and West. The whole spiritual life of the Russia of the XIX Century was filled with this theme, and it carried over into the XX Century as something basic, as a world-historical task set before us. And up to our present day there has dragged on the struggle between Slavophil and Westerniser principles within the Russian self-consciousness, all concentrated around this theme of East and West. Slavophilism says -- the East, Westernism says -- the West. But there ensue a time, when it becomes impossible still to choose, East or West, when for the very existence of Russia and the fulfiling of its mission it becomes necessary to affirm in it both the East and the West, to unite in it the East with the West. We are bound up with the Slavophil theme and the religious current in the resolving of this theme. But our generation is immeasurably different from the generation of the people of the decades of the thirties and the forties. They were idealists and romantics, in them was much that was idyllic and happy. We by the caprice of fate have become tragic realists. For us the problem of East and West is experienced apocalyptically, for us it is connected with eschatological presentiments and hopes. With the Slavophils, as we see, there was not this tumult, this anxiety, this tragic perspective, the soil under them did not shake, it did not burn, as it does under us. In the spiritual aspect of the people of the 1830's and 1840's I shall dwell upon detailing the characteristics of the person in Khomyakov. Then it will become clear, what differentiates the Slavophil generation from the modern generation. The Slavophils lived as people, having their own city, -- ancient Rus', we however live as though having not our own city, as though only but seeking for the Coming City. The first conceptions of Russian messianism are connected with the old idea of Moscow as the Third Rome. In this there was transplanted onto Russian soil a world-historical idea, an idea Roman and Byzantine. The Slavophils accepted the idea of Moscow -- the Third Rome as a fact of life, as an historical aggregate, as something empirical. For them the Third Rome was not something forward, but back behind. The idea of the Third Rome was based not so much on mystical hopes, as rather the Slavophil science, -- history, linguistics, ethnography. And it mustneeds be said, that this science was false, this history, this linguistics and ethnography was too often the stuff of fantasy. Religious messianism cannot depend upon historical science, and historical science ought not to be distorted to please religious messianism. The Slavophils made a jumble of science and religion, in that they imposed upon the City of God their own lifestyle sympathies, their own bonds with the historically empirical. All this will become clear in the analysis of the person and world-outlook of Khomyakov, to whom now also we shall turn.

Chapter II

Aleksei Stepanovich Khomyakov as a Person

I do not presuppose, in the precise meaning of the word, to write a biography of Aleksei Stepanovich Khomyakov. I seek instead to provide his psychological biography, his characteristics as a person. It is impossible to understand his teachings other than in connection with him as a person. Every remarkable teaching is the work of a remarkable person, from its depths it is created and by its depths only is it to be explained. Khomyakov was a very broad, very strong, very rounded man, and in him was reflected the best features of an entire epoch, of an entire way of life, since vanished into history and now perceivable by us in primarily aesthetic a manner. In Khomyakov's type there is a captivating and aesthetic completeness. Khomyakov was a man of a patrimonial way of way, and his psychological biography mustneeds begin with his ancestors and parents.

"Aleksei Stepanovich Khomyakov was born on 1 May 1804 in Moscow, at Ordynka, in Egor (St. George) parish, at Vspol'a. As regards his father and his mother, nee Kireevskaya, he belonged to the old Russian nobility.[1] Aleksei Stepanovich himself knew the array of his ancestors for back 200 years deep into the old days and he committed to memory "obscure legendary accounts" from the old days of Catherine and the time of his grandfather in general. All his ancestors were innately Russian people, and there is nothing in the history of the Khomyakov line derived of foreign a basis".[2] A fact of paramount importance in the biography of Khomyakov is the manner in which the Khomyakovs came into their landed wealth. "In the mid XVIII Century there lived nigh to Tula the landowner Kirill Ivanovich Khomyakov. Having buried his wife and only daughter, in his old age he remained the sole owner of a vast fortune: besides having the village of Bogucharov with estates in the Tula district,

---

[1] V. Z. Zavitnevich, "Aleksei Stepanovich Khomyakov", Kiev, 1902, Tome I, Book 1, p. 79.

[2] Ibid., p. 80.

Nicholas Berdyaev

Kirill Ivanovich had property also in the Ryazan gubernia and an house also in Peterburg. All this family wealth after him had to go he knew not where: and upon this the old man began to think, to whom he should bequeathe it. He did not want, that his ancestral holdings should pass out of the Khomyakov line; nor did he want, that his peasants should be left under the grip of some bad and negligent man. And so Kirill Ivanovich gathered at Bogucharov an assembly of the mir, the peasant commune, and he gave the peasants leave freely -- to choose for themself their landowner, whomsoever they might desire, only that he should be of the Khomyakov lineage, and whomsoever the mir might choose, he promised to bequeathe to that one all the estate. And with this the peasants dispatched their representatives to places near and far, to which Kirill Ivanovich had directed them -- to seek out the worthy Khomyakov. When these representatives returned, they again gathered the assembly and by common deliberation they chose a first-cousin nephew of their master, the young Sergeant of the Guards, Feodor Stepanovich Khomyakov, a man quite lacking in wealth. Kirill Ivanovich summoned him, and having gotten to know him up close, he saw that the choice of the peasant commune was the correct one, and that the one to be named his heir -- was a good and reasonable man. The old man therewith bequeathed him all his wealth and soon after he died, fully at peace, that his peasants would remain in good hands. And thus the modest young landowner came into possession of vast holdings. Reports quickly spread throughout all the gubernia, about his management and about the good order, to which he brought his affairs".[1] This Khomyakov, the favourite choice of the peasant mir gathering, was the great-grandfather of Aleksei Stepanovich. Family reminiscences concerning the exceptional manner of this coming into landed wealth had to have had an enormous influence upon all the entire spiritual outlook of A. S. Khomyakov, defining his attitude to the people's life, to the assemblages of the people, and to the responsibilities of landed property. Khomyakov was imbued with the sense, that his landed wealth was bestowed him by the people's assembly, that he had been chosen by the people, that the people had entrusted him to hold the land. And he denied any absolute rights of property ownership, as usually it is conceived of by legal jurists. All his life he thought, that the land belongs to the people and

---

[1] V. Lyaskovsky, "A. S. Khomyakov. His Biography and Teachings". Russian Archive, 1896, Book 11, p. 341.

ALEKSEI STEPANOVICH KHOMYAKOV

that as its possessor they but entrust it to hold for the common good of the people. Together with this, there was wrought within him a special attitude towards the people, an unique trust for the collective life of the people, for the deliberations of the people's assembly. He sensed his own blood connection with the people and the blood connection with his ancestors. And this feeling was not killed in him by the fact, that his father, Stepan Aleksandrovich, lost more than a million rubles playing cards at the English club. His wife, Maria Alekseevna, the mother of Aleksei Stepanovich, took matters into her own hands and set things right.

In the life of A. S. Khomyakov, his mother had an especial significance. "She, -- writes he to Mukhanova, -- was a noble and pure example of her times; and in her strength of character there was something, belonging to an epoch more assured and bold, than to the eras following. As for me, this I know, that in as much as I should become practically useful, I owe it indeed to her guidance, to her unshakable firmness in her aims, though she herself did not think that this was so. Happy the one, who has had such a mother and teacher in childhood, while at the same time such a lesson in humility whilst given such conviction! How little of that good, which is in a man, derives but from him? Both the larger complex of one's thoughts, and the direction of thought, are dependent upon one's initial upbringing".[1] For Khomyakov it was characteristic, that in him he had an organic, a blood bond connection with his mother, and by his mother -- the bond with the land. Khomyakov's mother was a woman severe, religious, with character, with discipline. We shall see below, what sort of a significance she had for her son. Khomyakov's father was a typical Russian landowner, a member of the English club, a cultured man, but full of the gentry's defects and weaknesses. The mother of Aleksei Stepanovich was stronger, than his father. "Following the footsteps of European enlightenment in the person of his father, in the person of his mother the Khomyakov family held strongly to the tradition of their native land, insofar as was expressed in the life of the Church and the lifestyle of the people".[2]

I have cited some characteristic facts from the childhood and early youth of Khomyakov. Aleksei Stepanovich studied the Latin language

---

[1] A. S. Khomyakov. "Collected Works", Tome VIII, p. 422.

[2] Zavitnevich. "A. S. Khomyakov", Tome I, Book 1, p. 84.

under the abbe Boivin, who lived at the Khomyakov home. The student noticed some sort of erratum in a Papal Bull and he asked the abbot, how he could consider the pope to be infallible, when the Holy Father is given to make grammatical errors. Aleksei Stepanovich got reprimanded for this. But the fact itself is very characteristic. Khomyakov began early his polemic against Catholicism and forthwith came to have an exceptionally critical attitude towards it. Another time, when Aleksei Stepanovich journeyed with his brother to Peterburg, then to the boys it seemed, that they were in a pagan city and that they would be forced to break with their faith. The Khomyakov brothers resolved firmly that it is better to suffer torture, than to accept an alien law. And all his life Khomyakov feared, lest whether he, as a Muscovite and Russian, might be compelled to change from the Orthodox faith, although the danger was no greater, than it had been in his childhood journey to Peterburg. There was danger, but not at all there, where Khomyakov thought it. The military nature of Aleksei Stepanovich found expression very early. At seventeen years of age he attempted to run away from home, in order to take part in the war for the liberation of Greece. He bought himself a bootleg knife, grabbed with him a small sum of money and secretly left home. They caught up with him at the Serpukhov gateway and returned him home. The condition of the soul of the youth in the moment of this military impulse is clearly outlined in the first verse of Khomyakov, "Missive to Venevitinov", of which I quote from the most characteristic parts:

> And so, there hath ensued the day of victory, of glory,
>   of revenge:
> And so, there hath come to pass the fanciful dream,
> Presentiments of soul, of golden dreams of youth,
> Desires ablaze for fulfilled a fate!
> From the Northern seas, eternally over-veiled by ice,
> To the Mediterranean waves, the gods delight,
> Of places, where sky, the azure swelling seas,
> The rocky crags, forests, fields, all dear for eyes to see,
> In all the age-old lands whence flourished peoples
> By laws beshielded, under the standard of freedom.

....

ALEKSEI STEPANOVICH KHOMYAKOV

Thus, friends, I go, I go into the bloody battle,
For the happy fate of a land, to my heart natal,
And, a new Leonides of Hellas reborn,
I shalt live through the ages in memory adorned.
I shalt thunder, like Perun! O, the charming sweet dream!
But never, alas, shalt it come to pass!
And would ye but bid me, as in bright days of yore,
To sing the fierce fight, the deeds of resounding glory?
All in vain: for by one dream is my soul filled.

....

O, that the voice of the Tsar should us summon
    to the dread fight!
O, that he should bid, that the Russian sword
    be steeled,
Saviour of weak realms, the hope, the fear universal,
To avenge sorrowing Hellas the oppressed!
Then perchance, heartened midst valiant warriors,
For the Greeks revenge, honour and faith of forefathers,
I be yet filled with swelling soul,
And anew befriend the good writ in Stone,
Upon the sweet lyre, in the embrace of friends,
I should sing of old times and battles of formers days.

    Everything, which was romantic in the nature of Khomyakov, always assumed the form of a military stirring. At eighteen years of age, his father sent Aleksei Stepanovich to a cuirassier-cavalry regiment under the command of Graf Osten-Saken, who has left behind a mention of him. "In his physical, moral and spiritual upbringing, -- declared Osten-Saken, -- Khomyakov was hardly the norm. His education was astonishingly excellent, and in all my life I never met anyone similar at that youthful age. How lofty the flight of his poetry! He was not attracted by the fad of the age in sensual poetry. With him everything was moral, spiritual, uplifting. He rode with distinction, and he bounded over the hurdle to the height of a man. At swordplay he fought superbly. He had the strong will, not of a youth, but of a man, tried by experience. He strictly kept all the fasts in accord with the ustav of the Orthodox Church and on feastdays and Sundays he frequented all the divine Services... He did not permit himself off duty the use of clothing of fine fabric even in his quarters and he refused the permission to wear a tin cuirasse [breast-plate] in place of iron ones of half-pud [i.e. 18 pounds] weight, despite his small stature and seeming weak build. Regarding endurance and perseverance under physical hardship, he was imbued to an utmost degree with spartan qualities".[1] And after a year Khomyakov was transferred into a Life Guards regiment. In 1828 was then realised the dream of the eighteen year old Khomyakov. He was sent off to war, entering into an hussar regiment and serving as an adjutant under the general Prince Madatov. He took part in many a military action. In the words of his contemporaries, Khomyakov as an officer distinguished himself "by cold brilliance of bravery". With him, there was a cheery and together with this also human attitude towards battle. From the theatre of military actions Aleksei Stepanovich writes to his mother: "I was in the attack, but although I was twice assaulted, I decided not to cut down the fleeing, for which now I am very glad; after this, I made my way up to the ramparts, in order to have a look up close. Here before me was my wounded white horse, over which I am quite sad. A flying bullet had hit right through both legs; though there is still hope it will recover. Before this it had already received a wound in the front shoulder from a saber, but this wound was basically a shallow wound. For this I was recommended for the Vladimir, but through various circumstances not dependent upon Prince Madatov, I received only the St. Ann with ribbon, and this perhaps is quite sufficient. Catching up, I journeyed hither: where once before in military actions the arrogance of the Turks was fiercely punished, but the second time to give our division a rest for all the grief and toil of the past year. Otherwise, I am in good spirits, well and very content during Pascha".[2] "And merry the bloody fighting", -- he exclaims in verse. Later on, when Aleksei Khomyakov had long already come to live in the countryside in tranquil a setting, every so often he got off onto the subject of the war, about the fighting, and he poured forth his experiences in militant verses.

---

[1] Zavitnevich, "Khomyakov", Tome I, Book 1, p. 101-102.

[2] A. S. Khomyakov, "Collected Works", Tome VIII, p. 5-6. Letter.

ALEKSEI STEPANOVICH KHOMYAKOV

Khomyakov was a contemporary of the Decembrists, he knew many of them, but he never felt any attraction to this remarkable movement, and always viewed it as the shallow-minded foppishness of youth. In a dispute with Ryleev, Khomyakov argued, that of all the forms of revolution the least just -- is the military sort. "What is the military? -- said A. S., -- This is but a gathered group from among the people, which the people has armed on its own account: it serves the people. Where indeed would it be right, if these people to the contrary of their purpose, should begin to deal with the people to instead its own whim".[1] And Khomyakov asserted to Prince A. I. Odoevsky, that this would not be a matter proper to liberals, but would rather presuppose a solely ruling tyranny of an armed minority. Aleksei Stepanovich's brother, Feodor Stepanovich, condemned the Decembrists precisely on this point, -- that they did not know *the soul of the people*. And thus also did Aleksei Stepanovich see it. The Decembrist movement to him seemed not a matter of the people. And it is moreover surprising, that this critical and only half-just opinion of Khomyakov should have coalesced already in his youthful years.

Khomyakov was first of all a typical landowner, a good Russian nobleman, a fine master, organically bound up with the land and the people. Aleksei Stepanovich -- was a noted hunter, and a specialist on various breeds of dogs. There is even an article by him about hunting and dogs. He likewise invented a gun, which shoots farther than ordinary guns; he invents an agricultural machine -- a seeding drill, for which he receives an English patent; he discovers a means for treating cholera. He sets up a distillery, he doctors the peasants, and is involved with questions of agrarian economics. This Russian landowner, practical and business-like, also hunter and technician, a man of dogs and an homeopath, was likewise a most remarkable theologian of the Orthodox Church, a philosopher, historian, poet and journalist. His friend, . N. Sverbeev, wrote of him:

> Poet, mechanic and philologist,
> Doctor, artist and theologian,
> Of the Russian peasant-commune the journalist,
> Thou art wise like the serpent, yet pure like the dove.

---

[1] Zavitnevich, Tome I, Book 1, p. 93.

Nicholas Berdyaev

Khomyakov -- was universal a man, a man of a series of manifest investigative interests, with sparks of genius, of wide accomplishments, and in all the spheres of life and thought having left remarkable traces. P. G. Pogodin provides an enthusiastic and naive characterisation of Khomyakov. In this description of his, there is the charm of a spontaneous and convivial acceptance of the person of Aleksei Stepanovich. "Khomyakov!, -- he exclaims, -- What was it behind this nature, so gifted, so amiable, so original! What a mind all-encompassing, what vitality, such profuseness in thoughts, which he had there locked up in his head, like an inexhaustible well-spring it would seem, having the key for any instance that might pop up, whether from the right or from the left! How many an account of matters most diverse, combined with an extraordinary gift for words, flowed from his mouth in a vital stream! What didn't he not know? And but listening to Khomyakov one might believe the fabulous tradition about Pico della Mirandola, set forth in the controversial treatise, *"De omni re scible"* [*"On everything knowable"*]. Both one and the other they are inexplicable... There was not a science, in which Khomyakov did not possess some broadest bit of knowledge, in which he could not but see some obscure points, which could not but lead to a prolonged discussion with the specialist or to put forth to him important questions. It would seem, that he had only to explain some misunderstandings, to fill in some of the gaps... And at the same time Khomyakov penned projects concerning the emancipation of the serfs many year prior to the mandates later drawn up, he proposed plans for land banks or moreover, or in context of newspaper accounts from the period, he considers borders for the American republics, he pointed the way to the legal system sought by Franklin, he analysed to the smallest detail the Napoleonic battles, he read and learned by heart whole pages of Shakespeare, Goethe or Byron, he expounded on the teachings of the Eddas and Buddhist cosmogony... And at the same time Khomyakov invents some sort of machine with a twofold motion, which he sends off to a British world exhibition and gains a patent privilege, he constructs some sort of gun, which shoots the farthest of all, he proposes new methods of viniculture and sugar-refining, as an homeopathologist he treats all the sick for some versts around throughout the surrounding district, he races round the fields with his swift dogs through the fresh-fallen winter snow after rabbits and he describes all the good points and the bad of the dogs and the horses like an experienced hunter, he receives first prize in a society of marksmen with his aim, and in the evening time he shows up with his then collection of anecdotes concerning some sort of wild prelate who had taken off into the Kostroma woods, about the zealousness of some Perm district policeman in spreading the Christian faith, for which he was recommended for the St. Vladimir, but could not receive it, in that he proved to be a musselman".[1] This sketch is charming in its naiveté and its enthusiasm, and in it there is much that is true, despite the embellishments. Khomyakov really was such an universal sort of person, and extraordinarily talented. In this regard, he might compare with Goethe. But Goethe was by his German nature disciplined, whereas Khomyakov was by his Russian nature chaotic. Khomyakov was, first of all, very much an idler, both on his own testimony and the testimony of his fellows.

In our epoch, religious thinkers and seekers do not invent guns, machines and methods of treating cholera, they do not ride off to the hunt, they understand little about dog-breeding. Khomyakov was as such a scion of the land, he was a man of the ancestral ways, in him there was not the airy aspect of the generations that followed. Vl. Solov'ev and people of his sort in the difficult moments of life wrote verses and in them poured out their most intimate feelings. Khomyakov in the difficult moments of life rides off hunting and in chasing rabbits solves his anguish. In one letter he says: "Where there are fields however and rabbits, and an happy mount, and the excitement of the chase, are not all my other delights of the quality of Nimrod's progeny (le grand chasseur devant le Seigneur)? I say moreover, does not this affinity give me a greater right to judge about matters of ancient Babylon, than it does for the Germans, those learned schmerzens, who don't know how to distinguish a dog's biting end from its tail end?".[2] Khomyakov -- was a man of robust character, with tremendous self-control. He concealed and did not like to open up with things he suffered, he was not intimate with this in his poetry and letters. It is impossible from Khomyakov's verse to guess at the intimate sides of his being, something in contrast which was possible as regards the verse of Vl. Solov'ev. In his verse, Khomyakov is the soldier, he shoots precisely to the point, he is aloof and reserved. Aleksei Stepanovich was a proud man, the haughtiness -- was a basic feature of his character. In his poetry he

---

[1] Zavitnevich, "Khomyakov", Tome I, Book 1, p. 100-101.

[2] A. S. Khomyakov, "Collected Works", Tome VIII, p. 15.

often employs the word *pride*, and this was a word of which he was fond. In him there was the pathos of pride. But this was not a spiritual pride in relation to the MostHigh, this was a worldly pride, in regard to people. And this character trait was expressed all the moreso in regard to women. Khomyakov happened to experience love as something inseparable, and here thus is how he experienced this feeling.

To ***

> I do thank thee! When with love tender
> Shone for me radiant thine eyes,
> Neathe the yoke of sweetness slept in breast turbulent
> > The passion of my soul!
> I do thank thee! When thy gaze severe
> On youthful songster with coldness fell,
> My proud spirit boiled forth, and the former bonds
> > I made bold to break!
> And wide aloft my flight, alive in winged power;
> All in breast aquiet, all in heart aflower;
> And song of thanks refreshed hath blest
> > The freed brow!
> Thus after violent storms the sea azure and quiet,
> The forest fragrant, the fresh valley pretty;
> Thus wounded lightly doth depart the eagle higher
> > To its native heavens!

One time Khomyakov hazarded the danger of growing fond of the famed Rosset-Smirnova, but pride conquered this emotion, since Rosset, in the opinion of Aleksei Stepanovich, represented something foreign for Russia.

A Foreignness

A. O. Rosset

> O, the charm surrounding her,
> All the South luxuriant doth breathe in her;
> From the very roses be her allure and name;

ALEKSEI STEPANOVICH KHOMYAKOV

From the stars be given her gleam of eye.

Riveted to her by magic a power,
The poet rapturous doth gaze;
But never he to maiden dear
His love to dedicate.

She perchance the clear heart's resounding,
The sublime in thought of beauty,
Of poets the joy and torment,
Of poets pure illusion;

She perchance for soul as flame thus vivid,
Midst rising smoke from candles prayerful;
Mayhaps some angel bright and beauteous
From birth hath blest her;

But foreign to her be my Russia,
My fatherland's wild beauty;
And for her be dear lands other,
Others preferred to heaven!

I sing her the song of my native land, --
She notices not, nor glances!
Whilst before her say I, "O Rus', the Holy!"
And the heart in her thrills not.

All in vain the rays of vivid light
From dark eyes do fall away,
And to her the proud souled poet
His love wilt not devote.

And very characteristic are likewise the verses of the "Elegy" --

An Elegy

When the evening dew doth descend

Nicholas Berdyaev

And into slumber the valed world, and cool breeze blow,
And the blue of dusk adorn the heavens
And moon beams kiss the drowsy earth;
Terrible for me becomes thought of worldly strife,
And woeful alone to be, and heart of hearts beseech,
And voice atremble then against fate doth murmur
Then the name of love involuntarily doth pronounce...

When however at morningtide the East awaketh
To lead forth in triumph the golden dawn
And sun its rays to shed, like a flaming torrent,
Upon the bright world of the heavens, upon earthly bustle --
I anew am alert and afresh. Upon the turgid coursing of people
Cast I the bold glare: a smile and cold contempt
Send I alone in answer to my threatened fate,
And in my aloneness do rejoice.
Readied for struggle and strong, like steel,
The soul flees the love of hapless desire,
And alone, loving but its sufferings,
Doth drink down the proud, the unvoiced sorrow.

This proud mindset is inherent in everything for Khomyakov. And quite in character he tends to speak also about a churchly pride: "By this right, this power, this might, I am bound only by good fortune to be a son of the Church, and nowise at all by any personal ability of mine. I say this boldly and not without pride, since it would be improper to regard as humble, that which the Church doth give".[1] While in another place he writes: "You cannot accuse me of pride, if I say, that I merely somewhat have brought back into human discourse our too much forgotten words of nobility of bearing".[2] The reservedness and self-control of Khomyakov is connected with a sense of his own worth, with a noble pride of character. In it there is nothing intimidating, nothing expansive merely for show, nothing lyrical, and he just did not want to open himself up defenseless before people. Aleksei Stepanovich was often accused of coldness, of lack

---

[1] A. S. Khomyakov, "Collected Works", Tome II, p. 223.

[2] A. S. Khomyakov, "Collected Works", Tome VIII, p. 318.

of feelings. And during moments of suffering he had the ability to speak on the most abstract of philosophic themes, nowise evidencing his agitation. Thus it was at the moment of Venevitinov's death. Mukhanov recollects concerning Khomyakov: "Particularly remarkable was his capacity for (philosophic) thought, which did not forsake him even in very deeply distressing circumstances, as though these circumstances lacked power to touch his heart. In such manner he continued to render quite clear judgements and calmly also about subjects most abstract, as though nothing troubling had occurred during this time".[1]

The mother of Aleksei Stepanovich was evidently a very remarkable woman and it is impossible not to take note of her influence regarding her children, and having great significance in the life of A. S. When the sons of Maria Alekseevna came to mature age, she summoned them to her and expressed her view in this regard, that young men, just like young women, ought to preserve their chastity prior to marriage. She made her sons give a vow, that they would not engage in sexual relations with a single woman prior to marriage. In the event of breaking the vow, she refused to her sons her final blessing. The vow was given and, accordingly, was fulfilled.[2] At twenty-six years of age, Khomyakov wrote:

A Confession

"Til now unknown to me is love,
And burning passion's fire unsettling;
Of fond glances, and endearments tender
Naught thereof agitated is my blood".
I harmoniously in sounds am arrayed,
And sing I of proud freedom
And in innocence of youth having trusted,
With hopes, with dreams of glory
And true friendship the riches,
I scorned of love the poison
And besought not its reward.

---

[1] Zavitnevich, "Khomyakov", Tome I, Book 1, p. 110.

[2] V. Lyaskovsky, "Khomyakov. His Biography and Teachings", p. 360.

From that time the soul knoweth torments,
Dashed hopes, the death of friends,
And sadly repeat the sound of songs,
Gathered forth from my youth.
I neathe eye-lashes bashful,
Encountered eyes of living fire,
And long silky curls playful,
And youthful bosom atremble;
A mouth with inviting smile,
Rouge red velvety cheeks,
And harmony of stature, like a supple palm,
And step with facile a grace.
Mayhaps, in the veins the blood hath stirred,
And fear, and full the joy,
With strong effect the bosom breathing;
And heart doth whisper: here is she!
But the bright wink of charm
Passed like in a dream, and vanished its trace:
To her be wild all my dreamings
And unknown to her the poet.
O when indeed?... And the heart doth ache,
And to the harp I flee anew,
And murmur, breathing gasping the breath:
Til now unknown to me is love.

Thus also A. I. Koshelev writes concerning A. S.: "Khomyakov was an amazing man: he carried through with his moral passion right down to his very last days. In both society at large and individually around the ladies he was uncomfortable. He had never the desire to become popular with them, lest the danger that it lead him into temptation".[1] Several times he came to feel love towards a woman, but each time he managed to vanquish it, subordinating it to his intellectual aims. Khomyakov was not by nature an erotic person. There is nothing of the erotic in his creativity. In this he is infinitely different from Vl. Solov'ev. For him, the reason and the will have the upper hand over feelings. He did not live under the

---

[1] N. Koliupanov, "Biography of Aleksandr Ivanovich Koshelev", Tome I, Book 2, p. 150.

ALEKSEI STEPANOVICH KHOMYAKOV

fascination of the feminine, and therefore perhaps some sides of Christian mysticism were foreign to him. Yet he had in him a strong ideal of the family aspect, the patriarchal ideal. But there were in him no traces of utmost eroticism, of mystical love. This can be felt both in his poems, and in his letters. And how characteristic indeed is this absence of the erotic for the Slavophils of this period. And how different they are from Vl. Solov'ev with his cult of eternal femininity. Whether in the person of Khomyakov or in the works of Khomyakov, in everything about him there is no place for the eternal femininity, for the world soul. We shall see this, when we speak about the philosophic world-view of Khomyakov. The Slavophil patriarchalism, the Old Testament family aspect, excludes any cult of the eternal feminine. In 1836 Khomyakov was joined in marriage with Ekaterina Mikhailovna Yazykova, the sister of a poet. This proved to be an uncommonly happy, untroubled and faultless marriage. And indeed it could not be otherwise for him, for otherwise his life should not have been so organically imbued. There was grief indeed that beset Khomyakov: they lost two children, at the death of which he penned his reknown verse. But an inward sense of tragedy, an inner sense of discontent, he did not know.

The military bearing -- is a characteristic feature of Khomyakov. This feature was evidenced also, in that he often lapsed off onto a war motif, both in his martial manner of writing, and in his love for dialectical skirmishes. His verses -- are almost exclusively militant, not lyrical, not woeful. In his creativity Khomyakov never opened up with his own weaknesses, his inner struggles, the doubts, the searchings, in the manner of most people. He is always the dogmatist. A dogmatic tenacity runs through all his nature. He had an ineradicable need always to affirm the organic and to struggle in the name of an affirmation of the organic. In him there are no traces of the softness and indefiniteness such as one finds in doubting natures, beset by wavering. He has no doubts in anything and goes off to the fight. It is impossible to go into battle beset by doubts, and inner discord. It is a poor warrior indeed, that fights with himself, and not against the enemy. Khomyakov always fought against the enemy, and not against himself, and in this he is very different from the people of our time, who too often engage in struggle against themselves, and not against the enemy. His contemporaries recognised Khomyakov first of all as a dialectical warrior, as a champion disputer, always on guard, always on the attack. In the heat of the dialectical fight Khomyakov loved to resort to paradoxes, to go to the extreme. Often this happened not deliberately, but sometimes he intentionally resorted to paradoxes in his aims of the fight. Khomyakov loved to poke fun and make a joke, he was forever joking around and his jest, evidently, annoyed certain people. It called into question his sincerity. Can a man forever joking around be indeed a believer? Is this not instead an indication of foppishness, a lack of seriousness and depth, and perhaps, of scepticism? Such a view concerning a man forever joking around is itself superficial. Jest -- is a complex thing, a profound matter, and too little investigated. In the element of laughter is perhaps a surmounting of the contradictions of existence and an uplift. A chaste sort of laughter veils over that which is intimate and sacred. Laughter can prove to be the self-discipline of spirit, its suit of armour. And the jesting of Khomyakov was an indication of his self-discipline, and perhaps also of his pride and reservedness, his sharpness of mind, but nowise is it as a scepticism, lack of belief or insincerity with him. The jest was first of all very intellectual. There can be laughter also in an utmost harmony. Too well-known is the opinion of Hertsen concerning Khomyakov, as expressed in "My Past and Thoughts". For many, this characterisation by Hertsen is the sole source for making a judgement on Khomyakov. But Hertsen however failed to understand Khomyakov, just as he failed to understand both Chaadayev and Pecherin; this was an unknown world for him. He was struck by the extraordinary talents of Khomyakov, he recognised him as a champion disputant and dialectician, but the inner core of Khomyakov was for him just as obscure, as was the inner core of all people of a religious spirit. Hertsen therefore is suspicious of the sincerity of Khomyakov, suspicious of the depths of his conviction, just as non-believers always are wont to do regarding believers. Hertsen made out Chaadayev to be a liberal, and Khomyakov he made out to be -- a dialectician, with his disputes veiling over an inward emptiness. But Hertsen perchance is not competent as a witness and judge of the religious coursings of Russian life and thought.

    The love for freedom was one of the taproots at the core of Khomyakov. We shall see, how Khomyakov's love for freedom finds expression in his theologising. Pervasive throughout all his life was an hatred towards coercion and compulsion, and his faith rests in an organic freedom, a faith in its graced power. The whole Slavophil doctrine of Khomyakov was the teaching about an organic freedom. Organism for him always was something liberating and free, only mechanism was coercively compelling. This passionate love for freedom finds beautiful expression in the verses of Khomyakov, devoted to Russia. He sees the mission of Russia to be first of all in this, that it reveal to the Western world the mystery of freedom.

> Thine all that, what spirit doth sanctify,
> In what be heard of heart the voice of heaven,
> In what life of days to come lies concealed,
> The principle of glory and wonders!...
> O, be mindful of thine portion on high,
> In heart the past to resurrect,
> And of the hidden depths within it
> Thou the spirit of life to question!
> Attend thou it -- and, of all peoples
> Having embraced with thine love,
> *Proclaim them the mystery of freedom,*
> To them pour forth the radiance of faith!
> And in glory wilt thou become wondrous
> Excelling all the sons of the earth,
> Like as this blue vaulted sky above
> Doth veil the beyond sight MostHigh!

In the verse, "The Judgement of God", he says:

> "*Warm them with the breath of freedom*".

And the same motif resounds in the verse, "Of Contrition for Russia":

> Go forth! Thee the peoples do summon.
> And, having made thine martial feast,
> *Bestow them the gift of holy freedom.*
> Bestow life -- thought, bestow the world -- life!

Khomyakov believed, that the principle of organic freedom is lodged first of all within Eastern Orthodoxy, and therefore also within the spirit of the Russian people, in the Russian village life, the Russian proclivities of soul and attitude towards life. The West does not know true freedom, since everything there has become mechanised and rationalised. The mystery of freedom is known only to the heart of Russia, undistortedly having preserved the truth of the Church of Christ, and only it can declare this mystery to the modern world, which has been subjugated by outward necessity.

His love for freedom excluded for Khomyakov the possibility of government service. He could not function within the official realm, organically he could not, nor could he stay even within the military, although he loved the military. He sensed the lifestyle of freedom only in the countryside, in the life of a landowner, dependent upon nothing and upon no one, bound up directly with nature. Khomyakov was a rich Russian nobleman, he did not know dependence under an administrative authority, nor did he know dependence upon his literary work, which was however the condition for many a Russian writer. Life smiled on him. And his particular lifestyle, the freedom of a country gentleman, presented itself to him as the freedom of the whole Russian people, of the whole extent of Russian life. Herein was a boundedness, connected with a way of life, with the historical conditions of place and time, but the very love for freedom with Khomyakov was unbounded. He wrote only by inspiration and therefore could little pretend himself to be a literary professional or specialist of a discipline, or the same with someone in civil service. Khomyakov was no less an hunter, than a writer, and he would not be one to turn down an hunt with hounds in the name of any duty to pen an article due under a deadline. With Khomyakov there was an unboundedness in his striving for freedom and a boundedness to the form of the lifestyle, with which he connected the realisation of freedom. Freedom, a vital and living freedom, was for him identical with a favoured lifestyle, such as might obtain in whatever the gubernia, in whatever the district. But he connected the Russian people as most freedom-loving too exclusively with the patriarchal lifestyle, with the family setting, with the domain of the land. And in this was his limitedness, which does not exist at large in the spirit of the Russian people, agitated and in anxiety.

Love for the domestic family setting was very characteristic for both Khomyakov and for all the Slavophils. The entirety of the societal relationships obtaining amongst people he regarded first of all to be modeled upon family relationships. Khomyakov was happy in his family life and upon this happiness he wanted to base his hope for societal happiness. He says about familial felicity, that "only it alone upon the earth merits the name of happiness". "Holy Rus' hath need of its own home, its own family for living".¹ The domestic social setting, on the model created by the family, is also that of a patriarchal lifestyle, in which all the relationships are such as those obtaining between fathers and children. With the family aspect of Aleksei Stepanovich was connected a certain miserliness on his part. It was not other people only, but he also considered himself stingy and in jest spoke ironically of this trait, calling himself *Papa Grandet*. "Papa Grandet did not forget to make a profit", -- he writes in one of his letters. Khomyakov was a genuine Anglophile, he love English Toryism, the English organic sense of history. He journeyed to England in his cap and peasant coat, he was fond of the English, and the English were fond of him. The English character seemed something kindred for Khomyakov. Khomyakov believed, that the fate of the world is decided in Moscow and London, and he thirsted for the uniting of Anglicanism with the Orthodox Church. His love for the English even went so far, that he seriously considered the English to be Slavs of a sort. In a letter of A. S. concerning England, there is a very vivid statement: "Whigism -- is a matter of daily bread; Toryism -- is all the joy of life, besides the debauchery of the taverns, or still worse the debauchery of the dance-halls; it is horse-races and boxing-matches, it is the frivolity at the ball and the dancing around the may-pole, or the yule-tide log and the merry Christmas plays; it is the quite and cozy shrine of the home circle, it is all poetry, all felicity. In England the Tories -- are every old oak with its long branches, every old steeple, which thrusts far up into the sky. Beneathe this oak was much merriment, in this old church was many a prayer of generations past".²

    Toryism for Khomyakov was not the political party, he saw in it the soul of the English people. Suchlike a Toryism, in his opinion, can be found, besides England, only in Russia. "If one doth seek to find the Tory principles outside of England, -- look around: one will find them, and the finest also, since they are not sealed away by any one person. For here is the gold-topped Kremlin with its cathedrals, and in the South the Kiev Caves, and in the North the Solovetsk shrines and the family household domestic shrines and, most of all, the universal community of an Orthodoxy subordinated to no one. Look further: for here is the power, once formerly summoning forth Kuzma Minin as champion of all the

---

[1] A. S. Khomyakov, "Collected Works", Tome VIII, p. 57.
[2] A. S. Khomyakov, "Collected Works", Tome I, p. 130.

Russian land, and the levies of Pozharsky, and as the crowning deed the choosing to the throne of Mikhail and all his line; for here, ultimately, is the countryside world with its one-mindedness of accord, with its judgement by custom of conscience and inner rightful truth. And hence the great, the fruitful benefits".[1] Khomyakov was indeed fond of England, but in turn he had little love for the Romance peoples, bound up with the spirit of Catholicism, and he could not endure France, towards which he was very unjust. Khomyakov however esteemed the Germans, although he poked fun at the Germans as "those Schmerzens". But he never asserted, that the West was in decay. For him, Europe was "the land of holy wonders".

Khomyakov was not a great poet, but in him there are powerful verses and his talents are beyond doubt. He however said on his own behalf: "Without pretense of humility I know for myself, that my verses, when good, depend on the thought, i.e. the prosifier everywhere peeks out, and consequently, one has to ultimately throttle the versifier". Aleksei Stepanovich was a talented versifier, and his verses are an indication of his extraordinary giftedness, but in them there is little of true poetry. For us foremost of all, the verses of Khomyakov are interesting as material for the traits of his person, for his psychological biography. In this regard, the absence of lyricism and of the intimate in his verse is very characteristic. Khomyakov not only was not a genuine poet, -- he also was not a genuine mystic. He can be termed a mystic only insofar as every Christian can be termed a mystic. He taught about the mystical Church, since the mystical itself is of the essence of the Church. But any especial mysticism within Khomyakov is impossible to find. In this regard he was too sober, too practical a man, too fine a landowner, he too much loved the hunt, his religion was too much caught up in his lifestyle, his familial setting. Khomyakov was robustly healthy a man, not inclined to ecstasies, nor knowing the pits of despondency. Foreign to him even was the Eastern Christian mysticism, -- asceticism. He accepted asceticism only in that minimum degree, to which every Christian accepts it, but the private mystical path of asceticism was foreign to him. Khomyakov was antagonistic towards too ascetic an understanding of Christianity, he had too powerful a taste for everyday life, and dear to him was the pagan side of the Russian way of life. The Western mystics he simply did not know. In

---

[1] A. S. Khomyakov, "Collected Works", Tome I, p. 137-138.

one place he says directly, that he had never read Jacob Boehme, the greatest of these mystics. Khomyakov made immeasurably bad use of denouncing all and everything in rationalism, but he himself was of a rationalist proclivity. He was a great dialectician, a powerful dialectician, and sometimes he criticised rationalism too rationalistically. In his life there was an element of judgemental reasoning. The intimate religious experience of Khomyakov, the prayerful experience, was veiled over by elements of rational judgement and rationalism. Khomyakov saw in mysticism an inverted side of the rationalistic sundering apart of the integrally whole life of spirit and therefore he reacted negatively towards it. But the integral wholeness itself of the life of spirit can be apperceived only as a life mystical, and not via lifestyle. Khomyakov however saw in the lifestyle a greater genuine faith, than in mysticism. This is very characteristic of him. Ivan Kireevsky became a believing Christian comparatively late in life, when he was already in his forties, but his religious life had far moreso a mystical hue, than with Khomyakov. Kireevsky interacted with the startsi-elders of the Optina Pustyn monastery, he became permeated by the spirit of Eastern asceticism. His nature was more mystical and contemplative. Of all the Slavophils, Kireevsky was the most mystical in temperament, and in the final years of his life he lived in the pervasive atmosphere of Orthodox mysticism, and intimate for him was the practice of mental activity. In general, however, the Slavophils were not mystics, they had no feel for mystical a trembling. And completely foreign for both Khomyakov and the other Slavophils was any sense of apocalyptic sort of mysticism.

 Khomyakov was not a genius, but in his nature there was an extraordinary giftedness, bordering on genius. His extraordinary giftedness did not find expression in any sort of finished works. Everything, that he wrote, is incomplete. Khomyakov is learned, but with the exception of the tome of theological articles, he tends to be read but little, since there are almost no books as such written by him for reading. This is a Russian trait: to be endowed with tremendous talents and yet not create anything complete. And in this, no little role was played by the genteel indolence of Khomyakov, his dilettante attitude towards the vocation of writer. Regarding himself, he attributed the words of a certain verse of his about the sins of Russia: "And laziness disgusting and disgraceful". Aleksei Stepanovich wrote that amidst his other affairs, writing was not the chief thing in his life. In his life, no less a role was played by the preoccupations of a country landowner, those of the hunt, inventions, projects for bettering the life of the peasants, and family concerns. He tried his hand even at painting, in Paris he did icons for a Catholic temple, but he did not follow through with his artistic concerns to the end. One time he was very taken up with viniculture and sugar-refining. He was an homeopath, he discovered some means for treating cholera, and he doctored the peasants during the time of an epidemic. His devotion to homeopathy was so great, that when he was dying from inflamation of the lungs and they besought him to accept treatment through the ordinary means, he resolutely refused any other sort of treatment, except for the homeopathic, since he regarded anything else as a fallacious idea. His extraordinary many-sidedness in combination with his lethargy and a certain dilettantism hindered him from doing anything to completion. Nonetheless, Aleksei Stepanovich was first of all a landowner, and only then a writer, and this could not but reflect on the character of his writings. His memory was extraordinary, he had the ability to devour a whole pile of books in a single day, he quoted citations from memory, and would write them out without reference notes. But in his writing there was no sort of discipline, there is no feel of attitude to his writing as a chief vocation, a primal task in life. His manner of writing was very scattered, chaotic. But everything that he writes is pervaded by a single idea, though it be an article about sports or about hunting. To characterise his manner of writing, I offer the Table of Contents from one of his articles. The article, "Regarding Humboldt", has the following Contents: "Confusion of Fact in his Reasoning. -- An Outline of Western History. -- The Book of Max Stirner. -- Ancient Russian Society. -- Peter I. -- The Insignificance of Russian Science.. -- The Person and Art. -- The Icon. -- The Absence of Tradition. -- The Peasant Assemblies. -- Our Whigism. -- The Return to Russian Life. -- Self-Education". Going through these Contents it becomes very difficult to say, about what the article was written on, since it seems to have been written about almost everything. But essentially, all the articles of Khomyakov are written about only one thing, -- about the vocation of Russia, all are pervaded by this single idea. In this was his strong side. That A. S. was lazy at writing, undisciplined, that he was not a professional writer, can be inferred from this fact, that his friends had literally to lock him away under key, in order to compel him to write his "Notes on World History", his *Semiramida*. Gogol had noticed, that Khomyakov was writing a large work, and he caught sight of the word "Semiramida" concerning Semiramis in the manuscript and then was wont to say, that Khomyakov was writing his Semiramida. This indeed "Semiramida", comprising three tomes of Khomyakov's "Collected Works", represents his rough note drafts. To read this "Notes on world History" is difficult, but only a remarkable thinker can pen such notes as these. Aleksei Stepanovich began to write prose work only in his early forties, prior to this he wrote only poetry and dramas.

A fascinating thing in Khomyakov is his knight-chivalrant attitude towards the Orthodox Church, his sense of fidelity. Khomyakov had a negative attitude towards Western knightly chivalry, but he himself was a genuine Orthodox knight, one of our but few knights. The knight chivalrant attitude towards the Church is rarely to be met with amidst us, whether amongst the Russian clergy, or in the Russian intelligentsia segment. For Russians there has not taken hold the feeling of a churchly dignity and honour, and all too rapidly Russians are wont to betray the sacred for them, in the name instead of every passing idol and statue. Khomyakov, in the words of Hertsen, "was like the medieval knights, standing guard the temple of the Mother of God, sleeping, in their armour". At whatever the moment day or night he was prepared fully armed to stand in defense of the Orthodox Church. In his attitude towards the Church there was nothing servile, nor wavering, inconstant. He was first of all faithful and steadfast, in him was the churchly solid stone. Khomyakov was born to the light of God religiously readied, churchly and firm, and all his life he bespoke his faith and fidelity. He always was pious, he always was an Orthodox Christian. In him there did not occur any sort of turnabout conversion, nor sort of transformation nor change. He -- was an untypical man for his era, withstanding the universal infatuation with the philosophy of Hegel, and not subordinating his faith to philosophy. His clarity of churchly consciousness accompanied him throughout all his life. All his life he observed the churchly rituals, he fasted, he was not afraid to be laughed at in the eyes of society, instead being indifferent and unconcerned with this. This was a lofty trait of character in Aleksei Stepanovich. He observed all the fasts and rituals, even when he was serving in the horse-guard regiment, and he wore his cap and peasant jacket, when he journeyed off to England. The integral wholeness of his nature for Khomyakov imbued also his religious life, and his life was organic. His religiosity was his lifestyle. He endlessly esteemed the Russian Orthodox mode of life, the whole emotional aspect of this lifestyle, right down to the trifles and details. In him there was no religious agitation, no religious anguish, no religious hunger. This was a religiously satiated man, calm and comfortable. In his type of religiosity the priestly prevailed over the prophetic, already possessing its city rather than seeking the city to come. And in this Khomyakov was profoundly distinct from Dostoevsky, from Vl. Solov'ev, and from us. In him there was not the yearning, there was not the hunger and thirsting. Calmly, firmly, assuredly throughout all his life Khomyakov voiced his Orthodox faith, he never had doubts, he never had desire for something moreso, he never strained his eyes peering off into the mysterious distance. He lived religiously, he was in the Church each day, and he lived each day without any sense of catastrophe, without the fear and terror. He lived an authentic and illumined Orthodox faith, he lived an organic life. The generation following began to live in the future and it was filled with terrified unrest. It would be in vain to seek out within the life of Khomyakov any inward sense of tragedy. He indeed had great grief, when his children died, and he had also a small grief, when there was circulated a decree by the Ministry of Internal Affairs to all the Slavophils, prescribing that their beards must be shaved off. But just read his reknown verse on the death of his children. What a resignation there is in it, the religious surmounting of the shock, the victory over the sense of tragedy. And thus it was in all and everything.

In the unanimous telling of his contemporaries, Khomyakov played a central and guiding role in the Slavophil circle. Khomyakov -- was the acknowledged head of the school, and already in any case its foremost theologian. Another theologically inclined Slavophil, Yurii Samarin, by his own testimony was but a student and follower of Khomyakov. From the correspondence of the members of the Slavophil circle there can clearly be seen the central role of Khomyakov in the question concerning the Church.[1] The other Slavophils sought from Khomyakov the resolution of their religious doubts, their wavering in the question on the Church. And all those who were wavering and doubtful, in their searching found in Khomyakov an unshakable firmness, a rock-solid faith, a solid rock of the

---

[1] Vide N. Koliupanov, "Biography of A. I. Koshelev", Tome II. In the appendice is printed a very interesting transcript of material from the Slavophils, characteristic of their attitude towards the Church and revealing what they were religiously fighting for. Insufficiency of space here precludes me from offering quotations from these transcripts.

ALEKSEI STEPANOVICH KHOMYAKOV

Church. Khomyakov in accord with his nature knew neither waverings nor doubts, since that is the way he was. There were times, when the question about the Church became acute for all the members of the Slavophil circle, acute to the point of loss of sleep, to tears. The comparatively sober and practical Yu. Samarin wept throughout an entire night, since he could not determine his own relationship to the Church. All these Russian people in those days were seduced by the philosophy of Hegel, and with it they considered it necessary to reconcile everything, including their faith. And herein Yu. Samarin arrives at the strange thought, that the fate of the Orthodox Church is dependent upon the fate of the philosophy of Hegel. This thought, very typical for those times, to Khomyakov seemed monstrous, since he was a staunch churchly fellow and had freed himself from the influence of the Hegelian philosophy, which he brilliantly criticised. It was only the spiritual influence of Khomyakov that freed Yu. Samarin from philosophic rationalism and led him to the Church. Under the influence of Khomyakov, Samarin reworked his dissertation, "Theophan Prokopovich and Stefan Yavorsky", and he developed it in accord with the concrete causality of Khomyakov's idea about the relationship of Orthodoxy towards Catholicism and Protestantism. And similar also was the influence of Khomyakov upon Koshelev, upon Aksakov and others. All those that were searching and in doubt got together with Khomyakov, they rode off to him in the countryside, they spoke with him whole days and nights and they left encouraged, and set upon the churchly path. Khomyakov was a very strong and very firm man within the circle. He spoke quite much, and he spoke moreso, than he wrote or did in life. He could argue throughout the entire day and night. And these endless disputes played a positive role in his time, since he contributed quite much to those round about, he did quite much to help matters along. He did far moreso by his word of mouth, than by his writings. He was the spiritual guide of the Slavophil circle and its militant defender from enemies. The theological genius of Khomyakov rendered him the head of the school, the world-outlook of which was predominantly religious. Khomyakov was the first secular theologian in Orthodoxy, the first free theologian. In this was his indubitable significance. The theological strength of Khomyakov flowed from the solidness of his nature, the foundation stone of which was the Church. Without Khomyakov the Slavophil world-outlook would not have received so vivid a churchly hue, it would have remained religiously indistinct and indefinite. Yu. Samarin, the faithful student of Khomyakov, proposed calling him a teacher of the Church. This exaggeration by his student and friend is quite characteristic, and it defines the role of Khomyakov. Even if Khomyakov be not regarded as a teacher of the Church, then still in any case, he was a churchly teacher of the Slavophils. Amongst the Slavophils there was no other man, churchly so steadfast, so faithful.

Khomyakov had vital an interest regarding societal life, the anguish over the ulcers of the Russian societal aspect. But he had no love for politics, he despised political passions. His dislike for politics, his apoliticism -- is a Russian national trait of Khomyakov. In Slavophilism was clearly reflected the non-politicalness of the Russian people. Khomyakov, just like all the Slavophils, saw the vocation of the Russian people to be not in political life, but in an higher life of spirit. The Russian societal aspect for him first of all a matter of lifestyle, of familial relationship. He wrote to A. O. Smirnova: "You know my perpetual deep repugnance at every political question, but now I am being pounced upon and gnawed at by politics. Wherever I go out, wherever I turn, whether in the society of men or of women, everyone is saying the same thing: "What about Lamartine or Ledru-Rollin, and what about the Prussians, and what Poznan?" Simply an obsession! It strikes me as sheer wickedness. If you as a young person, I think, were to go about in peasant coat and indeed the smock, you would be thinking about household and indeed family matters, and not about nonsense, about which you can do nothing, and in this you would be the smarter, and for me the less vexing".[1] And In a letter to Countess Bludova, A. S. says: "For me political questions hold no sort of interest; one thing only is important, and this is about societal questions".[2] How characteristic of Khomyakov, that his organic ideal should be first of all "about domestic households". He sensed the sweetness of existence and he had no sense for the allure of political power. The whole Slavophil teaching was an expression of the conviction, that the Russian people tends to love domestic life and is not fond of state-civil life. This -- is the psychology and philosophy of the landowner manor-houses, warm and cozy nests. Too great a disturbance, unrest, the catastrophic -- all this Aleksei Stepanovich found repulsive, and the only exception he made was

---

[1] A. S. Khomyakov, "Collected Works", Tome VIII, p. 411.

[2] Ibid., p. 391.

for the war. We have seen already, that Khomyakov the youth had a sharply negative attitude towards the Decembrists. Khomyakov as a mature man had likewise a negative attitude towards the revolutions of 1848. And this was not because Khomyakov was a reactionary. On the contrary, he desired progress and he sincerely loved freedom. But he desired a peaceful organic developement from grandfathers to their grandsons, a developement involving lifestyle, family, chiefly moral, without the storminess, without the political cataclysms. This attachment to an organic domestic lifestyle in the generations that followed passed over into, however, into class-partisan avarice, inertia and stagnation. Aleksei Stepanovich himself had a very fine attitude towards the peasants, and he concerned himself incessantly over their welfare. He loved his peasants and sensed his oneness with them. He wrote projects for improving their lot and he took steps towards emancipating the peasants long before the official steps in this direction. With him there was a sense of responsibility for the fate of the peasants. The peasants wept at the grave of Khomyakov and they said, that another suchlike master is not to be found, that he had not wronged even a fly. But Khomyakov had watched over his own interests as well, he was a thrifty man and left his children a large inheritance.

The official powers always looked upon the Slavophils with suspicion, although Slavophilism was the sole suitable ideology of the power, the sole sanctioning idea for autocracy, as something endowed of lofty mission. The absolutist bureaucracy did not however trust any sort of ideas, any sort of creative self-consciousness of free spirit. In the era of Nicholas I even the Slavophils, -- those conservative idealists, were under political suspicion. The Moscow governor-general, Count Zakrevsky, made the grandiose statement to his friend regarding the Petrashevsky matter: "Brother, what one can see is this: from the Moscow Slavs they have found no one in this conspiracy. What does this mean, as regards you? *It means*, all only this, they are indeed clever rascals, leaving no trace to catch". The infamous governor, Count Stroganov, quite disliked Khomyakov, and when the empress expressed a desire to see A. S., he advised against it, saying that Khomyakov was a dangerous man. To which Count Bludov then reckoned it necessary to put forth his defense of the Slavophils, saying: they are not dangerous, since all of them can sit down together on a single couch. A real persecution against Khomyakov began as regards his reknown verse, "Russia", which was considered almost treasonous to the

Nicholas Berdyaev

fatherland. They summoned him into the governor-general, he had to justify himself, and then he was dispatched to Count Bludov. In this poem, written before the Crimean Campaign, Khomyakov calls Russia to an awareness of its sins.

> Thou wast summoned to battle holy,
> Thee Our Lord hath loved,
> Unto Thee did give the power fatal.
> Yet preserveth thou a will evil
> Midst the blind, the foolish, the wild powers.
>
> Rise up, my native land!
> For brethren! God thee doth call
> Crosst the waves of the raging Dunaj --
> Thither, where, the land surrounding,
> Crash currents with roaring din of AEgean waters.
>
> Yet be mindful: be thou the instrument of God
> For earthly edifices be weighty;
> His servants He doth judge severely, --
> But on thee, alas! How many
> The frightful sins hath lain!
>
> In judgements black with black injustice
> And yoke of slavery branded;
> Of godless guile, of lie that rotteth,
> Of indolence deadly and shameful,
> And by every abomination filled!
>
> O, unworthy chosen,
> Thou wast chosen! Wherefore the more quickly hasten
> Thyself to wash with water of repentance,
> That the thundering of redoubled wrath,
> Come not upon thine brow!
>
> With soul prostrated,
> With head, lain into the dust,
> Pray thou with prayer humble,

ALEKSEI STEPANOVICH KHOMYAKOV

Let the wounds of conscience corrupted
By oil of lament be healed!

And stand then, true to the calling,
And rush into the thick of the bloody frays!
Fight for brethren strong the battle,
God's banner hold with firm the handgrip,
Strike with the sword -- that be the sword of God!

Khomyakov had a peculiar attitude towards the Crimean Campaign. He was almost glad at the defeat of Russia in this war, since he saw in this the chastisement for sin and the hope of the rebirth of his rodina, his native land.

Slavophilism was alarming and disturbing to the official powers, since they lacked the ability to control, let alone make sense of this phenomenon. The official powers understood better the liberals and the revolutionaries, and knew how to relate to them, and where it stood to this clear enemy. But the Slavophils adhered to the slogan, "Orthodoxy, Autocracy, Nationality", -- words that were quite familiar and dear to the ruling power, and yet somehow they remained foreign to it, remote, unintelligible. The Slavophils were free and were freedom-loving people, idealists, dreamers, in them was not the fawning subservience so near and dear to the heart of the bureaucracy of Nicholas I. All this was incomprehensible and disturbing for such people, as Count Zakrevsky and his ilk. Conservatism for such could make sense in terms of service and its fawning officiousness, but it remained incomprehensible as to how it could be as a free expression of the people's soul. For indeed, the Slavophils were not only autocraticists, they were also anarchists, and indeed their concept of autocracy reflected a peculiar anarchism. All the Slavophils -- were anti-state, haters of bureaucracy; the tsar for them was a father-figure, and not a formal power, and the social community -- was an organic union freely bonded together by love. All this seemed both incomprehensible, and dangerous. Such people as Khomyakov could themself occupy no place in the state mechanism, they could not serve in it. A.S. loved Nicholas I, but he could not bear the regime of Nicholas. He could only live off by himself in the countryside, in the family circle. And thus it was with all the Slavophils. The Slavophils and the bureaucrats were more foreign to each other, than were the Slavophils and the radicals to each other. The apoliticism of the Slavophils, their anti-statism and love of freedom -- were traits, impossible to be adapted to ends either political or statist. Khomyakov could not have any relationship to the real politics, although he was a very real man. This contradiction is very remarkable, in exposing the alienation of Slavophilism from the historical Russian official powers.

Aleksei Stepanovich died from cholera, far separated from friends at his Ryazan estate, on 23 September 1860. An evil fate pursued the Slavophil philosophy. When Ivan Kireevsky entered into a systematisation of the Slavophil philosophy, he suddenly fell dead from cholera. The same fate later befell Khomyakov, when he decided to continue the work of Kireevsky and entered likewise into a systematisation of the philosophy. The final moments of the life of A.S. -- are a remarkable testimony of the strength of his character and of the firmness of his faith. There have been left notes by a near-by landowner, Leonid Matveevich Muromtsev, concerning the final moments of Khomyakov. When Muromtsev arrived and asked Khomyakov, what was the matter with him, A.S. answered: "Yes, nothing special, though I happen to be dying. I am quite unwell. How terrible! How often I have healed people, but to heal myself I am unable". In the words of Muromtsev, -- "in this voice was neither any shadow of pity nor terror, but rather the deep conviction, that he was not a goner". "I reckon that I lost count repeating, -- reminisces Muromtsev, -- perhaps as many as ten times I besought him to accept my medical help and let me send for a doctor, and consequently, just as many times he answered no, and that amidst all this that he would himself undertake treatment from homeopathic compounds, on the one hand *veratrum* [hellebore], and on the other hand *mercurium*". "About one in the afternoon, seeing that the powers of the sick man were failing him, I suggested he be anointed. He accepted my suggestion with a joyful smile, saying: "I would be very, very glad of it". All the while the Sacrament was being made, he held in his hand a candle, and in a whisper he repeated the prayers and made the Sign of the Cross". After a certain while it seemed to Muromtsev, that A.S. was better, about which he was on the point of informing his wife: "I have a bit of good news. Glory to God, and all the best to you". "Faites vous responsable de cette bonne nouvelle, je n'en prend pas la responsabilité", -- said A.S., almost in a whisper. "Quite correct, and look, how you are getting warm and your eyes sparkle". "*And tomorrow how luminous it will be!*" These were his last words. More clearly than us he saw, that all these

ALEKSEI STEPANOVICH KHOMYAKOV

signs of an apparent recovery were only a final welling-up of life... For several seconds before the end, fully conscious, he firmly signed himself with the Sign of the Cross.[1] Aleksei Stepanovich Khomyakov died well; such as only people die, possessed of a rock-solid faith.

In his final years of life, after the death of his beloved wife, Khomyakov was joyless, and he devoted himself completely to his work. But in the past he had known the happiness of life, he knew personal and family happiness, as but few who do, his life was successful in all regards. He belonged to the sons, and not to the step-sons, of God. In him there was no sort of underhandedness, no sort of wounded egoism and malice. His spirit was strong and bright, captivatingly bright. In the reminiscences of the Westernisers he seems first of all a disputant, a dialectician, eternally jesting and poking fun, but his depths, his holy of holies, is not disclosed. And few there were who understood the unusual aesthetic completeness of this man. Khomyakov was not an aesthete, but his image ought first of all to be considered aesthetically.

*   *   *

A. S. Khomyakov was as though all of a single piece, chopped precisely out of granite. He was extraordinarily an integral whole, organic, manly, faithful, always cheerful. He was solidly of the soil, precisely grown of the ground, in him there was none of that being up in the air as with later generations, of being alienated from the land. He was not at all of the intelligentsia type, in him were neither the bad, nor the good traits of the Russian intelligentsia. In him was the Russian nobility, and together with this the Russian peasant, in him was an intense populism, in the spiritual and lifestyle mode of the people. It ought particularly to be emphasised, that Khomyakov was not an aristocrat in the western and usual sense of this word, in him was to be sensed not the aristocrat of refined manners, but rather a Russian landowner of the national type, grown up from the land. He was a man of lofty culture, but he was not a man over-cultured, in cultural refinement. In the figure of A.S., both as regards the spiritual and the physical, there was something robust, of the earth, organic: in him there was not that aristocratic and artistic refinement,

---

[1] A. S. Khomyakov, "Collected Works", Tome VIII, appendix, p. 50-52.

which passes over into fantasy. This was a realistic figure, his vital nourishment was not broken off, the connection with his vital taproots was not lost. Our nobility of the Slavophil type was always very strangely distinct from the nobility of the Western type. And the horseguard regimental Khomyakov, in observing all the fasts and rituals of the Orthodox Church, was very distinct from the ordinary type of the horseguard officer, typically faithful only to the ritual of drinking French champagne. A. S. Khomyakov grew out of the bosom of his native land just as organically, as grows a tree. And he wanted, that all Russia should grow with the very same organic growth, and he believed in this. He loved only all, that which showed of itself the same suchlike growth. Everything mechanical was for him alien and hateful. But the tree of Russian life grew not in accord with the Slavophil demands, and in this was the objective tragedy of Slavophilism. The Slavophils themself still little sensed this tragedy, and therefor in them was much the feeling that all was fine and well. Khomyakov calmly believed, that he was organically growing together with an organic growth of the tree of Russian life. In him there was little of the prophetic, there was not the presentiment, there was not the terror before the face of the unknown future. The absence of the prophetic spirit -- was a characteristic trait of the whole of Slavophilism. The propheticism of the Slavophils was something focused backwards, oriented towards ancient Rus', and not forwards, not oriented towards the City to Come. In the person of Khomyakov there was so little of the sense of tragedy, of catastrophe, almost no such process. He appeared to the world prepared, armed and armoured. In this was his strength, but all the same in this was his limitedness. Under him the earth did not burn, the soil did not quake. He grew up on the soil of a thousand year serfdom and as it were became encumbered, lost the capacity for flight. In Khomyakov's ideas, the earthly element too much prevails over the aerial element, with him there was much depth, but little striving upwards and afar. Mystical presentiments frequently were replaced by his moralism.

In Khomyakov, just like in all our Slavophils, just as in all the people of the decades of the 1830's and 1840's, there was no acute terror of the end, there were no apocalyptic presentiments, there were no eschatological themes. These people were genuinely alive, they prophesied about the past, they believed in the organic growth of the future. The national messianism of Khomyakov was not apocalyptic, it did not include within it any prophecy about the finish of history. I Khomyakov there was too much a lifestyle cheeriness, which passed over into a cheeriness regarding history. This lifestyle cheeriness in a fatal manner went by the wayside for the following generations, which discerned all less and less the capacity to be genuinely alive, in directing their gaze towards the frightful future. In the spiritual composition of such people as Khomyakov there is no anticipation of world catastrophes. In Khomyakov there is a series of verses, in which he expressed his faith in Russia, his national messianism. These verses are filled with a military vigour, in them there is no trembling terror afront the chastisings of God's judgement. How infinitely distinct these verses are from the verses of Vl. Solov'ev, from his "PanMongolism", so full of an apocalyptic terror. In Khomyakov there are verses of repentance, as for example, this remarkable verse:

>Do not say: "That was the past,
>T'was the old days, t'was the sins of the fathers;
>And our young tribe
>Knoweth not these old sins".
>No, this sin -- tis eternally with ye,
>In your veins and in your blood,
>Tis grown amidst your hearts,
>Within hearts, deadened to love.
>..........................
>Pray, repent, to heaven afar!
>For all the sins of bygone times,
>For your Cain-like bickerings,
>While still diapered infants;
>For all the tears of that terrible time,
>When, with hostile rapture,
>Ye called forth foreign allies
>To the ruin of the Russian side.
>For slavery to an age old captivity,
>For faintness of heart afront the sword of Lithuania,
>For Novgorod, betrayed,
>For duplicious Moscow;
>For the shame and sorrow of the holy tsaritsa,
>For decreed depravity,
>For the sin of saintly tsar-murder,
>For the laying waste of Novgorod;

Nicholas Berdyaev

For the slander against Godunov,
For the death and disgrace of his children,
For Tushino, for Lyapunov,
For the intoxication of frenzied passions;
For blindness, for malevolence,
For minds asleep, for hearts frozen,
For the arrogance of dark ignorance,
For a people held captive, and finally,
For this, and that, fully fatigued,
In anguish with blind doubtings,
Ye happen to implore healings
Not of That One, in Whose indeed Hand there be
Both sparkle of victories, and happiness of world,
And the fire of love, and light of minds, --
But rather of the soulless idol,
Of dead and blind gods!
And, besotted with the stench of pride,
Tipsy with earthly wisdom,
Ye have foresworn from all things sacred,
From the heart of natal the side!
For all, for every suffering,
For every reprehensible law,
For the dark deeds of the fathers,
For all the woes across the native land, --
Before the God of goodness and might,
Pray ye, with wailing and weeping,
That He forgive, that He might forgive!

Or then too the reknown verse, "Russia". But Khomyakov steadfastly believed in the might of Russia, in its invincibility. The eventual fate of Russia has not justified the faith of Khomyakov. He has proven to be a poor prophet, he did not foresee those blows, which Russia was to suffer.

In the basic mindset of Khomyakov and all the Slavophils there is absent any connection of a prophetic spirit, of an apocalyptic awareness, of presentiment of things eschatological. Christians do not have their own city, they seek for the City to Come. But Khomyakov, and together with him all the Slavophils, said: we have our own city, we have grown up organically with our own city and nothing has the power to tear us away from it. This city -- is ancient Rus', our land, our native land rodina, and it is the city of Christ, Holy Rus'. The city of the Slavophils -- is Holy Rus' and the cozyness of manor-houses, and fields of grain, and family, and patriarchal relationships. But this city -- is half pagan, this is not the city of Christ, this is not that city, for which Christians seek. The City of Christ has never and nowhere ever yet existed in history, the City of Christ is still forward, in the end-times. The Slavophils confused the nationally innate lifestyle, they confused the Russian pagan city with the City of Christ, the City to Come. They saw in Rus' almost that it was the onset of the thousand year reign of Christ, almost like chiliasm. And the veil of things future was hidden for them. Khomyakov was not at all an ascetic, he affirmed the flesh of history, he loved this flesh, but it was like a chiliasm in reverse, and not forwards. Earthquakes were needful, so that an apocalyptic consciousness might be begotten. And we live now in an era of earthquakes. But Khomyakov did not yet know the earthquakes, he did not foresee them, the ground under him was not yet shaken.

God deliver us from an ignoble attitude towards our fatherland, towards our ancestors. Howsoever great our difference from Khomyakov may be, still he belongs entirely so to our fathers, even perhaps, to our grandfathers. We have received from him an inheritance and we ought to esteem it. But for us there is no turning back to the Slavophil cozyness, to the lifestyle of the seigneurial manor-house. Our manor-houses are disposed of, and we have been torn away from any living bonds with the soil. But we are alive with a feeling for the beauty of these manor-houses and the nobility of some of the aspects, connected with them. The Slavophils were Russian nobility, with many of the deficiencies of that type. But with the nobility was connected also an aspect of chivalrant knightly feelings, with fidelity to the legacies of forefathers, fidelity to the sanctities of the Church. In Khomyakov there was a rock-solid faith, and in this he is dear to us. Our generation has need of his steadfastness and fidelity. The religious experience and the religious consciousness of Khomyakov were matters of reticence, were limits beyond which he did not go, and while there was much that he neither saw nor sensed, his fidelity to the sacred was unshakable. Christianity was for him first of all the sacerdotal, but his relationship to the sacerdotal was infinitely free, in him there was nothing servile. And everything prophetic, transcending the bounds of Khomyakov's consciousness, ought as with Khomyakov to be truly sacerdotal and sacred. Our generation is distinct from the generation of the Slavophils first of all by a cultus of creativity, by creative bursts of impulse. Yet creative bursts of impulse can also be godless, but the path itself of a religious creativity is the sole path for a new mankind. However fine, however splendid a type there was with Khomyakov, in its ultimate preservation it degenerates beyond recognition. Those, who at present reckon themselves such, as was Khomyakov, bear no resemblance to Khomyakov. For everything there is a time and a season, and everything is fine in its own time. A second such Khomyakov there can never yet be. There can never again be repeated the beauty of the old court nobility's manor-houses, but in this beauty, as in everything beautiful, there is something eternal, something deathless. The present-day style transforms these courtly manor-houses into new monstrosities, and only aesthetically can we call to mind their former beauty. And our fidelity to Khomyakov, just as to the fatherland, ought to be as such a source of creative developement, and not stagnation. Bad be that son, who increases not the wealth of his father, who goes forward no farther than his father. To return to Slavophilism, to its truth, cannot be for us calm a matter; in this return there is a creative unrest and dynamic. But to return to the figure of Khomyakov we necessarily must.

Chapter III

Khomyakov as Theologian, His Teachings about the Church

Khomyakov was first of all -- a remarkable theologian, the first free Russian theologian. In Eastern Orthodox theology, after the time of ancient teachers of the Church [i.e. the "Patristic Period"], one of the foremost places belongs to him. Yu. Samarin, his faithful student, says in his preface to the collected theological works of Khomyakov: "In those former times, whoever rendered to the world suchlike a service, as Khomyakov rendered it, to whom it was given by a logical explanation of this or some other side of churchly teaching to gain for the Church a decisive victory over this or that error, these they were wont to term as teachers of the Church".[1] In what does Samarin see as a source of the power of Khomyakov's theology? "Khomyakov in himself represented for us an original, almost unprecedented manifestation of *a fullest freedom within the religious consciousness*". "*Khomyakov lived in the Church*", "Khomyakov not only *valued* faith, but together with this he sustained a doubtless conviction in its *soundness*. Therefore he had no fear for it, and since he had no fear for it, he also always looked upon everything with the eyes wide open, he never closed his eyes to something, he never brushed aside something nor squinted at some perception. Totally free, i.e. entirely forthright in his convictions, he demanded that indeed selfsame freedom, as selfsame a right to be forthright also for others". "He valued his faith as *truth*, and not as a mere matter of convenience for him, as though it were apart from and independent of its truthfulness". Expanding on this aspect of Khomyakov's perception of the Church and teaching about the Church, Samarin expressed it thus: "I might *avow, be subject and humble myself* -- yet consequently still, I *might not believe*. The Church presupposes only

---

[1] Vide Yu. Samarin, "Preface to the 1st Edition of the Theological Collected Works of Khomyakov". In Tome II of the Khomyakov collection, or in the Collected Works of Yu. Samarin -- Tome VI.

faith, it evokes in the soul of man and permits of nothing less; in other words, it accepts into its bosom only the *free*. Whoever offers it a servile acceptance, not believing in it, that one is not in the Church and not of the Church". "The Church is not a matter of doctrine merely, is not a system and is not an institution. *The Church* is a living organism, an organism of truth and love, or more precisely: *it is truth and love as an organism*". In the opinion of Samarin, "Khomyakov was the first to have looked at Latinism and Protestantism *from the perspective of the Church*, which is to say, *from above*; wherefore also he was able to *delimitingly define* them". The remarks of Yu. Samarin are, perhaps, somewhat exaggerated, but in them there is much truth. The great significance of Khomyakov was in this, that he was *free* in his Orthodoxy, he freely sensed himself within the Church, and he freely defended the Church. In him there was no sort of scholasticism, there was no conditionally vested interest in his relation to the Church. In his theological work there were also no traces of the seminary mindset. There was nothing of the official, of the state's vested interests, in Khomyakov's theology. A veritable billowing stream of fresh air along with him entered into Orthodox religious thought. Khomyakov was the first secular religious thinker within Orthodoxy, he opened up the path of free religious philosophy, a path, choked with the clutter of the schoolish-scholastic sort of theology. He was the first to have transcended the schoolish-scholastic sort of theology. He showed by his example, that the gift of teaching does not exclusively belong to the clerical hierarchy, that instead it belongs to each member of the Church. Concerning Metropolitan Makarii, the author of the celebrated "Dogmatic Theology", which even up to the present time retains its seminary credentials, Khomyakov spoke thus: ""Makarii stank as a scholastic... I might even call him charmingly-stupid, if he had not written on such a great and important subject... It would be a shameful, if foreigners were to accept such pitiful drivel as the expression of our Orthodox theology, even in its present modern condition".[1] The Russian school-theology, scholastic in spirit, in its essence was not in the genuine sense of the word Orthodox, it did not express the religious experience of the Orthodox East as an unique path, it was not from experience, not from life. This theology slavishly followed foreign models and trended now towards Catholicism, now towards Protestantism. Khomyakov however was the first Russian *Orthodox*

---

[1] A. s. Khomyakov, "Collected Works", Tome VIII, p. 189.

theologian, standing on his own as a thinker, standing on his own in regard to Western thought. Within the theology of Khomyakov was expressed the experience of the Russian people, the indeed living experience of the Orthodox East, and not merely a schoolish formalism, always moribund. Khomyakov was more Orthodox in his theology, than many of our hierarchs and professors of the Spiritual Academies, he was more Russian. The dogmatics of Metropolitan Makarii seemed to Khomyakov but a revision of Catholic scholasticism. He indeed -- was an initiator of Russian theology.

The fate of the theological works of Khomyakov is very noteworthy. The most remarkable of Russian theologians could not even get his theological works published in Russia in his native language; the religious censor did not permit its printing. And the theological works of Khomyakov appeared, it occurred beyond the borders of Russia, in the French language. Such a monstrously absurd fact was possible only in Russia. The theological activity of Khomyakov, his militant defense of the Orthodox Church, seemed something hopelessly questionable, a matter for suspicion. They were unable to understand his freedom. Khomyakov wrote to Ivan Aksakov: "I permit myself the wherewithal not to concur in many an instance *with the so-called opinion* of the Church".[1] The "*so-called opinion* of the Church" seemed to him non-churchly, he saw in it only a partial theological view, whether of this or some other segment of the hierarchs. The churchly officials could not tolerate such a love of freedom. The professors of the Spiritual Academies, the official and the professional theologians, reacted very spitefully against Khomyakov's theologising, they saw in this an intrusion into an area monopolised by them exclusively. How dare some mere private man, an officer and landowner, a private literateur, dare to teach about the Church! Granted his ideas be very Orthodox, but an undertaking so very risky. Yet all the same, Khomyakov began a new era in the history of Russian theological awareness and in the final end he had also an influence upon the official theology. But this permeation and soaking-through of Khomyakov's ideas happened only slowly. Even the response of Nicholas I did not save him from the official hostility. V. D. Olsuf'ev writes Khomyakov on behalf of the empress, Maria Aleksandrovna: "Her Majesty the Sovereign Empress, having learned, that there was written a continuation of your collected work,

---

[1] A. S. Khomyakov, "Collected Works", Tome VIII, p. 356.

"Quelques mots etc.", wishes to peruse it... It has pleased her to direct me to report to you, that His late Majesty the Emperor with pleasure did read the aforementioned collection and was pleased with it".[1] His Highness the Emperor was pleased enough, but all the same they decided against its printing in Russia. The actual words of the Sovereign concerning Khomyakov are transcribed: "Dans ce qu'il dit de l'Eglise il est très liberal; mais dans ce qu'il dit de ses rapports avec l'autorité temporelle, il a parfaitement raison et je suis de son avis" ["In what he says of the Church he is very liberal; but in what he says of his relations with the temporal authority, he is perfectly right and I agree with him"]. The theological collection of Khomyakov's works was later translated into the Russian language by Yu. Samarin and Gilyarov-Platonov. Such was the fate of the Slavophil theology.

Khomyakov will be eternally remembered first of all for his setting of the problem of the Church and for his attempt to discern the essence of the Church, from within, and not from the outside. He first of all did not believe in the possibility to formulate a definitive concept of the Church. The essence of the Church is something inexpressible, not containable in any sort of formula, not reducible to any sort of formal definition, just as with every living organism. The Church is first of all -- a living organism, an unity of love, an unutterable freedom first of all, the truth of faith, not reducible to rationalisation. From the outside of the Church, it is neither knowable nor definable, it is grasped only by whomever is within it, whoever manifests themself as a living member of it. Scholastic theology has also sinned in this, in that it attempted rationally to formulate the essence of the Church, i.e. it transformed the Church from a mystery, knowable only to the believing, into something reduced to the cognition of objective reason. Khomyakov was an implacable foe against that intellectualism within theology, and against which at present also rise up LeRoy [Le Roy, Le Roi, Edouard, 1870-1954] and other Catholic modernists. This intellectualism always was more foreign to the spirit of Orthodoxy, than it was to the spirit of Catholicism. There was a far greater tendency towards intellectual scholasticism with Vl. Solov'ev. Khomyakov in contrast in his attitude towards the Church and dogmatics was moreso a voluntarist than an intellectualist, he inclines to that which at present the Catholic modernists term moral dogmatism. For him the sole source of

---

[1] A. S. Khomyakov, "Collected Works", Tome II, p. 90.

religious cognition and the sole guarantee of religious truth was love. And he ascribed significance to the dogmatic distinctions of Catholicism from Orthodoxy only insofar that within them was an infringement of love. The affirmation of love as a category of cognition comprises the core of Khomyakov's theology. He affirms first of all the living organism of the Church against every moribund mechanical aspect, against every rationalisation of it. The contemporary Catholic modernists, and indeed the Protestant modernists, themself often helplessly struggling against churchly dogmatic rationalism and intellectualism, -- could learn much from Khomyakov. In him the intellectualism and rationalism of theological scholasticism is surmounted not by some personal effort, but by the truth of the Orthodox Church, it is surmounted in a churchly manner. Khomyakov was first of all a man of the Church and he taught churchly about the Church. The modernists too often posit an opposition between freedom and the Church, and by the free effort of the person they want to set right the churchly deficiencies. Khomyakov however believed invariably, that only within the Church is freedom, that the Church also is freedom, and therefore a free theologising was for him a churchly theologising. Freedom for him is realised in sobornost' as communality, and not in individualism. In Khomyakov there was an infinitely free sense of the Church he freely sensed himself as within the Church namely, and not from the outside the Church. The Church was for him on the order of freedom. It seemed folly to him for any effort to seek for freedom outside the Church, to seek for a freedom from the Church, to see the source of freedom not in churchly sobornost' as community, but rather in the isolated person. If Khomyakov was by his genius successful in revealing the organic essence of the Church, then it is only because that he was nourished in the experience of Eastern Orthodoxy, in which there was no sort of intellectualism, no sort of external despotism. This could not be the work of an individual thinker. Even the biased Vl. Solov'ev acknowledges the tremendous significance of Khomyakov in the actual positing of the question concerning the Church. He was compelled to admit, that prior to the Slavophils in the history of Christian thought it was almost impossible to meet with an organic, and inward understanding of the Church.

  Khomyakov reveals his positive teaching about the Church in the form of polemics against the Western faith-confessions. And this negative polemical form has left its particular imprint upon all his theologising. Only in his catechetical essay, "The Church is One", amidst all of its twenty-six pages, is expounded in a positive form; in it, the Orthodox teaching of faith is set forth without a direct criticism of Catholicism and Protestantism. All the remaining theological works of Khomyakov bear a critical polemic character. His largest theological work was in the form of letters to Palmer, whom he attempted to convert to Orthodoxy. This critico-polemic form of an attack on Western faith-confessions, predominantly upon Catholicism, facilitated the defense of Orthodoxy for Khomyakov. To criticise Catholicism was not difficult; here for a Russian it was almost that it was movement upon a line of least resistance. True, Khomyakov does this with an especial acuteness and depth, and in this he sets forth a series of new arguments against Catholicism. But he is prone to find that almost all the singular human defects are there in the Western faith-confessions, while he finds hardly any defects in our Eastern Orthodox faith-confession. It is hardly just to imagine that everything of God relates to Orthodoxy, whereas all the human defects -- relate to Catholicism. There is that which is of God in Catholicism, and there is in Orthodoxy also the humanly deficient. Vl. Solov'ev was correct, when he reproached Khomyakov for this, that he constantly has in view an Orthodoxy -- in ideal a form, whereas the Catholicism -- is in real a form; amidst which in the ideal everything is pure, whereas in the real everything seems tarnished. The historical defects of Catholicism are too well-known, the human sin is too well visible in the historical judgements upon Catholicism. But indeed there is no little of this sin also in the historical judgements upon Orthodoxy. The unshakable sanctity of the Church is nowise affected by this, and this is this sanctity both in Orthodoxy, and in Catholicism. His dislike for Catholicism made Khomyakov biased favourably towards Protestantism. This inclination to side with Protestantism can be found in all the Slavophils. And this is understandable. The disdain for Catholicism, the reaction against Catholicism, assumes in fateful a manner the guise of Protestantism. This disdain for Catholicism with a tinge of Protestantism distorts the Orthodox position of Khomyakov. It would indeed be monstrous to assert, that the basic feature of Orthodoxy -- rests solely in a disdain for Catholicism. The entire Orthodox veracity of Khomyakov's theology is however not bound up with his aversion towards Catholicism, it remains in force even amidst otherwise different an attitude towards Catholicism. In Khomyakov's critique of Catholicism there is much truth, but there can thus be also a like critique of Orthodoxy, leaving untouched the unshakable sanctity of the Church, both Orthodox and Catholic.

ALEKSEI STEPANOVICH KHOMYAKOV

Khomyakov teaches about the sacred essence of the Church transcending any faith-confession aspect, he teaches this boldly and freely. And in this is his immortal merit.

I shall offer a number of citations by way of characterising Khomyakov's attitude towards the Church. His remarkable ideas are best of all expounded through his own particular wording. "Our law is not a law of slavery or for hire, toiling for repayment, but is rather the law of filial sonship and free a love".[1] "No sort of the head of the Church do we acknowledge. Christ is its head, and any other it knows not".[2] "But the Apostles allowed for a free investigation, they even imputed it an obligation; but the holy Fathers also by free inquiry defended the truths of the faith... Every belief, every meaningful sort of faith is an act of freedom and invariably issues from a preliminary free inquiry".[3] "The Church is not authority, just as God is not authority, as Christ is not authority; since authority is something external and on the outside for us. It is not authority, I say, but rather the Truth and the Life of the Christian, his inner Life".[4] "Whosoever doth seek outside of hope and faith for some other sorts of guarantee for the spirit of love, that one is already a rationalist".[5] Together with the Eastern Patriarchs, in responding to the Circular Missive of Pius IX, Khomyakov thought, that "infallibility resides solely in the *universality* of the Church, united in mutual love, and that the inalterability of dogma, equally just as with the purity of rite, is entrusted for guarding not only to the hierarchy, but to all the people of the Church, who are and who comprise the Body of Christ".[6] "The Church knows brotherhood, but it does not know subjection".[7] "The unity of the Church was free; more

---

[1] A. S. Khomyakov, "Collected Works", Tome II, p. 21.

[2] Ibid., p. 34.

[3] Ibid., p. 43.

[4] Ibid., p. 54.

[5] Ibid., p. 59.

[6] Ibid., p. 60.

[7] Ibid., p. 69.

precisely, the oneness was a freedom itself in an harmonious expression of its inward agreement. When this living unity was repudiated, churchly freedom had to be sacrificed for the attainment of an unity of the artificial and the volitional, outward signs or tokens had to be substituted in place of the spiritual feel for truth".[1] "We confess the Church to be one and free".[2] "The cognition of Divine truths obtains by the mutual love of Christians and possesses no other safeguard, besides this love".[3] "The clergy in the *Christian* actuality is invariably a free clergy".[4] "Christianity itself is nothing other, than freedom in Christ... I assert that the Church is more free, than do the Protestants: since Protestantism avows in Holy Scripture an infallible authority which at the same time is *external* to man, whereas the Church in the Scriptures avows its own particular witness and looks upon it as upon an inward fact of its own particular life. And thus, it would be extremely incorrect to think, that the Church demands a compulsory oneness or a compulsory obedience; on the contrary, it loathes both the one and the other: since *in matters of faith a compulsory oneness is a lie, and a compulsory obedience is death*".[5] "The mystery of moral freedom in Christ and the unification of the Saviour with the reason-endowed creature can be in a worthy manner revealed only in the freedom of human reason and in the oneness of mutual love".[6] "The mystery of Christ, with the creature being saved, is a mystery of oneness and of human freedom in the incarnated Word. The cognition of this mystery was entrusted to the unity of believers and their freedom, since the law of Christ is freedom...Christ was *visible* -- this would be on the order of a truth binding and irrefutable, but it pleased God, that the truth should have transpired *freely*. Christ was visibly seen -- this would have been on the order of an external and outward truth; but it pleased God, that it should become for us inward,

---

[1] A. S. Khomyakov, "Collected Works", Tome II, p. 72.

[2] Ibid., p. 112.

[3] Ibid., p. 157.

[4] Ibid., p. 181.

[5] Ibid., p. 192.

[6] Ibid., p. 219.

through the grace of the Son, in sending down the Spirit of God. Such is the meaning of Pentecost. Hence truth ought to be for us ourself in the depths of our conscience. There is no sort of visible sign that limits our freedom, nor that should provide us a measure for our self-determinations against our will".[1] "No sort of token, no sort of sign limits the freedom of the Christian conscience: the Lord Himself teaches us this".[2] "We would be unworthy of the comprehension of truth, if we did not possess freedom".[3] "The oneness (of the Church) is nothing other, than the concurrence of the freedom of persons".[4] "The entire history of the Church is the history of *human freedom enlightened by grace*, in the witnessing concerning Divine Truth".[5] "Freedom and oneness -- such are the two powers, by which was worthily entrusted the mystery of human freedom in Christ".[6] "Neither the hierarchical might, nor the significance of the clergy as such can serve as a guarantee for truth; the knowledge of truth is bestown only by mutual love".[7] "It would be better, if amongst us there were rather less of the official, the political religion, and if the government could be persuaded of this, that Christian truth is not needful of a constant protector, and that immediate attention over it tends to weaken, rather than strengthen it. The spreading of intellectual freedom could help much towards doing away with the countless schisms of the worst sort".[8] "As members of the Church, we -- are bearers of its majesty and dignity, we -- within the whole world gone astray are the sole preservers of the truth of Christ. Keeping silent, while we were bound to proclaim the voice of God,

---

[1] A. S. Khomyakov, "Collected Works", Tome II, p. 230.

[2] Ibid., p. 231.

[3] Ibid., p. 232.

[4] Ibid., p. 235.

[5] Ibid., p. 243.

[6] Ibid., p. 244.

[7] Ibid., p. 363.

[8] Ibid., p. 364.

we accept upon ourself the judgement of being cowardly and inattentive servants of That One, Who suffered abuse and death in His service to all mankind; but we would be worse than cowards, we would become betrayers, if we gave thought to reply on our own ability in the preaching of truth and if, having lost faith in the Divine power of the Church, we began to seek the assist of deficiencies and dishonesty. Howsoever high a man might stand on the social ladder, be he our leader or ruler, if he be not of the Church, then in the area of faith he can be only our student, but by no means the equal to us, and not our co-toiler in the matter of preaching. He can in this instance render us only one service -- to be converted".[1] "The orators, the wise men, the examiners of the law of the Lord and the preachers of His teaching spoke often about *the law* of love, but never did they speak about *the power* of love. The people heard the preaching about love as about *a duty*; but they forgot about love as a Divine *gift, by which there is secured for love the knowledge of absolute truth*. What is not known by the wisdom of the West, is taught it by the folly of the East".[2] How amazing this thought concerning the gift of love, as securing the knowledge of truth! "To us is given to see in the Scriptures not dead letters, not some object external for us nor a churchly-official document, but rather the witness and the word of all the Church, and moreover, it is our own particular word, inasmuch as we are of the Church. The Scriptural writing is ours, and therefore this cannot be taken away from us. The history of the New Testament is our history; the stream of Jordan has rendered us in Baptism co-participants in the death of the Lord; by bodily Communion, we have become co-united with Christ in the Eucharist of the Last Supper; for us at His feet, and worn down over the expanse of the ages, Christ God the hospitable Master, hath poured forth water; upon our heads on the day of Pentecost in the sacramental-mystery of myrh-anointing Chrismation hath descended the Holy Spirit of God, so that the greatness of our love sanctified by freedom should serve God more fully, than the servility under ancient Israel was able to do".[3] Suchlike were the lofty concepts of Khomyakov concerning the people of the Church.[1]

---

[1] A. S. Khomyakov, "Collected Works", Tome II, p. 86.

[2] Ibid., p. 108.

[3] Ibid., p, 151.

ALEKSEI STEPANOVICH KHOMYAKOV

It would be difficult to find more free an awareness of the Church. There is nothing compulsory with Khomyakov. In his attitude towards the Church there is nothing that comes from the outside, everything -- is from within. The Life of the Church is for him also life in freedom. The Church -- is not an institution and it is not authority. Within the Church is nothing of the juridical, there is not any sort of rationalisation. According to Khomyakov, where there is an authentic love of Christ, freedom in Christ, oneness in Christ, there is also the Church. No formal signs delimit the essence of the Church. Even the OEcumenical Councils are therefore genuinely ecumenical and therefore authoritative, in that they are freely and with love sanctioned as such by the people of the Church. The free Sobornost' of a community of love -- herein is where there is the true churchy organism. A very bold conception of the Church, but one which could well frighten the official theologians. This conception is perhaps foreign to theological scholasticism, but it is quite near to the spirit of Sacred Tradition and Sacred Scripture. Khomyakov ascribes a special significance to Sacred Tradition, since that within it particularly he sees the spirit of Sobornost'. Holy Scripture for him is but an inward fact of churchly life, i.e. since that it is grounded upon Sacred Tradition. Khomyakov saw a confirmation of his understanding of the churchly spirit of Orthodoxy reflected in the "Circular Missive of the Orthodox Church", in its reply to Pius IX.

Khomyakov's definitions and formulae are in truth ecumenical, and universal. With his teaching on the Church, every free son of Christ's Church has to be in agreement, and only the slaves would want to rise up against it. But Khomyakov spoiled his efforts through his apparent bias. He taught about the Church in polemical a manner, he defended Orthodoxy by means of an attack upon the Western faith-confessions. And he came out suggesting, that everything sacred within the Church of Christ -- freedom, love, organicity, oneness, -- all these are lodged only within Eastern Orthodoxy, whereas in the Western Catholicism there is none of this, only deviation and sin. An insufficiency of love towards the Western Christian world -- is indisputably a failing in Khomyakov. He all the while

---

[1] In LeRoy's book, "Dogme et critique", there can be found a tendency towards an orthodoxly Catholic conception of the Church akin to the concepts of Khomyakov.

held to the view, that in Eastern Orthodoxy, in the local Russian Church there were no sort of historical downturns nor human sins. Faced with the impious West, everything was just fine and good in the Russian and the Greek Church, everything in it was Divine, with the human subordinated to the Divine. His disdain towards Catholicism was an hindrance for Khomyakov, as it was also for all the Slavophils in following him, and it led to an avowed preference for Protestantism over Catholicism. And in such an attitude towards Catholicism was rooted a blunder of the Slavophils.

    I am least of all inclined to deny the great and mystical primacy of Orthodoxy, in having spotlessly preserved the truth of Christ. But the mystical essence of the Church, the oneness in love and freedom is also there within Catholicism. In the Catholic Church there are celebrated genuine sacraments, the Apostolic Succession remains unbroken, Holy Tradition is preserved, and there exists a mystical Community of the Living and the Dead. One mustneeds distinguish the Catholic Christian world from papism, with its tendencies, and from the sins of the hierarchy. These tendencies in Catholicism -- are however all relative trends, and not absolute. Khomyakov quite misconstrued Catholicism and the whole of Western religious thought with his accusations of rationalism, whilst he himself was not entirely free from rationalism. And in him at times there is to be sensed a Protestant-like moralist tendency; this tendency impairs his Orthodox theologising. Khomyakov did not at all know, he did not understand nor did he appreciate Western mysticism, both as a mystical aspect that is Catholic, and a mysticism that is free. He is all the while focusing his view exclusively on the official Catholic theology while he little senses the mystical life of Catholicism, the mysticism of the Catholic saints, of the Catholic religious experience. It would indeed be impossible to understand Orthodoxy based merely upon the official theology, and it is necessary rather to penetrate into the intimate religious life of the people, into the Eastern asceticism, the mysticism of the Orthodox saints. The same also has to be said concerning Catholicism. Catholicism is not exclusively its scholastic theology and papism. In Catholicism there is its own deep and mysteried life, its own mystical trembling, its own sanctity. Khomyakov did not want to see this. Instead, he identified Catholicism too exclusively with the school-rote dogmatic theology and canonical rules, with papal politics, with moral Jesuitism. This essential error of Khomyakov and the other Slavophils is bound up in this, that their religious consciousness failed to dig down to the primary mystical foundations. Khomyakov deals little with religious mysticism; he says almost nothing about Catholic and Protestant mysticism; he does not know Jacob Boehme. It would be a fatal mistake to identify the whole of Catholicism with rationalism and juridical formalism, whilst denying in the West any aspect of mysticism.

In the chapter concerning Khomyakov's philosophy of history, I dwell in detail on a basic aspect of his world-view, the division of religion into the Kushite and the Iranian. In the Kushite he sees a religion grounded upon necessity, of nature, of magic; in the Iranian -- a religion of freedom, a religion of the freely creative spirit. Western Catholicism is thus -- in the legacy of the Kushite spirit; while Eastern Orthodoxy -- of the Iranian spirit. Hence Catholicism is infected with an ugly magic taint, and by Roman juridical formalism and rationalism. Khomyakov fails to see freedom within Catholicism. Catholicism for him is not a spiritual religion. This is, as it were -- a natural and magic-based religion enclosed within Christian an attire. The Western world has essentially not accepted Christianity, in it lives on the spirit of Rome, the Kushite spirit. Even the sacraments within Catholicism Khomyakov views as magic an aspect, almost a sorcery. The Western world is weighed down with its pre-Christian, pagan cultural past. In the Russian people however there was a virginally untouched soil, the Russian people accepted their first culture in Christian a form. And therefore it is pre-eminently a Christian people. The deep division of the Orthodox East from the Catholic West for Khomyakov is seen first of all to be in the moral sphere. Dogmatic differences, in the opinion of Khomyakov, are of secondary and derivative a significance. Eastern Orthodoxy, which in the Russian people has found its most pure expression, was faithful to Christian morality, to Christian love. The West betrayed Christian love, it deviated off from the Eastern Christian world, and apart from it introduced new dogmas, and convened councils, which it passed off as ecumenically universal. The insertion of the filioque clause into the Symbol/Creed of faith was therefore a bad thing, since it was done without the mutual love of the entire Christian world. Herein was expressed the of old self-affirmation of the West, its pride, its contempt towards the East as towards an inferiour. In these thoughts of Khomyakov there is much truth. A lack of love seems characteristic of the Western Catholic world. But is the Eastern Christian world so without blame? Is there sufficient love in it for the Western

Christian world? And first of all, Khomyakov himself displays a lack of love. This is a double-edged sin, the blame for which ought to be shared. The responsibility rests both upon the Western Catholics, and upon the Eastern Orthodox. This -- is a sin which is human, of human hostility, of human self-affirmation, of human pride. The Church as the Body of Christ, the Church Catholic and Orthodox is not reflected herein in all this. For the Church there exists neither West, nor East, to it are applicable no sort of geographic categories. With us there is less catholicity, less universality, than with the Catholics. With then there is less orthodoxy, less fidelity, than with the Orthodox. But in an exclusive affirmation of self and one's own there is something ugly, humanly ugly, something not connected with the Divine sanctity of the Church. The image of Christ and the truth concerning Him is preserved both in Orthodoxy, and in Catholicism, and both there and here are made the sacraments, through which we are in communion with Christ. This -- is the chief thing, all else, the human, the empirical, pales before the sanctity of the Church.

Khomyakov, just as with all the Slavophils, reacted negatively towards our Synodal churchly governance; he did not see a genuine Sobornost' within the structure of this Russian Church, he saw rather a degeneration of the Church under the state, a bureaucratisation of the Church. But in the face of the West he gave the appearance, that in the East everything was just fine. He constantly feels some sort of awkwardness for the problems of the Russian Church. He well understands, that the actual reality does not correspond to the ideal concept. But the sacredness of the Orthodox Church has been shaken no little by the defects of the Russian reality, by human sins, and these sins ought not to be veiled over in a defense of Orthodoxy. Khomyakov was indeed a churchly radical, apprehensive of both churchly might and state might. For him the proper subject of the Church was the Church's people. The Sobornost'-communality of the Church, a fundamental idea within all the entirety of Slavophilism, and in which the Slavophils considered as the essence of Orthodoxy, did not include within it an acknowledgement of matters formal and rationalistic; -- in Sobornost' there is nothing of the juridical, nothing suggestive of state power, nothing of the external and compulsory. Although Khomyakov himself would not have loved to employ this word, but the Sobornost' of the Church -- is mystical, on the order of that which is of mystery. Synodal governance, and indeed any sort of governance, cannot be an adequate expression of the mystical Sobornost'. Sobornost' -- is reflective of a living organism, and within which live the Church's people. In reality, it is within the OEcumenical Councils that there was expressed most clearly of all the spirit of communality of the Church. But the authority of the OEcumenical Councils is not external, not formal, not rationally expressible, incapable of a transference over into a juridical language. The OEcumenical Councils are authoritative only because that within them was disclosed the truth for the living communality of the organism of the Church. The Church -- is not authority, the Church rather instead -- is the life of the Christian in Christ, in the Body of Christ, a life of freedom and grace. Khomyakov does not acknowledge any other head of the Church except for Christ himself. With indignation he rejects the typical charge made against the Russian Orthodox Church, that it is Caesaropapist. "When, -- says he, -- after many catastrophes and misfortunes the Russian people in a general assemblage chose Mikhail Romanov as their hereditary sovereign (for such was the lofty origin of imperial power in Russia), the people entrusted to their chosen one all the power, with which they themself were endowed, in all its aspects. The chosen one thus empowered, the sovereign became the head of the people in churchly affairs the same, as he was in matters of civil administration; I repeat: *the head of the people in matters churchly*, and in this sense, the head of the local Church, but solely in this sense. The people did not transmit nor were they able to transmit to their sovereign such rights, as they did not themselves possess, and hardly can anyone presume, that the Russian people once upon a time esteemed itself as called to govern the Church. From the beginning it had, just like all the peoples comprising the Orthodox Church, a voice in the selection of its bishops, and this its voice it could transfer to its representative. It had the right, or more precisely the duty to watch, that the decisions of its pastors and their councils were carried out in full; this right it could entrust to its chosen one and his successors. It had the right to defend its faith against every hostile or forcible assault upon it; this right it could likewise transfer to its sovereign. But the people did not possess any sort of power in questions of conscience, of general churchly decorum, dogmatic teaching, churchly administration, and therefore it could not transmit such a power to its tsar".[1] And further on: "The sovereign, being the head of the people, in the many matters relating to the Church, has the same rights as is given to

---

[1] A. S. Khomyakov, "Collected Works", Tome II, p. 36.

everyone, to the freedom of conscience in his faith and to the freedom of human reason; but we do not consider him a prophetic figure, stirred by an unseen power, as the Latinate bishops of Rome purport themselves to be. We think that, in being free, the sovereign, like every man, can fall into error, and that if, God hindering it not, suchlike a misfortune were to occur, despite the constant prayers of the sons of the Church, then and therein the emperor would not lose a single one of his rights to the obedience of his subjects in secular matters; and the Church would not suffer any impairment in its majesty or in its fullness; since never there be replaced its true and sole Head. In this supposed case it would but have one less Christian in its bosom -- and only this".[1]

It is impossible to find in Khomyakov any religio-mystical conception of autocracy. Suchlike a concept could sooner be found in Vl. Solov'ev with his teaching about the high-priest, the tsar and the prophet, about the tripartite theocracy. Khomyakov was an adherent of autocratic monarchy, he considered this form as solely corresponding to the spirit of Russian history, as solely akin to the Russian people. Yet in Khomyakov's autocracy there was a strong anarchic tinge, which gave expression to the Slavophil disdain towards politics, towards matters of the state, towards the exercising of power. This anarchic tinge did not exist in Solov'ev, since the Western and the Catholic spirit was too strong in him for this. Khomyakov justified autocracy not so much religiously, as rather nationally and historically. This was first of all a national ideology. Khomyakov did not see any sort of a churchly mysticism in autocracy nor was he able to see it as such, since the Orthodox Church was not for him the City upon earth and was sharply contrary to any suchlike City. To Khomyakov was foreign the idea of a theocracy of the Church holding power and militant, whether through a tsar or high-priest organising the earth, as with Solov'ev's theocracy. And therefore Khomyakov stubbornly denied any historical Russian connection towards Caesaropapism. For a mystical autocracy also is Caesaropapism. Khomyakov did not avow this sort of mysticism, for him the Russian monarchy was not of a sacred societal flesh. The idea of a sacred flesh in general was foreign to Khomyakov and to Slavophilism. The complex and tormentive problem of the relationship of the Church and the state was decided by Khomyakov moreso in a spirit of the national lifestyle, than in religio-mystical a spirit.

---

[1] A. S. Khomyakov, "Collected Works", Tome II, p. 37-38.

ALEKSEI STEPANOVICH KHOMYAKOV

He considered the forms of the state to have been created by the spirit of the people, and he was proud of this, that the tsar's power had issued for us from the people. The people themself live however the churchly life, and therefore everything for him was sanctified by the Church. But in the opinion of Slavophilism, imperialism was foreign to the Russian people, just as theocratic illusions were foreign, since all this was Western an impulse, and not Russian.

I have spoken already and shall speak some more about the Anglophilism of Khomyakov. This Anglophilism was expressed also in a love for the Anglican Church, with which Khomyakov sought closer relations and which he hoped to unite to the Orthodox Church. In Anglicanism namely Khomyakov saw least of all any impediment for union with Orthodoxy. He entered into active relations with the English theologian Palmer. The letters to Palmer -- comprise quite the largest portion of Khomyakov's theological work. Palmer inclined towards a transition over into Orthodoxy, and Khomyakov ultimately wanted to persuade him in the truth of Orthodoxy. In this matter of bringing Palmer over into Orthodoxy he got involved quite actively, he pleaded with the highest hierarchs of the Church, to facilitate this transition for Palmer. He hoped in the depths of his soul, that in the footsteps of Palmer, the entire Anglican Church would join itself together with the Orthodox Church. Khomyakov with indignation spurned the very idea of a churchly *unia*. An unia is possible only in secular matters, political matters, and an unia therein involves bargaining, compromise, mutual concessions. But *the Church -- is one*, in the Church is the fullness of truth. There is nothing in the Church to be yielded away, and there can thus be no sorts of bargaining to engage in. Khomyakov explains the propensity of the Catholic Church towards an unia as deriving from its political-state character. The unia -- is a product of political intrigues, and political intrigues are an unworthy basis for the Church as the preserver of the truth of Christ. In principle, Khomyakov is profoundly correct in this, profoundly churchly. In the strict sense of the word there cannot even be talk about a re-union of the Church, since the Church -- is one and can never be divided. There can be re-united and ought to be only broken off portions of Christian mankind. With the Anglicans it would have been easiest of all to unite with the Orthodox, since Anglicanism is not overall the Church, but merely a nationally united collection of Christians, positioned amidst Catholicism, Protestantism and Orthodoxy. But the subordinated position of the Russian Church, its lack of independence from the state power, troubled Palmer. Khomyakov himself sensed, that things here were not as they should be, but he attempted to smooth over the difficulty and bypass it. Khomyakov's position would have been stronger, if he had looked the empirical reality in the eye and had not posited it dependent upon the sanctity of Orthodoxy.

Another impediment stood in the way concerning Palmer's coming over into Orthodoxy. Palmer sensed himself already a Christian, having been baptised, and so he could not consent to a new baptism, demanded of him by the Eastern patriarchs. The Russian Church seemed more flexible and had agreed to accept Palmer into its bosom without this condition, but the Greek Church remained obstinate. And here Palmer was left in confusion over this, into what Church he was to go. He wanted to enter into the universal OEcumenical Orthodox Church, and before him stood two local, national churches, the Russian and the Greek, divided on the principal question. This was a great quandary. The Russian Church repulsed him by its subjection to the state. The Greek Church made a demand, contrary to his religious conscience. Wherein then was the Church catholic? Khomyakov was not able to overcome these difficulties, and Palmer then went over into Catholicism, he saw in Catholicism the Church universal, and not merely national. The history with Palmer presents a tormentive question for the Orthodox East.

Khomyakov had a negative attitude towards the Old-Ritualism, the Old Believers. At one point each Sunday he would dispute with the Old Ritualists at church in a portico. But in essence Khomyakov also, just like the whole of Slavophilism, fell into that selfsame sin, which obtained with the Old Ritualists. The sin of the Old Ritualism was in this, that it nationalised the Church, it tended to subordinate the universal Logos to the national element, it fell into an hapless provincialism and particularism. For the Old Ritualism, the national Russian flesh overshadowed the universal churchly spirit. They considered the local Russian Church identical with the Church universal, and everything not Russian they regarded as not churchly, not Christian, pagan and impious. This Russo-national rituality down to its very trifles, right down to the cut of its garb, was taken to be the very essence of the Church. For Nikon the Orthodox Church was first of all the Greek Church, i.e. all however still national, still local; whereas in contrast for the Old Ritualists the true Church is only the Church Russian, likewise national, likewise local. This churchly nationalism was the result of a prevailing of the feminine national element over the universal Logos, a non-submission to the Logos. In the Russian churchly nationalism there can be found clear traces of paganism, of a pagan national self-affirmation, of a pagan lack of enlightenment by the Logos. There are elements of Old Ritualism also in Slavophilism, and these elements cannot in any strict sense of this word be termed churchly. For Khomyakov, certainly, with his profound understanding of the essence of the Church, the cruder forms of Old Ritualism and the Old Believers seemed foreign, but he also went astray with churchly nationalism, and for him the national element at times overshadowed the universality. The attitude of Khomyakov towards Catholicism is explainable by his churchly nationalism, in regard to Catholicism his was an Old Ritualist psychology. The Slavophils in a certain sense can be termed cultural Old Ritualists, Old Ritualists who have emerged though higher an awareness, having come to terms with the complex results of the culture. The Slavophils were faithful sons of the Orthodox Church, the ruling Church, but they introduced into the Church a national spirit, akin to Old Ritualism. The attitude of the Slavophils towards Peter I, towards the bureaucracy, and to certain sides of our Synodal administration, was culturally Old Ritualist. Yet alongside the weaknesses and sins of the Old Ritualism they appropriated for themself also the truth of the Old Ritualism, its better sides: they affirmed churchly Sobornost' against churchly bureaucratism, and they posited the centre of gravity within the people of the Church, within the people's religious life. In the Old Ritualism there was preserved the people's religious life, there was a direct participation of the people in churchly life, where there is the parish and the real manifestations of Sobornost'. The Slavophils dreamed about all this for the entirety of the Russian Orthodox people. Slavophilism by the very fact of its existence confirms, that the schism [caused by Nikon] was a most profound tragedy in Russian history. The Slavophils tended to denounce the falsehood of the Old Ritualism but together with this it was with a respectful esteem that they looked upon the strong religious life of the Old Ritualists, which they could not find among the Orthodox. The very existence of the schism discloses, that in the Orthodox East not everything was felicitous, and it was not as felicitous, as Khomyakov was wont to portray it before the face of the Western faiths. Khomyakov was helpless facing both the problem of re-union with the Old Ritualism and the problem of re-union with Catholicism. Slavophilism fell caught between the extreme nationalism of the Old Ritualism and the extreme of the universality of Catholicism. But

Nicholas Berdyaev

Khomyakov was the first to have given our theology such a direction, that it became possible to consider both these problems with decisions religious and inward. Though he himself did not detect all the inferences from his radical theological outlook.

The significance of the Slavophil theology in Russian religious thought is tremendous. One mustneeds remember the stuffiness of that theological atmosphere, into which the religious thought of the Slavophils brought in fresh gusts, thinking that was from life and not from the schools. The Slavophils introduced into Russian philosophy and Russian literature religious themes, they conjoined theology to Russia culture as a theme of Russian life. For the Slavophils, Orthodox theology was not Byzantine rhetorics, but rather a matter of life. In the official theology, even the moral side of Orthodoxy had meaning primarily rhetorical; in the religious thought of the Slavophils it became alive. The Slavophils were, to use a current expression, pragmatists in theology, their religious philosophy was, in a certain sense, a philosophy of action, it was directed against the intellectualism in theology. Contemporary Catholic modernism in much comes nigh to Khomyakov's understanding of the Church. Regarding Khomyakov, there was almost nothing new in Catholic modernism that was not there already in him. That which LeRoy terms moral dogmatism, contrasting it to intellectualist dogmatism, Khomyakov had also essentially affirmed. And for Khomyakov the dogmas have first of all a significance that is vitally-moral, and not intellectually-theoretical. Khomyakov sees the source of dogmatic cognition in the mutual love of Christians, i.e. he apperceives this source as pragmatically actual. It is also in a pragmatically real way that Khomyakov interprets the source of the dogmatic division of East and West, he sees this in an insufficiency of love between West and East, in a vital-moral defect. Christian dogmas are disclosed within the life of the Church, within religious experience. Khomyakov -- is no less an enemy of the scholastico-intellectualist theology, than are the contemporary modernists. In the following chapter we shall see, that the philosophy of Khomyakov was a philosophy of action, but more religious and therefore more profound, than what generally passes for the modern philosophy of action. With a sense of satisfaction we can say, that the most current forms of theology and philosophy in the West come down to this, that long ago already they had been asserted and developed by our Slavophils. And the foremost among the Slavophils was Khomyakov, he -- was the head of the Slavophil churchly philosophy. We have seen already,

ALEKSEI STEPANOVICH KHOMYAKOV

that he played both religious and churchly a guiding role. In the fighting skirmishes, which transpired in the circles of the decade of the 1840's, Khomyakov remained invincible. The core idea of Khomyakov, which he had in common with all the Slavophils, was this, that the source of all theologising and all philosophising ought to be the integrally whole life of spirit, organic life, that everything ought to be set relative to the religious centre of life. This idea manifests itself as the source of the Slavophil philosophy and likewise of all Russian philosophy. Towards this idea approach various paths in the West. The integral wholeness of the life of spirit obtains only within religious life, only in the life of the Church. With faith in the true life of the Church are bound up all the hopes of Russia for the realisation of a type of culture, rather higher, than the Western, and in the fulfilling of its worldwide mission.

Howsoever great the theological merits of Khomyakov, howsoever dear he be for us, his religious consciousness overall was limited, was too neat and incomplete. There is little in him of a prophetic spirit. Khomyakov denied dogmatic developement within the Church, he did not perceive in the Church a theologic process. Orthodoxy for him was complete, "received in total", the revelation of God had been acquired in full. Khomyakov did not await a new revelation in Christianity, he did not allow for such a possibility. The Orthodox Church was for him foremost of all a guardian of matters sacred. He discerned little of the prophetic and creative side. The eschatological problem, the problem of the end did not occupy any place in the theology of Khomyakov; in all his religious philosophy there is nothing about this, not even an hint. Khomyakov did not connect his Russian messianism with anything apocalyptic. Neither is there any apocalypsis in his philosophy of history. Apocalyptic presentiments, apocalyptic apprehension, an apocalyptic sense of tragedy, all this was foreign to Khomyakov. I have said already, that this was characteristic of all his generation, and likewise for all of Slavophilism. These people had not yet come into the cosmic atmosphere of the apocalypse, they had not yet come into the new religious epoch. The Slavophils were innovators, almost revolutionaries in theology, and their love for freedom was striking; this was a free discerning of the truth of Christ. But they all nonetheless belonged to the old religious consciousness. The new religious consciousness, firing up into a new religious epoch, does not alter the unshakable sanctity of the Orthodox Church, but it does acknowledge not only the priesthood, but also propheticism, it is filled with presentiments of witnessing the revelation of the Holy Trinity, full of the tragic sense of the end of history. For the new religious consciousness the Church -- is a Divine-human process, which cannot yet be at its finish, which will transpire in its fullness only at the end of history. The denial of the possibility of a new Christian revelation is a boundary line, at which Khomyakov and the entirety of Slavophilism stops short. And at this limiting boundary line -- is the source of the eventual degeneration of Slavophilism, its uncreative fate. The priesthood is assured, but where is the Kingdom and prophecy? The incompleteness of Khomyakov's religious consciousness is evident already in this, that in him there is almost nothing of a religious cosmology.

Out of his fear of a Catholic magicism, Khomyakov falls at times into a Protestant moralism. The sacraments find in him moreso a spiritually moral, rather than cosmic sense. The religious consciousness of Khomyakov shows primarily on the side of those sacraments, which are connected with a spiritual renewal, and for him are almost hidden those other sides, connected with a cosmic transfiguration. That in the discerning of the cosmic nature of the sacraments there is revealed the mystery of God's creation -- this is something that Khomyakov does not sense, this is foreign to his consciousness. In the sacraments obtains not only a spiritual and moral renewal of the human soul, in the sacraments obtains also a prefigurative image of the transfiguration of the Creation, a new Cosmos, in which the nourishment will be by the Eucharist, the coming together will be by wedlock, and the fearsome watery element will become baptism. The sacraments -- are the foretype of a new life in a new cosmos, and all the fullness of life ought thence to be sacramental, to be by grace, and every activity ought thence to be theurgic. That the sacraments -- are the path to cosmic transfiguration, the transfiguration of all the flesh of the world, -- it is impossible to find anything about this in Khomyakov. He was afraid even to ascribe an objective-cosmic nature to the sacraments, since he feared this to be a tendency towards the pagan magic, of which he always accused Catholicism. But too great a protest against Catholicism readily leads to Protestantism. To him it seemed more Orthodox, more accurate to emphasise the subjective-spiritual side of the sacraments. Herein, perhaps, was expressed an insufficient sensitivity of Khomyakov towards the mystical side of Christianity. The cosmic mystery does not stand at the centre of Khomyakov's understanding of Christianity. In the religious philosophy of Khomyakov overall there is almost absent a religious cosmology. How strange the cosmic mystery of J. Boehme would have seemed to him! He had little sense of any world soul, of an eternal femininity, of anything, that was so dear to Vl. Solov'ev. With him there was no place for Sophia the Wisdom of God. The religiosity of Khomyakov was one-sided, exclusively masculine. He was entirely in the Logos, within the Logos he thought and taught, and not in the world soul. And he was not given over to the trembling and agitation of the world soul. The limitedness of his exclusively masculine consciousness shielded from him that apocalyptic apprehension, which has filled the world soul in the new cosmic epoch, in that apocalyptic newness, which was engendered in the consciousness of the new epoch. In Khomyakov there is not any sort of mystical sensitivity. He was too solidly a man and too solidly a noble. He did not want to be given over to any sort of forebodings, nor would it have delighted him to plunge into the abyss of the world soul. He knew the world soul only from the side of the hunt and the country landlord, he knew only the land, bearing grain, and a wife, bearing children. Other land, other femininity he did not know nor want to know. The mystique of sex to him was foreign and unneeded. For him was wrought the old marriage on the old land. He neither wearies nor languishes for a new marriage upon a new earth.

    The religious consciousness of Khomyakov did not yearn for the City to Come, and in his religious philosophy there is no place for a theocracy. Orthodoxy never confused the Church with the City. In this aspect is a tremendous difference of Orthodoxy from Catholicism, which identified the Church with the City of God, with the Kingdom of Christ upon earth. For the Catholic consciousness the City of God has been realised already in the life of the Church, and therefore the consciousness of striving for the City to Come, an apocalyptic consciousness, is not readily engendered upon Catholic a basis. Orthodox do not sense this belonging to a realised City, and therefore it is easier upon an Orthodox basis to engender an apocalyptic search for the City to Come. Orthodoxy -- is moreso an Johannine Christianity, whereas Catholicism -- is moreso Petrine. But in historical Orthodoxy there is no chiliasm, no apocalypsis, and while there is sacredness and the priesthood, there is no propheticism and kingdom. Khomyakov confesses historical Orthodoxy as a religion of the priesthood, without prophecy about the City. And he knows only one City -- Holy Rus'. This City was sanctified for him by Orthodoxy, and it is only about the historical Russian theocratic kingdom that he wishes to know. We shall see, that Khomyakov grounds the idea of Holy Rus' moreso upon a nationally-historical, rather than mystical basis. Khomyakov sees the temptation of the Catholic confusing of the Church with the City, with the Kingdom. Orthodoxy for him in contrast was without power, it did not strive towards a kingdom of this world, and in this he saw all the greatness of Orthodoxy. Khomyakov quite justly criticised Catholicism, but he quite unjustly denied for Christianity any striving towards this City. Here was the limitation in his old Orthodox consciousness. The Russian realm was for him the Orthodox realm, since that it was the realm of the Orthodox Russian people. Through the spirit of the people was sanctified this realm. But holy flesh, the holy corporeality was not in this kingdom, it was not the mystical City. The Slavophils cleansed the truth of Orthodoxy from every defilement, they were at the ideal summit of the Orthodox consciousness and by this they cleared the path for a new religious consciousness. The new religious consciousness starts then, when the Church of Christ is conceived of as a cosmic kingdom. The sacred within Orthodoxy ought to become a dynamic power of history. The Slavophils wanted to sanction forever the Orthodox powerlessness, passivity, the lack of will as a trait of the Russian people. The Church -- is freedom, the Church -- is love, but the Church -- is not power nor might. And the Russian people wants not the power of might, it wants only freedom and love. The Russian people does not desire a kingdom, it desires only the Church. The prophecy concerning this, that the Church will become the City, was however still obscured for the Slavophil consciousness.

Chapter IV

Khomyakov as Philosopher.
His Gnosseology and Metaphysics.

Khomyakov and Ivan Kireevsky -- set in place the foundations of the Slavophil philosophy, which also can be called a national Russian philosophy, reflecting all that is unique in our national thought. Sudden death prevented both these Slavophil thinkers from further working out their philosophy. The founders of Slavophilism did not leave us any large philosophic tracts, nor did they create systems. Their philosophy was left fragmented, and has passed down to us merely in some articles filled with profound intuitions. Kireevsky had just barely set about the fundamentals and developing of the Slavophil philosophy, when he died from cholera. The same fate overtook Khomyakov also, in hoping to continue the work of Kireevsky. There was something providential in all this. And perhaps, *suchlike* a philosophy ought not to be a system. The Slavophil philosophy -- represented an ending of abstract philosophy, and therefore already could not be a system, like other systems of abstract philosophy. This was a philosophy of an integrally whole life of spirit, and not of detached intellect, nor of abstract reason. The idea of an integral knowing, based upon an organic fullness of life, -- is the departing point of Slavophil and Russian philosophy. Following upon Khomyakov and Kireevsky, the original and creative philosophic thought with us has always posited itself the task of discerning not an abstract, intellectual truth, but rather truth as both pathway and life. This unique form of Russian philosophising was expressed also in the camp of the opposing position, and even in our positivism, always thirsting to conjoin pravda-truth which is true with pravda-truth which is just. Russians cannot grant, that truth be discerned purely by intellect, by way of reason, that truth is but a judgement of reason. And no sort of gnosseology, no sort of methodology has evidently the power to shake this pre-rational conviction of Russians, wherein the apperception of the existent obtains only by means of the integrally whole life of spirit, only in the fullness of life. Even our quasi-Western and quasi-positivist philosophy has striven towards this synthetic religious wholeness, though it be helpless and incapable to express this Russian thirst. But our creative philosophic thought, having Slavophil sources, consciously has set itself the task to affirm, against every rationalistic dissociation, an organically and integrally whole religious philosophy. Ivan Kireevsky, with whom Khomyakov has to share the glory as a founder of the Slavophil philosophy, says: "For us philosophy is something *necessary*: the total developement of our mind demands it. By it alone lives and breathes our poetry; it alone can grant the soul an integral wholeness also to our infant sciences, and our very life, perhaps, is due to its elegance and harmonious order. But from whence cometh it? Where to seek it? Certainly, our first step towards it ought to be by appropriation of the mental riches of those lands, which in their speculations surpass all nations. But foreign thoughts are useful only for the developement of our own. German philosophy cannot take solid a rooting amongst us, for *our* philosophy ought to develope from out of *our* life, to be crafted from out of the impelling questions, from out of the governing interests of *our* national and private manner of life".[1] These words can be taken as a slogan for every Russian aspiration in philosophy. I. Kireevsky and Khomyakov did not ignore German philosophy, they made their way through it and creatively surmounted it. They surmounted German Idealism and the Western abstract philosophy by a faith in this, that the spiritual life of Russia would beget from its loins an utmost comprehension of the existent, an utmost and organic form of philosophy. The first Slavophils were convinced, that Russia would remain faithful to the integrally whole truth of the Christian Church and would therefore be free from the rationalistic dissociation of spirit. The Russian philosophy should thus be a continuation of the philosophy of the patristic fathers. The first intuitions of this philosophy were born within the soul of Kireevsky. Khomyakov was however its most powerful dialectician.

Independent Russian philosophy began with a critique of the abstract idealism of Hegel and passed over to *a concrete idealism*, to an original fruition of Russian thought. The surmounting of Hegelianism, of that titanically arrogant and titanically powerful philosophy -- herein was the task, posited by Kireevsky and Khomyakov. The surmounting of

---

[1] I. V. Kireevsky, "Complete Collected Works", under redaction of M. Gershenzon, publisher "Put'", Tome II, p. 27.

ALEKSEI STEPANOVICH KHOMYAKOV

Hegelianism had at the same time to be the surmounting of every abstract and rationalist philosophy, by appealing to the whole spirit of Western culture. According to Kireevsky's thought, in the Western nations there occurred "a split within a most basic principle of the Western teaching of faith, from which there had at first the Scholastic philosophy within faith, then the Reformation in faith, and finally, philosophy external to and outside of faith. The first rationalists were the Scholastics; their descendants are termed Hegelians".[1] Khomyakov saw within Hegel the Kushite spirit, repudiating free creativity. Hegelianism -- was the apex of the whole Western path of developement, the final stage, beyond which -- was the empty void. The dashed wreck of Hegelian philosophy represented a crisis of philosophy in general. Khomyakov lived within the spiritual atmosphere of classical German Idealism and he pondered deeply over the contradictions of this idealism and the fatal reasons for its failure. "*The existent,* -- says Khomyakov, -- had completely to be set aside. The very concept, in its fullest abstraction, had entirely instead to be reborn from its own bosom. Rationalism or the logical judgements of reason had as though found its crowning moment and a Divine sanctification in a new sort creation of the entire world. Such was the enormous task, which the German mind set for itself in Hegel, and it is impossible not to be astonished by the boldness, with which he proceeded towards its resolution".[2] "It follows therefore to term the logic of Hegel as *the in-spiritising of abstract being* (Einvergeistigung des Seyns). Such, it would seem would be its fullest, never as yet expressed definition. Never before had man set himself so awesome a task, so bold an undertaking. An eternal creation begets itself from the womb of the abstract concept, while not possessing in itself any sort of essence. There is a self-effectuated passing over from bare possibility over into all the manifold and intellectual existence of the world".[3] In Hegel there reached an end-point of that cycle of developement in that "philosophy of rational judgement", which "regarded itself the philosophy of reason". Khomyakov tends thus to formulate the boundary-line, to which the philosophic movement in

---

[1] I. V. Kireevsky, "Full Collected Works", Tome I, p. 226.

[2] A. S. Khomyakov, "Collected Works", Tome I, p. 267.

[3] Ibid., p. 268.

Germany had come nigh: "It is the re-creation of the integral reason (i.e. spirit) from the conceptualising aspect of rational judgement. As soon as the task had defined itself in such a manner (and particularly suchlike is the sense of Hegelian activity), the path had to cease: every step forward had become impossible".[1] "The common mistake of all the schools, still not clearly obvious in its founder -- Kant, but sharply characteristic to its completion -- in Hegel, consists in this, that it constantly assumes the dynamics of a concept within the personal understanding to be identical with the dynamics of all actuality (of all reality)".[2] "It would be impossible to initiate developement from that substrate, or better said, from that absence of a substrate, from which Hegel started out; from this results a whole series of mistakes, the confusion of personal laws with worldwide laws; from this likewise is a confusing of the critical concept with the movement of the world of appearances, despite their opposition; from this likewise results the collapse of the entire titanic effort. The root of Hegel's mistake lies however in the mistake of the whole school, in the accepting of rational judgement as an integral wholeness of spirit. The whole school failed to notice, that in this accepting the concept as the sole basis for all thinking, one destroys the world: since the concept turns every activity underlying it into but pure, abstract potentiality".[3] Khomyakov foresees the inevitability of Hegel's abstract idealism passing over into materialism. The search for a substrate will snatch hold upon matter: it is impossible to live and to think in a substrateless, non-existing abstraction. Khomyakov predicts even the rise of dialectical materialism. "Criticism brought into focus one thing: the overall unsustainability of Hegelianism, in having endeavoured to create a world without substrate. His disciples did understand this, that in this particularly consisted the whole task of their teacher, and they very simplistically imagined to themself, that there needed only to be introduced into the system this missing substrate, and the matter would be settled. But from whence to seize hold the substrate? Spirit, evidently, would not do, first off because, that the very task of Hegel directly expressed itself as a searching process, creating spirit, and

---

[1] A. S. Khomyakov, "Collected Works", Tome I, p. 291.

[2] Ibid., p. 296.

[3] Ibid., p. 110.

secondly also because, that the very character of Hegel's rationalism is to an utmost degree idealist, and totally not spiritualistic. And here the most abstract of human abstractions, -- Hegelianism, -- will have grabbed hold upon matter and pass over into the purest and most coarse materialism. Matter would become the substrate, and then the system of Hegel would be preserved, i.e. there would be preserved the terminology, a large portion of definition, the transitions of thought, the logical exercises and the fabricating process of the Hegelian mind. The great thinker would not have tolerated such an humiliation; but perhaps, his disciples would not have taken the liberty to decide upon such an humiliation, if his threatening brow were not already hidden beneathe the grave".[1] Hegel did not survive to see the dialectical materialism of Marx, though he also was the source for it. Khomyakov indeed predicted the appearance of Marxism, in which would be preserved "the fabricating process of the Hegelian mind". The philosophical sham of dialectical materialism was chastisement for the sin of rationalism.

In Western philosophy, only A. Trendelenburg has given a critique of Hegel, akin to the Slavophil critique, but not creative, not constructive. I offer for comparison two citations: "Without a living contemplation, -- Trendelenburg says in his "Logical Investigations", -- for the logical method it would follow indeed all decisively to do away with the idea -- with the eternal oneness of the subjective and the objective. But the method does not do this, whilst aware, that the logical world in the abstract element of thought is only a "realm of shadows", nothing more. To it certainly it would seem, that there is another, a fresh and vibrantly-alive world, but certainly likewise -- not purely from intellection".[2] And still further on: Dialectics purported to demonstrate, that self-contained intellection actually encompasses all the whole world. But this demonstration is not given. Everywhere the seemingly closed circle is broken stealthily, in order to adopt from the outside, what does not suffice it from the inside. A shut-in perspective ordinarily sees before it a single phantasmagora of images. Human thought lives by contemplation and dies from starvation, when it is compelled to feed off its own empty belly".[3]

---

[1] A. S. Khomyakov, "Collected Works", Tome I, p. 302.

[2] F. A. Trendelenburg, "Logical Investigations", Part I, p. 81.

Nicholas Berdyaev

Kireevsky and Khomyakov perceived, that German idealist philosophy -- was a product of Protestantism, that Kant -- was one of the moments in the developement of the Protestant splintering, and Hegel -- was the completer of a Protestant rationalism. The falling away from the Church as a living organism, as an ontological reality, led to a disintegration of the integral life of spirit, to a falling away of logically-judgemental thought from the integrally whole reason. "Germany vaguely recognised in itself a complete absence of religion and this carried over, little by little, into the bosom of philosophy all the demands, which prior to then was answered by faith. Kant was a direct and necessary continuator of Luther. It would be possible to discern in his twofold critique of pure and practical reason a character fully Lutheran".[1] The sins of Protestantism were inferred by the Slavophils however to derive from the sins of Catholicism. Catholicism already had permitted the prevailing of abstract rational-judgement within the Scholastic philosophy and theology, there already had begun the disintegration of the integrally whole spirit and integrally whole reason. But one must note, that Khomyakov ignored too much the Western mysticism and its significance for philosophy. The mystic, Meister Eckhardt, was indeed a source for Protestantism and German philosophic idealism. And in still yet another vein, the mystic, Jacob Boehme, had an influence upon Franz Baader and Schelling, -- to figures, akin to Slavophilism. With Boehme and Baader there was a spiritual wholeness, their philosophy was a philosophy of the Logos, and not of rational-judgement. There was this integral wholeness also within Catholic mysticism. But as regards the thought of Khomyakov and Kireevsky, however, this spiritual wholeness is preserved only in the Orthodox Church, only in Orthodoxy lives the Logos-Reason. And from the East only do they await a rebirth of philosophy, of a victory over the rationalistic emptiness, an egress from the blind alley. Within the Eastern teachers of the Church it then is necessary to seek out new principles for philosophy. Khomyakov sensed the meonic aspect of European philosophy, the triumph of the spirit of non-being. Being, the existent, is abolished by the rationalistic judgement of reason, by abstract philosophy. This is most clearly of all evident in the titanic genius of an effort by Hegel to reconstruct the existent by way of a dialectical path emerging from out of

---

[3] Ibid., p. 110.

[1] A. S. Khomyakov, "Collected Works", Tome I, p. 300.

the abstract idea. The existent is given only to a philosophy of the integral spirit, only to a reason which is organic, non-fragmented. Khomyakov foresaw the ultimate triumph of the meonic aspect and the illusionism in the ultimate developement of European philosophy. In the most recent forms of transcendentalism and immanentism, being is abolished without a trace, it is transmuted into a contemplation of consciousness and into forms of an existential judgement. Against this triumph of the spirit of non-being within rationalistic philosophy, Khomyakov affirms ontologism. But for him the Hegelian Pan-Logism was not an authentic ontologism. The identification of logic with ontology was only one of the forms of the sundering of logic-judgemental thought apart from living being. Only in Russia, within the consciousness of the Slavophils did the surmounting of the Hegelian abstract idealism beget a concrete idealism, affirming the concrete and integrally whole spirit as the existent. The Slavophil philosophy consciously turned to a religious source and there it found the substrate, it found the existent. Western thought after the collapse of Hegelianism instead finds the existent within matter, in the sensually tangible, in positive science. Russian thought finds the existent within mystical a receptivity, in religious experience.

Western philosophy amongst us is banal and derivative, it is a Western thought transplanted onto Russian soil, primarily German, and this thought lacked the power to be independently creative for us, howsoever creative it may have been in the West. Only the Slavophil philosophy for us was creative, full of the creative spirit. This philosophy proved original for us, because at its base lay the religious experience of the Orthodox East: it is the integral life of the spirit, which the Slavophils demand for philosophic investigation, and it is an experience religiously Orthodox. The gnosseology of Khomyakov passed through German idealism, and it surmounted Kantianism and Hegelianism. This surmounting was accomplished not by way of some sort of new philosophy on the Western model, but by way of a philosophy of the integral life of spirit. The gnosseology of Khomyakov does not separate subject and object and does not rend asunder the spirit. Khomyakov on principle affirms the dependence of a philosophy of cognition upon the religious life, upon religious experience. But this does not at all mean, that for Khomyakov philosophy is merely in the service of theology. The Slavophil philosophy -- is not theological, but rather religious. The Scholastic understanding of the dependence of philosophy upon theology, the Catholic subordination of philosophic thought to churchly authority -- all this was foreign and repugnant for the Slavophils. Khomyakov affirms the freedom of philosophy, a free philosophy, but philosophy ought freely to recognise, that the religious fullness of experience and the life of spirit is a source of cognition for the existent. The philosophic spirit of Khomyakov is very profoundly different from the philosophic traditionalism of Joseph de Maistre, of Louis de Bonald and other French Catholic thinkers of the beginning XIX Century. Here, among the Slavophils, was the genius of freedom, and there, among the traditionalists, was the genius of authority. In the German philosophy of the XIX Century stood Franz Baader with a kindred point of view. But the Slavophils evidently did not know Baader, and he exerted no sort of influence upon them. Khomyakov, however, well knew Schelling and highly esteemed him. With Schelling the Slavophil philosophy has points in common, and here and there in both -- is identical a philosophy. But there is also a principal difference. Schelling was a gnostic, which cannot be said of Khomyakov. Schelling philosophically asserted the identity of subject and object, and the philosophical aspect in him prevailed over the religious. Khomyakov reacted critically towards the final period of Schelling's philosophy. "A reconciler of inner discord, -- says Khomyakov, -- the restorer of rational relationships between appearances and consciousness, consequently, the recreator of the integrality of spirit, -- Schelling gives a rational justification to nature, recognising it as the reflection of spirit. From rationalism he passes over to idealism, and finally he passes over to a mystical spiritualism. His final epoch has, moreover, a significance of still more consequence, than the philosophy of practical reason in Kant, or remotely yields to it in the sense of genius. However, the first and actually fruitful half of Schelling's activity remains, in its most important conclusions, a most lofty and beautiful effort in the history of philosophy up to our time".[1] It would however be a great mistake to think, that the Slavophil philosophy was simply a transposition of Schelling's philosophy into the Russian language. Schelling to his very end had not turned with any vital intensity to the Christian faith, he remained a romantic, and therefore in his philosophy there could not be a genuine image utilising the religio-Christian experience. And the Eastern Christian experience, upon which

---

[1] A. S. Khomyakov, "Collected Works", Tome I, p. 292.

ALEKSEI STEPANOVICH KHOMYAKOV

Slavophilism was grounded, was foreign to him. Pr. V. F. Odoevsky was a Schellingian, but not Khomyakov.

With the Slavophil philosophy there is a point in common with modern pragmatism, as a philosophy of action. The first point of congruity is already in this, that pragmatism also issues forth from life, it affirms knowledge as being a fact in life, it denies intellectualistic and rationalistic criteria of truth. The Slavophil philosophy as such was a philosophy of action, of anti-intellectualism. For Khomyakov, truth is discerned through action, in religious experience, within the practical activity of the integrally whole spirit. The disciple of Bergson and foremost philosopher of Catholic modernism, LeRoy, having adopted a pragmatic point of view towards dogmatics, comes so nigh close to Khomyakov's point of view, that there is almost nothing more that we might learn from him. But the pragmatic philosophy is distinct from the Slavophil in this, that it does not know a positive religious experience,[1] it does not know the Logos within action, within the practical action of life. The anti-intellectualism of this philosophy was apparently a reaction against intellectualism, and therefore it assumed a form of alogism, of irrationalism. Khomyakov's philosophy of action finds the Logos within the integral life of spirit, it issues forth not simply from life and its needs, but from religious life. But the element of anti-intellectualism, the vital pragmatism was already there in the Slavophil philosophy. This philosophy sought out criteria of truth within the integral life of spirit, and not in the intellect, not in abstract logic, i.e. it sought out active criteria. The dynamic of the Logos -- herein was what this philosophy was alive with.

The whole unique aspect of the gnosseology of Khomyakov was in this, that he affirms it *in terms of Sobornost'-communality*, i.e. a churchly gnosseology. The existent is given only through Sobornost', a churchly consciousness. The individual consciousness is powerless to apprehend truth. Together with this, the self-affirming individual consciousness represents always a sundering apart of the integral life of the spirit, a splitting apart of the subject from the object. The integrally whole spirit, which only also attains to the highest Reason, is always connected with Sobornost'. "All the most profound truths of thought, all the utmost truth of the striving of the will is accessible only to the reason, which within it is set in full moral accord the all-existent reason, and to it alone are disclosed

---

[1] I am speaking not of LeRoy, but concerning James and Bergson.

the invisible mysteries of matters Divine and human".[1] Only in religious life can there be a source of true philosophy, since only in religious life is there found the Sobornost' consciousness. However, in a religious splitting apart the spirit is hewn asunder, and the individual judgemental reason prevails in place of the Sobornost' reason. Khomyakov sees in love, in the churchly community of Christians, to be the source and criteria of knowledge. This -- is a thought very deep and daring. In the previous chapter concerning Khomyakov as a theologian we have seen, how for him community in love manifests itself as the source of religious cognition. He carries over this idea also into his philosophy. "Of all the worldwide laws of the volitional reason or the reasoning will, -- says he, -- the first, the supreme, the most perfect is manifest to the undistorted soul as the law of love. Consequently, an accordance with it can excellently strengthen and broaden our mental perspective, and we ought to submit to it, and in accord with its structure to build upon the stubborn failure of our mental powers. Only amidst the accomplishing of this effort can we hope at the fullest developement of reason".[2] And further on: "The community of love is not only useful, but fully necessary for the apprehension of truth, and the apprehension of truth is dependent upon it and impossible without it. That which is inaccessible for an individual's pondering of truth becomes accessible only by conjoined thought, united by love. This feature sharply differentiates the Orthodox teaching from all the others: from Latinism, standing upon an external authority, and from Protestantism, relegating the person to freedom within the wastelands of abstraction in judgemental reason".[3] *This particularly mustneeds be stressed, that Sobornost', as a community within love, was not for Khomyakov a mere philosophic idea, a borrowing from Western thought, but was the rather a religious fact, taken from the living experience of the Eastern Church.* Only by being mindful of this, can one understand the Slavophil philosophy. Sobornost' has nothing in common with a "consciousness in common", with some sort of "supra-individual subject" type of thought from armchair philosophers, Sobornost' rather is from life, from actual being, and not something off the top of one's head, or from books. The Sobornost' community of love is also

---

[1] A. S. Khomyakov, "Collected Works", Tome I, p. 282.
[2] A. S. Khomyakov, "Collected Works", Tome I, p. 283.

[3] Ibid., p. 283.

an ontological prerequisite of Khomyakov's gnosseology. The whole of his gnosseology rests upon this fact of being, and not upon a mere teaching about being. The point of contact with the existent, the intuition of the existent is possible only within the integral life of spirit, within the Sobornost' community. Which leads further to this, that faith is revealed to be at the foundation of cognition.

    Faith is more primary, moreso preliminary than is cognition. In the initial, the non-rationalised consciousness, reality is taken on faith. The philosophy of Khomyakov leads to an identity of knowing and faith. "I have termed *faith* that capacity of reason, -- says Khomyakov, -- which apperceives the actual (real) given, transferring it over to the discernment and consciousness of rational judgement. Only in this area does the given bear within itself the fullness of its character and sign of its origin. *In this sphere, prior to the logical consciousness and fully within the vital consciousness, needing neither proofs nor deductions, man is conscious of what appertains to his mental world and what appertains to the external world* (italics mine. -- N.B.). Here, on the touchstone of the will, there is bespoken for him, what in his object (objective) world was created by his creative (subjective) activity, and what is independent of it. Time and space, or better said, the appearances therein in these two categories is apperceived here independent of its subjectivity, or at the extreme, dependent upon it in very little measure".[1] "Reason lives by the acceptance of the appearance based on faith".[2] "The fullness of the human reason or spirit perceives all the appearances of the objective world *as being such*, but having either come from such itself, or not from such. In both instances it still accepts them unmediatedly, i.e. by faith... Amidst all the possible circumstances the object (or appearance or fact) is by faith, and only by the effect of consciousness is it transformed fully within the awareness, and the measure of the awareness never exceeds the limits, or better said, does not alter the character, with which the object initially is apperceived".[3] The difference between the real and the illusory, and likewise between the subjective and the objective, is established only by an act of faith, which is

---

[1] A. S. Khomyakov, "Collected Works", Tome I, p. 327.

[2] Ibid., p. 279.

[3] Ibid. p. 328.

prior to the logical consciousness. The existent is taken on faith, it obtains prior to the rationalistic sundering of the integral life of spirit. The triumph of the rationalistic consciousness leads to this, that there is lost the distinction between the real and the ideal. Therefore, in modern philosophy there tends to triumph also illusionism and meonism. Only in faith, preceding all rationalisation, obtains the identity of subject and object wherein the existent is grasped. "The totality of reasoning, -- says Khomyakov, -- is a matter of re-creation, i.e. a converting of the reason-perceived into a fact of our particular life".[1] This is almost the same thing, but with other words, as expressed by Franz Baader, when he said, that to know truth means to be truth. Only in faith does a man become truth, and turn the reason-perceived into a fact of his own particular life. Faith however is first of all a function of the will at the core of our integral spiritual existence. The teaching about the will, about the volitional reason and the reasoning will comprises the core of Khomyakov's gnosseology and metaphysics. Khomyakov was uniquely a volitionist, and he was such a long while before voluntarism had become popular in European philosophy. But the volitionism of Khomyakov was in principle distinct from almost all the forms of the eventual voluntarism of European philosophy. His voluntarism was combined with logism, i.e. with an acknowledgement of the reason-aspect of the will, of the Logos as being, whereas the voluntarism of modern philosophy is alogicised, it denies the Logos, and from the time of Schopenhauer it possesses the tendency towards an acknowledgement of the will as irrational, blind, mad. The voluntarism of Khomyakov was not an abstract principle, the will was not cut off from the integrally-whole reasoning spirit. Khomyakov surmounts the modern opposition of voluntarism and rationalism.

Khomyakov was a voluntarist not only in his metaphysics, but also in his gnosseology. His philosophy is a philosophy of the freely willing spirit, it is contrary to every determinism, to every force of necessity. But again I stress, that his metaphysical and gnosseological voluntarism has nothing in common with the alogism and irrationalism of Schopenhauer or Hartmann, and likewise it is distinct from the modern voluntarism of James and Bergson, Wundt and Paulson, Windelband and Rickert. The voluntarism of contemporary European philosophy is a result of the loss of the Logos. This -- is an alogos/alogical consciousness. Not so in

---

[1] A. S. Khomyakov, "Collected Works", Tome I, p. 330.

ALEKSEI STEPANOVICH KHOMYAKOV

Khomyakov. Khomyakov proceeds from the integrally whole spirit, in which the will and reason are not fragmented apart. Reason for him -- wills, and the will -- reasons. In German rationalistic philosophy, in Hegel, Khomyakov does not find the will, and he does not find freedom. In such is not a dynamic reason, there is only a static reason. For Khomyakov, "*freedom in a positive show of power is the will*".[1] "The whole great school of German rationalism, just like its decrepit offshoot, materialism, contains within itself unconsciously the idea of non-volition (necessitarianism)".[2] "For man, the will belongs to the sphere of *the pre-objective*. Amidst this, philosophy up to the present has known only the reflection of the object within rational-judgemental knowledge, and if there has eluded for it the actual efficaciousness of the object, transferred over into this knowledge, then all the moreso altogether impermissible for it would be the sphere of powers, not transferred over into the objective image; consequently, the will also would be impermissible. Of this in particular one finds no traces in German philosophy".[3] Only the will, only the willing reason, posits the distinction between the I and the not-I, between the inward and the outward. "The will in an healthy condition discerns the autonomous object from the external world".[4] "The will ascertains some things as I and of-me, and yet other things, as I, but not *of-me*, evidencing a variance of origins, from which flow the existence or modification of the known objects themself".[5] And just how far foreign to Khomyakov was the blind alogistic voluntarism is evident from the following passage: "Of worldwide laws concerning the willing reason or reasoning will (since such is a definition of spirit itself), the primary, the utmost, the most perfect one for the undistorted soul is the law of love". The Logos indeed -- is the Meaning of the world -- and is Love. And Khomyakov sees this principle manifest in "*free thought, i.e. in the will of reason*". "The will -- this is the final word for the consciousness, just as it is the first one for action. The will of

---

[1] A. S. Khomyakov, "Collected Works", Tome I, p. 276.

[2] Ibid., p. 313.

[3] Ibid., p. 276.

[4] Ibid., p. 277.

[5] Ibid., p. 278.

reason, and -- I might add -- of reason in its fullness, since the change in appearance is a change in the apperceived, but the apperceived as such, -- as already presupposes, or better said, contains in itself already the pre-existing existence of the pre-objective consciousness, of that first degree of thinkable being, which does not transfer and cannot pass over into the appearance, always antecedent to it. And thus, the change itself of the appearance, wrought within the apperceived, becomes already a fullness of thinkable being, and therefore only in the fullness of reason do we find the principle of appearance and its change, i.e. power".[1] "No one would be doubtful of their will, although one be unable to receive the concept of it from the external world, the world of necessity; therefore upon the consciousness of the will are based whole categories of concepts, since that in it, as I have already said, lies the distinction between the objects of the world of the existing and the world of the imagined; and therefore finally it is, precisely that reason *thus cannot be doubtful in its creative activity -- by the will, as also in in its reflective receptivity -- by faith, or the finalative consciousness -- by rational judgement*".[2] For Khomyakov "*necessity is a foreign will*", "*necessity is manifest will*".[3] "Whichever the way we might have come, whether from our own personal subjectivity and consciousness, or whether from an analysis in their world totality, one thing enters into the final conclusion -- *that of the will in its identity with reason* (italics mine. -- N.B.) as its efficacious power, inseparable either from the concept concerning it, or from the concept of its subjectivity. It establishes everything existing, rendering it from the possible, or elsewise, *rendering the thought from the thinkable* by its free creativity. It essentially is reasoned, since the reasoned is everything that is thinkable, and it -- is reason in its activity, just as the consciousness is reason in its reflectivity or passivity or, if one prefer, receptivity. Both these aspects, with the mediating of objectivity or objectness, is where the will posits itself the object for consciousness, and is pre-existent to the reason and constitutes its fullness, the integral wholeness of its inward

---

[1] A. S. Khomyakov, "Collected Works", Tome I, p. 340.

[2] Ibid., p. 343.

[3] Ibid., p. 344.

churnings".[1] Khomyakov saw the existent in the aspect of will, but it is the reasoning will, in the will, identical with reason. In the volitional reason, in the rational will there obtains an identity of thought and being. The will assumes a central place in the gnosseology of Khomyakov, but his gnosseology -- is ontological. The will for Khomyakov is not a psychological concept. His metaphysics and gnosseology cannot be explained away as a psychologism. Psychologism always is begotten of an alienated and solitary individual soul. Sobornost' however is of a position opposite to every psychologism. The philosophy of Khomyakov can be termed a concrete spiritualism, concrete namely, and not abstract. His spiritualism -- is not the traditionally dualistic sort. The idea of a freely creative spirit -- is a basic idea of the whole of Russian philosophy; it can be found not only with the philosophers, tied in with Slavophilism, but also with philosophers, not directly connected with Slavophilism. Thus, for example, the philosophy of Lopatin is all pervaded by the idea of the freely creating spirit, all in opposition to necessitarianism, to involuntarism. And in this Lopatin is akin to Khomyakov and faithful to the fundamental ontological traditions of Russian philosophy. The same can be said also for A. Kozlov.

Khomyakov together with Kireevsky mustneeds be acknowledged as having set in place the foundation of an unique tradition within Russian philosophy. Russian philosophy possesses a character predominantly ontological; in it gnosseology always occupies a subordinate position, and the logical problems are not especially worked out. *The concrete existent* -- herein is what the Slavophil and Russian philosophy strives after. But can there exist a national philosophy, ought not philosophy to strive towards this, that it be true, rather than national? Certainly, philosophy ought to strive for truth, in love for the pathos of its wisdom. But truth is not revealed in mankind minus flesh and blood. In the great matter of the revealing of truth, always singular, there can be various missions and destinies. Various nations in various epochs are entrusted to reveal various sides of the truth. This is connected with the grasped mindset of a nation, with the fundamental striving of its spirit. The grasped mindset of the will of the Russian people, the integrality of spirit of its direction to the revealing of the mystery of the existent, posits ontological tasks for Russian thought. The religious nature of the Russian people sets before the

---

[1] Ibid., p. 345.

Russian consciousness the task of the creating of a synthetic religious philosophy, the reconciling of knowledge and faith, and towards this aspect it directs our creative power. The ontological and religious strivings of Russian philosophy are not a subordination of truth to nationality, but are rather the revealing by our nationality of the ontological and religious side of truth.

Khomyakov pondered a path of a creative Russian philosophy, he set in place the fundamentals of the tradition. But the gnosseology and metaphysics of Khomyakov were so little elaborated, just as with Kireevsky, that they remained fragmentary. In Khomyakov there was no working out of the cosmological side of his metaphysics. With him cosmology is almost absent, there is no nature-philosophy. This is because, in the religious consciousness of Khomyakov cosmology was likewise almost absent. With him there was no teaching about the world soul. The absence of a cosmology -- was a major blank spot within the Slavophil philosophy. In this Slavophilism was indeed behind, and not ahead of Schelling, who so involved himself problems of nature-philosophy and cosmology. The great idea of Sobornost' in Khomyakov has no connection with any teaching about the soul of the world. And his religio-philosophic consciousness was quite repulsed by an undying truth of paganism, the truth about the earth. *It*, mother-earth, eternal femininity, is almost absence in the philosophic and religious consciousness of Khomyakov. And with *it* only is connected the cosmological side of religious philosophy. Christian cosmology is also a teaching about the soul of the world, about eternal femininity, about mother-earth. This bridge, connecting Christianity with paganism. Within paganism was provided the earthly-feminine foundation of the Church, that *she*, with which the Logos is united. The absence of a cosmology in the consciousness of Khomyakov led to a spiritualistic tendency; with him psychology takes precedence over cosmology. Russian philosophy, religious in spirit, in its ultimate developement in the figure of Vl. Solov'ev, dealt with the cosmological problem, the teaching about the soul of the world. And this was a great step forward.

The Slavophil philosophy, although limited to fragments, although neither Khomyakov nor the other Slavophils left behind large philosophic treatises, nonetheless still provided visible fruition within the history of Russian thought. A Russian philosophic tradition took form, and there was traced out the possibility of an unique philosophic school. Among direct continuers the Slavophil tradition in philosophy was the greatest Russian philosopher Vl. Solov'ev, and thereafter Pr. S. Trubetskoy. Two major philosophic tracts of Vl. Solov'ev, "The Critique of Abstract Principles" and the "Philosophic Principles of Integral Knowledge", are pervaded by the Slavophil spirit. Vl. Solov'ev received from Khomyakov the idea of a critique of abstract principles and the idea of the affirmation of integral knowledge, although he himself recognised this insufficiently. Khomyakov had already surmounted all the abstract rationalism and all the abstraction, by means of his philosophy of an integral knowledge, the knowledge of an integrally whole spirit. Khomyakov asserted an integrally whole, organic reason. Solov'ev brought the fragmentary thoughts of Khomyakov into a system. But in his own method of philosophising, Vl. Solov'ev left the imprint of indirect traces of Hegelianism. It might be perhaps, because it was easier for Solov'ev to render the Slavophil philosophy into a systematic form. Khomyakov was rather more free of Hegelianism. But I am not wont to say, that the philosophy of Solov'ev was simply a repetition of Slavophil ideas. In Vl. Solov'ev there was a great creative mind, and he likewise creatively transformed all the influences. A total critique of abstract principles had not been accomplished by Khomyakov, but only hinted at. Solov'ev brilliantly produced this critique. With Solov'ev there was a philosophic scope and universal breadth, lacking in Khomyakov. He was the sole creator among us of universal a philosophic system, on the order of the great systems of the West, Germany chiefly. This was his contribution to Russian culture. Khomyakov left only philosophic fragments; Solov'ev however left philosophic treatises. But he too, as a Russian man, was too agitated by the spirit of life and therefore he could not devote himself exclusively to the private chamber sort of philosophic studies. Likewise, one must stress the nuances, differentiating Vl. Solov'ev from Khomyakov. Khomyakov's spirit of philosophising was voluntaristic and pragmatic, whereas the spirit of philosophising in Solov'ev was more intellectualistic and logicalist. And in this Khomyakov was closer to us, than was Solov'ev. After Solov'ev, Pr. S. Trubetskoy has continued the Slavophil tradition in philosophy. His remarkable work, "Concerning the Nature of Consciousness", was pervaded with the Slavophil spirit and it developes the Slavophil idea of Sobornost' in its gnosseological aspect. The whole of creative Russian philosophy tends to struggle against individualism, against fallen reason, and for the Sobornost'-communality of consciousness, for the acquiring of the Logos. In Russia there is a surmounting of philosophy as an abstract principle, and therefore it has provided the way for an exit from out of the blind alley, which modern European philosophy has gotten itself trapped in, thus providing an the possibility for surmounting the crisis of philosophy.

Russians are called to create a religious philosophy, a philosophy of the integral spirit. Our whole national aggregate bespeaks this, the ingrained and age old striving of our mentally-grasped will. The will posits the tasks of thought, and by our thoughts our will always posits the tasks of an integral grasping of the meaning of being and of life. Our creative thought is not directed at the solving of special problems of gnosseology and logic; moreso rather is it innate and necessary for us to solve problems of religious ontology, the philosophy of history, of ethics. This is a fact, with which it is impossible not to reckon. Khomyakov therefore also can be regarded as the founder of Russian philosophy, in that he penetrated into the most intimate aspects of Russian thought, and he philosophised about that which tormented the Russian spirit. In Russia, philosophy does not start with the same end-purpose, with which philosophy is initiated in Germany. And this is, first of all, a difference of life and not of logic, for these are different world-perceptions. Russia cannot renounce its own world-perception and by doing so seek for the wellspring of its philosophy. We begin our philosophising from life and we philosophise for life; in this sense we are born to be pragmatists prior to any "pragmatism". But our pragmatism is not relativistic nor is it of the sceptic sort, since it is connected with religious experience, in which obtains given absolute life.

Even the irreligious, the atheistic Russian intelligentsia, confessing various forms of a distorted positivism, unconsciously has striven towards a philosophy of an integral wholeness of spirit and only in regards to its fatal splintering was it hostile to the Slavophil philosophy. It is especially important to note the connection of Russian philosophy with Russian literature. The Russian national spirit has found its perfect expression in the creativity of the Russian great writers. Our literature -- is the most metaphysical and the most religious in the world. It suffices but to call to mind Dostoevsky, in order to sense, what philosophy can and ought to be in Russia. Russian metaphysics becomes transmitted into the philosophic language of Dostoevsky. Just as with Richard Wagner, through whom can be unriddled a clew to the spirit of German philosophy. Russian philosophy values its connection with Russian literature. And this connection, always witnessing to an organic belonging to the soul and body of Russia, cannot be sundered by any sort of gnosseology, logic or methodology. An abstract

ALEKSEI STEPANOVICH KHOMYAKOV

logic is powerless to prevail over the spirit of life, which possesses its own organic logic. Khomyakov questioned the spirit of life, the first one of all he questioned it, and in this was all his significance. The initial point of view of Khomyakov's philosophy, which appears also as the initial point of view of the whole of Russian philosophy, neither demands nor allows of a "gnosseological" basis in the sense of a Kantian critique of philosophy. This philosophy from the start does not recognise the primacy of suchlike a gnosseology, for it is instead ontological in origin, it begins with life, with being, with givenness, nor does it surrender the will to the splintered off rational-judgement and its pretensions. Gnosseologism is a philosophy of abstract rational-judgement, whereas ontologism is a philosophy of the integral reason. The integral reason, however, discovers not abstract categories, but rather concrete realities. Whereas the dispute of the critical gnosseologists against the Slavophil philosophy is represented by them as a dispute logical, scientific, cultural, -- the protagonists of the Slavophil philosophy understand however, that this is a dispute vital, volitional, religious. The Slavophil path, that of Russian philosophy, presupposes a choice, of Eros, with the exertion of the whole of spiritual existence. This path is akin to that of the finest philosophical traditions of Greece, with the traditions of the philosophy of Eros.

In Khomyakov's time, creative thought stood facing the tasks of surmounting Kant and Hegel, while now at present, creative thought strands facing the tasks of surmounting Neo-Kantianism and Neo-Hegelianism, gods of a lesser grandeur, but no less mighty. The whole cycle of the German Idealism has continued on still into a modernised form, with the addition of a "neo" prefix. Khomyakov and the Slavophils had to struggle against a classical idealism. At present the struggle is against an epigonal derivative idealism. That armament, which was forged out in the struggle with the classic German idealism, against the summits of Western philosophy, can be of use also in the struggle against the modern idealism. Modern thought cannot rest content with the philosophy of Khomyakov, -- in it there is much of the archaic, with its own times it is too much immeasurably entangled. But sub specie aeternitatis there is in the philosophy of Khomyakov also something enduring and unalterable. The idea of the philosophy of integral spirit is bestown us for all time. And for all time is evident the self-decay of abstract rational-judgement, of fallen reason. Fallen reason ought to be brought back up, to restore its lost wholeness, its organicity. Then only will become possible a philosophy of the existent, and only a philosophy of the existent is an essential philosophy. But I have pointed already to this, that in the philosophy of Khomyakov there is almost completely absent a cosmology and nature-philosophy. A philosophy, faithful to the legacy of the Slavophil spirit, ought first of all to work out a cosmology. This was partly done by Vl. Solov'ev, but in too dialectical a method. And yet this fact, that the nature-philosophy motif had not been basic for Khomyakov, further confirms that the Slavophil philosophy was not some mere Schellingism upon Russian a soil, but was rather a phenomenon organic and original. This was a phenomenon, akin in spirit to Franz Baader, but quite independently of him, nor nourished by the mystic Jacob Boehme, whom Khomyakov on his own admission altogether did not know, but rather instead, the mysticism of Eastern Christianity. I want to stress once more, that the philosophy of Khomyakov in its spirit -- is a churchly philosophy and cannot otherwise be understood. This was a philosophy faithful to the truth of the Church, it is sustained by a mystical acceptance of concrete realities, and is possessed by reasoning not abstract, but rather organic. Only fidelity to the basic tradition of the philosophy of Khomyakov and Kireevsky, only the consciousness of its paternity can lead to a philosophic rebirth of Russia. Creative culture is impossible without tradition, without a succession, without an uniqueness. Only by its own national culture does each nation serve world culture, render in its flesh and blood universal a deed. This was profoundly understood by Khomyakov and he pointed out for the Russian consciousness a path, on which it could serve towards a worldwide renaissance. We certainly ought always to learn philosophically from the West, to love western culture, on the example of Kireevsky, but we ought certainly to return our obligation to Western thought, with which we have many connections. At present we are entering into an epoch, when Russian philosophy both can and should lead western philosophy out of its blind alley, to save it from meonism and illusionism. And now we pass over to the most developed part of Khomyakov's philosophy -- to his philosophy of history.

Chapter V

Khomyakov's Philosophy of History

In the philosophy of Khomyakov the area most elaborated is the philosophy of history. The problems of the philosophy of history in particular were of concern to the Slavophil consciousness. Along with a series of articles of philosophico-historical significance, three tomes of Khomyakov's collected works are devoted to his "Notes on World History". The philosophy of history -- is the most worked out part in the philosophy of Khomyakov, and indeed of any of the world-views of the Slavophils. This is explicable by the exceptional concern in the problem of history, as the problem over the future of Russia. The philosophy of the integral life of the spirit also had to be of interest into the problem of the meaning of history. Within Slavophilism there had been wrought an act of national self-consciousness, and already therefore the fate of history, the fate of East and West had to evoke an exceptional interest. National self-consciousness always finds its philosophic formulation in the constructing of a philosophy of history. This selfsame interest involving a philosophy of history occurred also in Germany in the period of the end-XVIII and beginning-XIX Centuries. But here also, within the sphere of the philosophy of history, neither Khomyakov, nor any of the other Slavophils, created systems, and they could neither create it nor should they have created it. In this regard, their attitude towards history was too alive, and their contemplation of history was too concrete. Khomyakov's "Notes on World History" -- consists of raw notes. And this -- was a notebook, the diary of a thinker. These were thus mere notes and remained in the rough, and in such form they were not intended for publication. From them there might be compiled a genuine book for reading, but in such a raw form these notes would be unsatisfactory, and in the strict sense of the word they could not be called a literary product. Only specialists read these notes. Within this unsystematic heap of raw material are scattered about precious thoughts, brilliant intuitions, precise critical jottings on the most varied questions. Khomyakov always indeed wrote simultaneously about everything, not differentiating his material, not fixing upon a particular subject. With him there was always a very definite striving, a beloved thought, which he expressed from all the angles. In one article, as I have already pointed out, he speaks simultaneously concerning Max Stirner, and about the ancient Russian society, and about Peter the Great, and about the insignificance of Russian science, and about the person in art, and about the icon, and about the mir peasant-assemblies; throughout all these angles he expresses one dear thought. The outward chaotic aspect of exposition in him is connected with a tremendous inward concentration of thought. The "Notes on World History" from the outward side present an impression of complete chaos, an heap of raw materials, slovenly rough drafts. But inwardly the notes are united by a single idea, with everything touched on in succession.

Khomyakov did not love scholarly processes of research, he was not at all of that studious sort. He sometimes makes factual errors. He quotes always by memory, which was always an astonishing thing about him, and he never makes a citation. All his "Notes on World History" was written from memory, without references from books, and they abound still with facts. There is even too much factual material from him for a work dealing with the philosophy of history. The abundance of historical facts, those of purely concrete material, renders the "Notes" particularly antiquated for our times, not corresponding to the standards of our contemporary historical science. But the "Notes on World History" well bears examining not as history, but as a philosophy of history. In facing the court of historical science the "Notes" of Khomyakov do not hold up under criticism, but they have not lost their interest and significance as an attempt at an uniquely original philosophy of history. A philosophy of history can never become so outmoded, as might an history, as might a scientific historical investigation. Khomyakov himself did not perhaps provide clear methodological boundaries between the philosophy of history and historical science, but for us this is not so very important. His philosophy of history remains a landmark in our national thinking. The problem of East and West -- here was the central concern of all the Slavophil thought; around this problem was created the Slavophil philosophy of history. The problem of East and West -- is basic not only for the Russian philosophy of history, but also for Russian history, -- it is a basic task of our history.

Khomyakov's philosophy of history sprouted up within the atmosphere of the worldwide Romantic spirit at the beginning of the XIX Century. It is impossible to deny the influence of the Romantic historicism upon the Slavophils, and this influence nowise diminishes the originality of Slavophilism as a "Romanticism" purely Russian. For the rationalism of the XVIII Century there existed nothing historical, organic, irrational, nothing clothed in flesh and blood. Only in the bosom of the Romantic movement was there begotten an interest in "the historical". There was thus put forth the problem of history, and it was acknowledged to be organic, national, irrational. They sensed the value of the traditional, connected with the life of the people. Thereupon was born the idea of developement and the idea of an organic understanding of history. This Romantic movement, which as I have already said before, was not only "romantic", but "realist" also, and it was worldwide in character. Within the bosom of this movement was born both the philosophy of history, and also modern historical science. The historical school could not arise prior to the romantic encounter with the spirit of history, with the national spirit. Khomyakov was not a romantic by nature, and this was sufficiently explained in the chapter, dealing with the traits of him as a person. But in his philosophy of history there is a whole series of romantic motifs. There is in him a romantic idealisation of the past, and an acknowledging of the importance of an artistic intuition for history, and an organic understanding of the process of history. In the very first "Note" Khomyakov says: "Within science there is still a poetry, because science is a friend of truth".[1] And further on he says: "Poetry is needful, in order to know history; there is necessary an artistic sense, i.e. with human truth purely, in order to divine the might of one-sided an energy, inspiring millions of people".[2] History for Khomyakov was the developement of a living, concrete organism. In his attitude towards history there was a profound acknowledgement of father and mother, of a blood connection with the past, the present and the future. "Everything of the present has its roots in the past".[3] The rationalistic denial of the legacy of the fathers, of the legacy of history, was for him deeply alien and contrary. He recognised the inevitability of a conservative element within historical developement, he demanded a noble attitude towards one's fatherland. Every lapse was intolerable for him. We

---

[1] A. S. Khomyakov, "Collected Works", Tome V, p. 6.

[2] Ibid., Tome V, p. 71.

[3] Ibid., Tome V, p. 22.

have seen already his organic love for English Toryism. A love for the "historical" being such for the fatherland was very characteristic for Khomyakov. He wants first of all to be faithful to his own land, to his own soil, and impelled by this sense of fidelity, he constructs his own philosophy of history. In essence, in his scientific proclivity Khomyakov himself belonged to the historical school, although he polemicised against individual representatives of this school. He recognises the legitimacy of organic developement within history. He wants not only to be a religious thinker, but also an erudite historian.

Khomyakov's philosophy of history mixes together two points of view: the religio-mystical and the scientific-positive. It is difficult to determine, from whence derive the basic positions of Khomyakov's philosophy of history, -- whether from a scientific, or from a religious source. A large portion of the philosophico-historical assertions of Khomyakov possess twofold a meaning, not quite scientific, not quite religious. In this is a fundamental defect of Khomyakov's philosophy of history. He has little of a clear methodology of historical knowledge. At the basis of his philosophy of history stand two ideas: the first, is the idea that the moving principle of the historical life of peoples is faith, while secondly is the idea of mutually antagonistic principles in the history of mankind -- of freedom and necessity, of spirit and of materiality. Both ideas are derived by Khomyakov via a religio-philosophic, and not a scientifo-philosophic path. Behind the historical science of Khomyakov is hidden a religious idea: the acknowledgement of faith at the mysterious origins of the histories of peoples and the free spirit as the creative principle of history. Khomyakov deeply despises the biases of erudite historians, their insipidness, their formalism and schoolish mentality. "From beneathe the tumultuous heavens, from out of the life of God's world amidst the bustle of their brother people, the scholarly bookmen arrogantly strode off into the stuffy solitude of their libraries, surrounding themself with evidences of their own self-conceit and blocking entry to the great lessons of existence and truth".[1] Khomyakov begins his "Notes on World History" with the words: "Man, the king and the slave of earthly nature, recognises within himself an higher, spiritual life. He has empathy with the world, he strives towards the source of every event and every truth, he is uplifted with thoughts about godliness and in it he finds the

---

[1] A. S. Khomyakov, "Collected Works", Tome V, p. 42.

crown of all his existence. Whether dark, or whether bright be his concept, whether it be eternal truth or a transitory phantom that he brings his generation, in any case faith comprises the limit of his inner developement. From its circle he cannot emerge beyond, since faith is the highest point of all his ponderings, the secret condition of his desire and action, the extreme bound of his knowing. Within it is both his personal and social future, in it is the ultimate conclusion of all the fullness of his intellectual and worldly existence".[1] Further on he says concerning this: "Faith is the most perfected fruition of a people's culture, the furthermost and utmost limit of its developement. Be it false or true, it includes within itself the whole world of human thoughts and feelings".[2] Khomyakov sets religio-philosophic preconditions to his philosophy of history. But together with this, his philosophy of history makes pretension to being scientific, within it a large place is occupied by ethnography and linguistics, and great significance is ascribed to a racial aspect. The basic intent with Khomyakov's philosophy of history -- is as a basis for Slavic and Russian messianism. But herein he seeks to ground this messianism scientifically, ethnographically, linguistically, and not religio-prophetically nor mystically. He seizes upon faith and the creativity of the free spirit as constituting empirical facts of history and he wants empirically to demonstrate the great pre-eminence of the Slavs and Russia. In such a manner, science easily becomes falsified, fantastic theories on the special significance of the Slavic language and the Slavs are created, the English are avowed to be Slavs, etc. There cannot be a Slavophil science, and it would be impossible to posit a Russian messianism dependent upon such a dubious science. It is impossible to ground any sort of messianism upon faith of its being an historical and ethnographic fact, i.e. upon faith as an object of historical knowledge; messianism can only be based upon faith as an inward fact of revelation and insight, upon faith as a subject of cognition.

Khomyakov posits the prophetic problem of East and West as grounded within the Russian philosophy of history and within Russian history, but he does not resolve it in prophetic a spirit. With him there is no prophetic interpretation of history and frequently we meet with a moralising over history. In his philosophy of history ethics prevails over

---

[1] A. S. Khomyakov, "Collected Works", Tome V, p. 8.

[2] Ibid., Tome V, p. 168.

the mystical. In it there is a religio-moral appraisal, but there are no religio-mystical insights. In Khomyakov there are no mystical insights into the times and aeons of world history, there is no eschatology in his philosophy of history, there is not the idea of the end. There is no apocalypsis in his Christian philosophy of history; and only within an apocalypsis can there obtain a prophetic mysticism of history. The Slavophils were men reflecting their way of life, and the spirit of their way of life pervades all their philosophy of history. Hence there is no sense of catastrophe in Khomyakov's conception of history, there is no trembling nor dread in the face of mysterious historical destinies; much in their way of life was happy. And therefore Khomyakov's philosophy of history cannot thus be termed as conclusive and sustainable within a religio-mystical spirit, since in it there is no catastrophic end, there is no tragic struggle of the spirit of Christ against the spirit of the Anti-Christ. In the history of Khomyakov there is not sensed the power of the spirit of the Anti-Christ: his life was lived too comfortably in his Russian lifestyle, on his landlord estate, in the family setting. And thus the whole of history presented itself to him in this lifestyle mode, this familial and estate light, and it was the same moreover with the Russian history, the Slavic history. The philosophy of history for Khomyakov and the Slavophils consists no little of the happy and felicitous. And Khomyakov deduces Russian messianism from out of Russian history as a fact of life, as something empirical. In this messianism there are no tasks entrusted to human freedom, and there is nothing of the tragic such as is connected with freedom. The mystical aspect of history, the messianic aspects of propheticism with Khomyakov stand in too great a non-reliance upon science, upon linguistics, ethnography etc., with an empirical lifestyle. But the mystical aspect all the same cannot depend upon science, just as science ought not to be dependent upon the mystical. Still, Khomyakov writes his notes on world history, such as though history were not subject to the uninterrupted activity of Divine Providence, -- there is no realisation of the prophetic in it and in it there is no tragic clash of creative freedom with the decrees of God. For mysticism, history is a revelation. However, the moralising over history contains within it the danger of a tendency towards Deism. The struggle of freedom with necessity, of the spirit with materiality, which Khomyakov sees everywhere in history, can transpire within the bounds of the Creation and not lead to a clash with Divine Providence. It remains unclear, whether the historical process for Khomyakov, was it a matter of the revelation and the realisation of the prophecies? It is unclear from his philosophy of history, what sort of role within the historical process the Church plays as an ontological reality. Within history, he has as it were no feel for the life of the world soul. For him it is as though he senses only the revelation in individual souls, but not in the soul of the world. Nor with him is there the great mystery of the correlation of the masculine and the feminine within history (not in man, but in mankind).

Chaadayev's philosophy of history was consistently more religious than Khomyakov's philosophy of history; in Chaadayev there was less a pretension to a scientific basis of the religious meaning of history. Within Catholicism there was a traditional philosophy of history, there was the teaching about a providential plane of history, and also about the acting of Divine Providence within history. There is a philosophy of history in Blessed Augustine, in Bossuet, in the French theocratic school of the early XIX Century. An Orthodox philosophy of history did not exist. The Catholic drift of Chaadayev helped him assert a religious philosophy of history, whereas Khomyakov's exclusive Orthodoxy made it difficult to create a religious philosophy of history. Within Orthodoxy there was not that active attitude towards history, such as was in Catholicism. Therefore either there can nowise be an Orthodox philosophy of history, or else there could be an apocalyptic philosophy of history, with acute a positing of the eschatological problem. The Catholic philosophy of history exists, however, also outside the apocalyptic perspectives. But we have seen, that Khomyakov has no apocalypsis, that the eschatological problem is not raised by him. His philosophy of history therefore cannot precisely be termed Orthodox and religious, in it there are religio-moral premises, but there is no providential plane to history. In Chaadayev there is a providential plane to history, and his philosophy of history can be called religious, though Catholic in spirit. In contrast, Khomyakov decides the philosophic-historical problem of East and West on the aegis of his own reason, not that of churchly reason, and in his resolution of the matter the religious aspect gets mixed up imperceptibly together with the scientific and positivist mannerisms. With Vl. Solov'ev the philosophy of history gets defined more religiously and mystically, than with Khomyakov, and this is due to the prophetic spirit of Solov'ev. In his "History and Future of Christian Theocracy" there is a genius of mystical insights, there is an astonishing understanding of prophecy. Vl. Solov'ev recognised a mystical subject within history, and he penetrated into the mystery of its world historical fate. Solov'ev stands at the boundary line of a new world epoch, when the apocalyptic consciousness has been born within Russia. For Khomyakov there was neither a world soul, nor an apocalyptic consciousness, and in this is his limitation, his boundary. The weak sides of Khomyakov's philosophy of history were further on developed by such echoes of Slavophilism as, for example, Danilevsky. Danilevsky's philosophy of history is already nowise religious nor mystical, -- this is a quasi-scientific and quasi-positivist philosophy of history. The "Slavophil science" gets reborn into a sort of inadmissible naturalism. Danilevsky openly bases the great vocation of Russia upon naturalistic grounds, his Slavophilism is gets justified not religiously, but rather upon natural-science, upon ethnography, linguistics, on a teaching about races and types of developement. This naturalistic Slavophilism is also there in Konstantin Leont'ev, in whom a false naturalism is combined with mysticism and with religious dread. In the Slavophil philosophy there were admittedly elements of a pagan naturalism, and these have led to a reborn and wild nationalism, altogether not religious. In Khomyakov the naturalism was combined with moralism, but in the later period the naturalism was freed of any sense of morals; both these aspects have impeded the creation of a religious philosophy of history. But all these deficiencies should not prevent us from acknowledging Khomyakov's philosophy of history as a remarkable effort, in places almost of genius.

* * *

The most remarkable, the idea of Khomyakov nigh closest to genius, set at the foundation of his "Notes on world History". Is this -- his division of the powers acting within history, the Kushite and the Iranian. From the Kushite element there comes forth the religion of necessity, of the might of nature, of magic. From the Iranian element there comes forth a religion of freedom, of the creative spirit. In almost all the pagan religions Khomyakov sees the triumph of the Kushite element. The Iranian spirit was most of all expressed in the Jewish religion. Christianity is however the ultimate triumph of the Iranian element, of the religion of freedom, the religion of the creative spirit, victorious over all the religions of necessity, -- the religions of the magic of being. "The first and chief object, upon which historical criticism ought to turn its attention, is the faith of the people... The measure of enlightenment, the character of the enlightenment and its sources are determined by the measure, the character and the source of faith. In its myths live traditions about the ancient stirrings of the tribes, and in the legends -- is an image of their moral and societal mode of life, and in their mysteries -- is a whole world of their mental composition. The faith of primitive peoples determined their historical fate; history was converted into religious myth and only in it has it been preserved for us. Such is a general rule, with which all the investigations of antiquity ought to start with".[1] The view that mythology is also ancient history, that the history of a religion is also a record of primitive history, -- this is a thought that Khomyakov shares with Schelling.[2] And therefore a philosophy of primitive religion is also for Khomyakov a principle of the philosophy of history. The views of Khomyakov on pagan mythology are quite outmoded, but his fundamental division of matters into the Kushite and Iranian includes within it thoughts of a religio-philosophic character, and therefore it stands above and apart from the developement of the historical science concerning religion. The Fall led to a loss of freedom, with a subjection to necessity, to materiality. Iranianism is based upon the tradition about freedom, the Kushite -- upon the triumph of necessity. In an Iranian religion there obtains the knowledge about freedom, in the Kushite -- the knowledge about necessity. "All the ancient faiths divide into two categories: as a worshipping in spirit as creative freedom, or to the worshipping in life as eternally-necessary fact. We have found a sign of this in making a god of the serpent or alternately in an hatred towards it".[3] "The comparison of faith and enlightenment, which is singularly dependent upon faith and is included within it, leads us to two root principles: to the Iranian. i.e. to the spiritual reverencing of the feely creative spirit or towards the primal-origin monotheistic utmost deity, or the Kushite -- the acknowledging of an eternal organic necessity, effected under the power of the logical inevitability of laws. Kushitism divides down further into two segments: to Shiva-ism -- the worship of the material domain, and Buddhism -- the worship of enslaved spirit, finding its freedom only in self-annihilation. These two principles, in their unceasing clashes and

---

[1] A. S. Khomyakov, "Collected Works", Tome V, p. 131.

[2] Vide "Schelling's Werke", Dritter Band, 1907, p. 588.

[3] A. S. Khomyakov, "Collected Works", Tome V, p. 324.

comminglings have produced that infinite manifold of religions, which the human race disgraced itself with prior to Christianity, and especially the theatrical and anthropomorphic ones. But, in spite of a bit of commingled confusion, the innate basis of faith is expressed by the general character of enlightenment, i.e. by the oral instruction, by the tone of the literature, by the simple aspects of the common lifestyle, by the spiritual prayer and scorn towards the body, expressed through consigning the corpse to burning or as food for animals in Iranianism, or by a contrived education, a symbolic literature, by a stipulative ordering of governance, by conjurative prayer and reverence for the body, expressed either by embalming, or by cannibalising of the dead, or by similar rituals, within Kushitism".[1] Khomyakov sees in the Gnostics a Kushite principle, for which a characteristic symbol is the serpent. "The hostility between the Jewish principle and the Kushite found expression throughout all the developements of Israelite life. And after the fall of Israel itself, a long while after the fall of Egypt, it was expressed still more vividly in the teaching of the Gnostics and namely of the Ophite-Serpent Gnostics, direct and indisputable inheritors of Egyptian and Phoenician thought. Although they were already ashamed of their former crude concepts, although in part they spurned the organic duality, the too nakedly offended human sense, but the former Master/Vladyka of the people of Israel (Sabaoth)became nevertheless represented by them as an evil principle, and evil namely because, that it was creatively free, and therefore, that it summons its creation to a free spiritual life. Whereas for them the serpent, summoning people to a life of the material, to submission to the laws of the world of necessity, the serpent is for them the messenger of an higher, a good principle. Gnosis is knowledge, but not knowledge of freedom, rather instead a knowledge of necessity. Its production from the Egyptian-Phoenician systems is needless to demonstrate: it is clear and indisputable; in it namely is the noted symbol of the serpent. In all the religions purely Iranian the serpent is presented as evil, but in the Kushite -- as good".[2] The Iranian leads to theism, it affirms the free creativity of the Personal Spirit, whereas the Kushite leads to pantheism and to the teaching about emanation. The Iranian expressed itself in the word, and this is a religion of

---

[1] A. S. Khomyakov, "Collected Works", Tome V, p. 530-531.

[2] Ibid., p. 219.

the word; the Kushite expressed itself in architecture, in memorial materiality, and this is a wordless religion. "The key to the developement of the Kushite, is its engrained tendency of the purely material, the erecting of so very gigantic monuments in architecture and sculpture and not bequeathing us a single word, either of inspired poetry or pervaded by life-creative thought. Buddhism reaches an high degree of spirituality, but only in the sense of an abstraction from materiality. In this spirituality there is no self-initiating and living impulse; it is naught else than negation, elevated up to a religious significance... The teaching of the Buddhists was and is a cult of non-being... It hid away the crude materiality, from which it was born, and it substituted a replacement for the distinct form of birth with the phantom of emanation... The original archetype was preserved obdurately and indelibly. Buddhism is subordinated exactly the same to necessity, is exactly the same bereft of moral impulse, as in Shiva-ism; but that, which was manifest in materiality under the phantasm of life, has exposed its own lifelessness, when it passed over into the sphere of creative spirit and failed to acknowledge within itself the freely creative principle".[1] The triumph of the Kushite is traced down by Khomyakov in the ultimate fate of philosophy. "Those very appearances, which we meet with amidst the study of the Kushite materiality cult, have to repeat themself and actually do repeat themself within all the philosophies, which historically and logically have arisen from materialism or from consideration upon the inalterable consequences of visible nature or of the cognitive mind, which is naught else than the mirror-image of the cognitive world. The mysterious teaching about necessity has peeped through and persisted in all the diverse philosophic forms, be they scepticism or dogmatism, analysis or synthesis. A refuted system would arise anew within a refuting system in accord with a law of direct antagonism; and after endless nuances concerning essence, being, the knowable, the knowing and knowledge, all the effects of bold reason itself could only reach the deduction of the negative, of the self-annihilation of necessity within cognition. But since the negation has not satisfied all the demands of the mind, negative freedom has declared seeming rights as proper to the will and has termed itself the free consciousness of necessity: a woesome logical subterfuge, derived by the tenacious toiling of German thought from logical, i.e. necessary laws of the material-mental world. Correct or

---

[1] A. S. Khomyakov, "Collected Works", Tome V, p. 224.

incorrect, this philosophy received its own full and lawful developement; but the egoistic mentality of our times ought not to overlook the profound meaning of the ritualism of ages past within history. Kushitism, in its abstract tendency, was wont already from of old to pass over into modern impersonalism, into pantheism".[1] Khomyakov sees this as all one and the same Kushite principle, be it in the Phoenician religion, or in Buddhism, or in materialism, or in Hegel. "Iran based its faith on the tradition concerning freedom or upon the inward consciousness of it. The Kushites we have to guess about, whereas the Iranians tell about themselves. Foremost amidst their testimonies in antiquity, in its definiteness and simplicity, is occupied by the writings of the people of Israel; second place indisputably belongs to Brahmanism, in spite of a thoughtless admixture of other religions; and a third place finally of a clearly expressed concept of moral freedom is contained in the books, ascribed to Zerdushta (Zarathustra). The areas however, in which it was lost into a characterless syncretism, -- Babylon, Assyria, Phoenicia and Hellas, permit of criticism only on a few aspects of the primordial faith, but they do not contain in themselves anything truly organic. Elemental Shiva-ism was depicted as dualistically derived, a crude symbol of necessity; contemplative Buddhism assumed the form of a capricious emanation, hence of necessity. Starting off clearly and decisively from the principle, completely foreign to the Kushite system, the Iranian religion elevates everything visible and particular within life towards the eternally-existent spirit, giving it various names, whether though locale, the character of the language, or the trend of the infantile thought of man. God in the sense of Creator is the fundamental characteristic feature of Iranism. Freedom is posited as a principle, a moral good -- the highest value of every fragment of being".[2] And thus, factually within the history of pagan religions there has occurred the syncretic admixture of Iranism, preserving the Divine tradition on freedom and the creativity of the personal spirit, an admixture together with Kushitism, with subjection to necessity and materiality. Upon the basis of this admixture was also created the system of emanation, in which was distorted the idea of the Divine creativity. "The free power of spirit does not tolerate of any sort of limitation, it cannot share the worldly sphere with the other

---

[1] A. S. Khomyakov, "Collected Works", Tome V, p. 225.

[2] Ibid., p. 230.

principle, which seeks domination, and not freedom. The world is foreign to it and it is foreign to the world, if the world as such possess in itself any sort of self-sufficiency, any sort of germ of independence, not thus recognised as the manifestation of the freely manifesting spirit. The least corner of the world, not dependent upon spirit, suffices for necessity. How quickly its rights are preserved, in it is acknowledged some sort of autonomy, self-sufficiency: from the easy admixture of the spiritual world into a thoughtless caprice thus exhausts itself in a fruitless struggle against unyielding matter. Necessity is a fact and naught else than a fact. The fact's independence is a triumph of necessity. Spirit struggles and suffers; whereas fact lives without meaning, without consciousness, without suffering".[1] "Within historical times, the Iranian teaching belongs already to the Jews alone".[2] "The sacred for Iran was everything, even the materiality, in which was manifest the free and creative spirit; the sacred was the sound of the word, a thought enclothed, and the sacred was the letter, a conditional form, given to this sound. To the Kushites however the sacred was coarse matter, elemental and unthought, the sacred was artistry, the natural form of its being, and hieroglyphics, the half-natural form of its action".[3] Iranianism created world literature, poetry, sacred lettering, the word. In Iranianism is the Logos. Kushitism created prodigious material memorials, in architecture and sculpture. In Kushitism there is not the Logos. This is an innate idea of Khomyakov.

    The views of Khomyakov on antiquity, on the Greek religion are very outmoded and out of date. After Nietzsche, after E. Rhode, after Vyach. Ivanov it is impossible to speak thus about Greece, as Khomyakov speaks. Only now in the present period has there been revealed within Greece, within paganism, both the world soul and the tragedy wrought within it, preparing for the coming of Christ. Khomyakov failed to appreciate the great significance of paganism for Christianity. Paganism provided the foundation for the Church -- the earth, the soul of the world. In paganism, in Greece especially, there was revealed the world soul for the reception of the Logos. In Judaism, in the Old Testament, there was

---

[1] A. S. Khomyakov, "Collected Works", Tome V, p. 322.

[2] Ibid., p. 323.

[3] Ibid., p. 368.

only the revelation of God. Khomyakov does not sense this revelation of the world soul in paganism, nor does he know, that in the soul of Greece trembled the soul of the world in its coming to Christ. Khomyakov sensed but weakly the eternal-feminine basis of the Church, mother-earth, the Mother of God. The traditional theology, the seminary attitude towards paganism all the while has been poisoning the Christian world, hiding away a great mystery, and it has to be surmounted in the interests of churchly renewal. Khomyakov was free of the seminary theological mentality. But in him there was no insight into the truths of paganism, he had no feel for the mystical in Greece, and therefore he went astray with the traditional theological view. And indeed not only the history of Greece, but the entirety of world history ought to be reconsidered, in it there ought anew to be discerned a religious meaning, religious, and not theological. But here is what Khomyakov says about Greece and Rome: "If Rome once upon a time displayed a but dim presentiment of a cognition of God, if the creative thought of the Hellenes sought to unwravel the being of the Supreme Spirit or its reflection in the human soul, then in these rather late appearances there might be seen but the influence of the Iranian East or the awakening of a particular awareness of an enlightened philosophy. Never whether in Hellas, or in Rome, did the philosophic perspective lift up to religion. It always remained on the lower rungs of logical deduction or instinctive conjecture, or of school thesis, of the strange in life and the incapable of outward clarification. We have seen the Eleusinian and other mysteries could contain within them weak intimations of the Iranian living cognition of God; we might also make bold to say, that the Kushite worship of elemental necessity was preserved in the mysteries of Dionysos".[1] Mystical Greece in Khomyakov's time had not still been adequately investigated and he therefore lacked real personal insights into it. The religious consciousness of Khomyakov was not oriented towards the feminine element as an eternal and independent principle, without which there be no Church nor the appearance of Christ in the world. Khomyakov's "Iranianism" is also a principle exclusively masculine, and "Kushitism" -- the feminine principle. The exclusive affirmation of the Iranian spirit is also an exclusive affirmation of a masculine religion, a solar religion. But Christianity is indeed a masculine-feminine religion, a religion of the uniting of the two principles, the uniting of the Logos with

---

[1] A. S. Khomyakov, "Collected Works", Tome V, p. 331.

the world soul, of the Light-Bearing Man with the feminine earth. The Kushite element was the source of slavery and chaos, but in it lived the feminine, capable of being enlightened. In this abasement of femininity as being the earthly and earthly basis of the Christian Church -- is the chief defect of the whole teaching of Khomyakov about Iranianism and Kushitism. The triumph of truth represented itself to Khomyakov as the exclusive triumphing of the Iranian masculine. "Spirit triumphed over matter, and the Iranian tribe takes hold over the world. The ages have passed, and its force does not weaken, and in its hands is the fate of mankind. The descendants reap the fruits of the service of their ancestors, of services, expressed and testified with the immutability of the word. The greatness of Iran is not a matter of chance and conditional circumstances. It is the direct and necessary manifestation of spiritual powers, alive in it from time immemorial, and as a reward for this, that of all the human families it has longest of all preserved the feeling of human worth and human brotherhood, a feeling woefully lost by the Iranians in the frenzy of their victories and evoked anew, but already not by the power of their own particular reason".[1] The mystique of the world soul was foreign to Khomyakov and there is nothing in it within his conception of world history. He insufficiently recognised, that within Christianity there has been preserved the mystery of Divinised-matter. Iranianism was exclusively "spirit-worship", whereas with Christianity there is likewise a sanctification of the flesh, a transfiguration of the earth. In Khomyakov there was still that traditional theological view, under which revelation was given only to Israel, whereas the other Iranian peoples preserve only the memory of the primordial fate of man, as related in the Bible. This view does not hold up under scientific criticism and bears upon itself the seal of a religious limitedness. But these words of Khomyakov are characteristic: "The lofty significance of the creative spirit is apparent in many, especially in the gods, though almost never in the goddesses, in which (since they are completely foreign to Iran) the Kushite principle predominates".[2] Herein the eternally feminine has failed to entice, just as occurs with Khomyakov.

The division into Iranism and Kushitism lies at the crux of Khomyakov's philosophy of history. With this division is connected also

---

[1] A. S. Khomyakov, "Collected Works", Tome V, p. 528-529.

[2] A. S. Khomyakov, "Collected Works", Tome VI, p. 40.

the resolution of the basic problem of the philosophy of history, the problem of East and West. With indeed the very first words of his philosophy of history, when Khomyakov speaks about the Iranian and Kushite religions, he readies the soil for the basis of the mission of the Orthodox East, of Slavism and of Russia. In the West, in European culture, in Catholicism evidently there has had to triumph the Kushite and Christianity be distorted. Therein -- is the obdurate magicism, the might of material necessity, the dominion of the logico-rationalist principle within the consciousness. In Catholicism the Kushite spirit was inherited from ancient Rome. In the East, in Orthodoxy, in Russian culture there happened to triumph the Iranism, the pure Christianity, the integral wholeness of spirit and its free creativity. Only Orthodox Russia preserves, according to Khomyakov, the tradition concerning the freedom of the spirit, and in it the spirit of Iranism has been expressed most purely. Therefore Orthodox Russia ascribes so little significance to everything external, material, formal, juridical; for it the chief thing -- is the spirit of life. The struggle of the Christian East and the Christian West is also a struggle of the Iranian and Kushite elements within the Christian world, the struggle of spiritual freedom and material necessity; of the moral versus the magical. Concerning Rome, Khomyakov says: "Of necessity there arose and was strengthened personal freedom, the sense of law and the one-sided trend of mind, which transformed each Roman into a legislator and a lawyer, at the same time killing within the soul all his striving for spiritual freedom, all the lofty intents of thought and all the existence of inner life. Such a developement of personal freedom and sense of family, although already distorted, the sense of an outward truth and the apotheosis of the state itself, the benefit of which was the supreme of all laws, gave Rome a might incontestable, an untiring constancy, an haughty consciousness of its own superiority over all the other, the less organised societies, and undoubtable victory in all the struggles with other tribes and powers. But the one-sidedness of developement purely external readied the ruin for Rome in its very triumph, by taking away all the spiritual foundations of morality, replacing all the innate principles with conditional and capricious principles and annihilating the possibility of a religious and peaceful life".[1] "Rome gave the Western world a new religion, a religion of the societal accord, elevated to a degree of unconditional sanctity, not demanding any

---

[1] A. S. Khomyakov, "Collected Works", Tome VI, p. 359.

sort of an affirmation within, a religion of law, and amidst this a new sanctity bereft of all high demands, but guaranteeing the material lifestyle in all its aspects, it humbled the world, having lost any other, most noble or better sort of faith".[1] Khomyakov perceives this spirit of ancient Rome within Roman Catholicism and with the European culture connected with it. The spirit of Rome is first of all the spirit of the state, the spirit of material necessity, -- the Kushite spirit. "The uniting of people into the artificial form of the state, into a form purely external, this unity was foreign to the Iranian spirit. It was accepted as an outward necessity, as a means as a check against the totality of Kushite powers".[2] Khomyakov thus lays the groundwork for the stateless character of the Slavs and the Russians, -- the bearers of the Iranian element.

His dislike for Rome -- is a motive force throughout all of Khomyakov's philosophy of history. He displays a clear preference for Byzantium, although he also is critical in regard to Byzantium. He sees the authentic Iranian spirit only in Slavism, only in the Russian people. "In the victory over the state and the outward religion, it (Christianity) took on the character of the conquered religion, a character external and civil. It demanded not love, but rather submission, not faith, but instead ritual. The true and living unity, the unity of spirit, expressed in an unity of visible forms, was substituted for by an unity of the material norm, and the concept concerning this norm little by little passed over into the concept about a dominating might, having become the norm, in a concept about the caste, of controlling spiritual affairs, about the clergy, recognised by order of preference for the church, and ultimately, concerning a single bishop, the bishop of Old Rome, endowed with the full oneness of teaching, and the full oneness of spiritual power, and its unconditional infallibility. The idea of law lay at the basis of Roman life, and Roman life, passing on a new principle of enlightenment to the German conquerors, bestowed them the idea of a strict logical law not only in matters of civil life, which would be conditional and consequently impossible without subjection to logical law, but also in spiritual and religious life. The Kushite principle of logical necessity penetrated into the teaching, which had been bequeathed by the Iranians to the Jews, and this in turn bestowed the relationships of man to

---

[1] A. S. Khomyakov, "Collected Works", Tome VI, p. 402.

[2] Ibid., p. 36.

God the significance of an eternal legal affair, and to prayer and the sacraments -- the sense of a conjuring, and to faith by love -- the character of a compulsory law".[1] "For the Roman, having created the mightiest of all states and the science of law, led to its most possible completeness of logical conclusion, faith was a law, and the Church -- a manifestation earthly, societal and civil, subordinate to the supreme will of the indivisible world and its head in Christ, but at the same time demanding a conditional unity and visible symbols of this governing oneness. The symbol of unity and the constant expression of its legal might had to be situated in the Roman bishop, as pastor of the universal capital".[2] "Ancient Rome left its mark on the new Christian West. The pride of their former might and the former lost grandeur was a legacy, not to be refused by the Romans of later times, nor by their spiritual pastors".[3] "The emperorship was, evidently, incapable of adapting all the presuppositions of the ancient Roman idea of a law-legitimate state to the new Christian era: it did not contain within itself the principle of self-sanctification, which the Christian thought demanded; *since the West still failed to comprehend the impossibility of conjoining Christian concepts and the concepts concerning the state, i.e. the embodiment of Christianity within the state-civil form* (italics mine -- N. B.)".[4] "Christianity was the continuation and the final conclusion of the tradition concerning the freely creating spirit and spiritual freedom. Its triumph dealt, visibly, a decisive blow to the Kushite religions -- to the worship of an organic necessity, in whatever the form it had appeared, and to all the religions, based upon a provisional intellection or conditional symbolisation. But it was difficult to preserve the inviolability of its initial strictness and purity in the commotions of civil life, determined by conditions both intended and unintended, and in movements of thought, drawing upon their materials of knowledge from science, worked out by the world, fully in accord to the Kushite system. The Western peoples, conceiving the Church itself as a state-civil faith, introduced their former principles into the very core of the teaching, which they had received from

---

[1] A. S. Khomyakov, "Collected Works", Tome VII, p. 43.

[2] Ibid., p. 197.

[3] Ibid., p. 198.

[4] Ibid., p. 424.

the first preachers of Christianity. The integral wholeness of the free spirit was shattered by rationalism, but a rationalism, concealed beneathe a juridical form... Christians seemed as subjects, subordinated to the decisions of this domain of might. The representatives of the Church were essentially separated from its subjects and were wont to receive the title, corresponding to its new significance -- as the religious or churchmen, in distinction from the people".[1] The Catholic Church for Khomyakov was the *imperium romanum*, a creation of the Kushite spirit. He did not see either freedom or love in the Roman Church. And the whole of Western Christianity presented itself to him as inauthentic, as counterfeit. He denied, that Christianity lies at the basis of European Western culture, he saw there only paganism both Kushite and Roman. And in this consists an innate error within all of Khomyakov's philosophy of history.

The attitude of Khomyakov towards Byzantium is complicated. He understood, that "the life of political Byzantium did not correspond with the greatness of its spiritual life".[2] He perceived the innate dualism of Byzantium, which preserved the dogmatic truth of Christianity but failed to realise the societal truth of Christianity. In Byzantium "there was acknowledged the enlightening power of Christianity, but there was not the awareness of its constructive power". In the opinion of Khomyakov, Byzantium received from Rome its bowing before the state, the absolutism of the state. And thus it remains incomprehensible, why for him Byzantium was better than Rome. Christian Rome never stooped to such thralldom before the state power, as did Byzantium. Khomyakov quite well understood, that Russian Orthodoxy is very distinct from Byzantine Orthodoxy. For the Slavs, the state was never such an idol, as it was for the Byzantines. But all the same, Khomyakov praises Byzantium to the detriment of Rome. He perceives quite justly in Eastern Orthodoxy the spirit of Sobornost' and he opposes it to the spirit of absolutism in Roman Catholicism. In the East, the Church Councils were the expression of the consenting opinion of the people of the Church. But Byzantium herein was not the same thing. The spirit of Byzantium -- was the spirit of state absolutism. In Byzantium there occurred a sort of fatal deadening of Christianity, its dynamics ceased, its spirit of life was extinguished and

---

[1] A. S. Khomyakov, "Collected Works", Tome VII, p. 448.

[2] Ibid., p. 50.

there remained only the icons, only the dark faces, only the stasis. The Second Rome had thus to fall, it had become impotent to fulfill its Christian vocation. With Khomyakov there was too soft an attitude towards the Iconoclasts, and he was afraid, lest icon-veneration might pass over instead into idol-veneration, idolatry, -- a characteristic tendency for the Byzantine spirit. But he insufficiently failed to recognise, that the iconoclastic spirit contains already within itself the rationalistic abstractness.

Khomyakov was not fond of the Romance peoples and the Romance culture, and this dislike distorted his philosophy of history. He failed to sense the plasticity of beauty of the Romance and Latin spirit. Neither did he comprehend, how profoundly Christian is the blood of the Romance peoples. Khomyakov loved England, he believed in England, he expected of it a great future. England -- was his weakness and his whim. The Protestant culture of the Anglo-Saxons and the Germans he holds higher than the Catholic culture of the Romance peoples. We have seen already, that he preferred Protestantism over Catholicism, and he regarded Protestantism an inevitable chastisement for the sins of Catholicism. Khomyakov failed to notice, how deeply hostile the Pan-Germanism is to Pan-Slavism, he did not sense the world-historical Germanic movement in the direction of the Germanisation of the Slavs. England and Germany in their blood were always insufficiently Christian, and therefore in these lands there was played out the tragedy of Protestantism. The Germanic spirit, having created a great culture, -- is nonetheless insufficiently of a Christian spirit as regards the racial-blood of its predispositions. This is evident as regards the pantheistic mysticism of Eckhardt, and characteristic of all the currents of German culture. This is clearly visible also in that national genius of XIX Century Germany, Richard Wagner, who wanted to return to Christianity, but remained moreso a Buddhist, more faithful to the spirit of India, than to Christianity.

From Rome, in the opinion of Khomyakov, the Catholic culture of the Romance peoples received the spirit of rationalism and juridical formalism. The Germanic peoples, however, imparted to the foundation of European society the principle of the feudal-like retinue-fealty, the spirit of conquest and the aristocratism connected with it. The spirit of conquest, according to Khomyakov, poisoned the European societal order, and split it into conquerors and the conquered. The European aristocracy, in the opinion of the Slavophils, is very characteristic of the West, and it developed out of the retinue-fealty, out of conquest. The aristocracy therefore has no inner connection with the people, and is foreign to it. The European societal order is not of the people, in it there is no organic democratism. And Khomyakov sees in this non-organic character of the European societal order a source for the eternal possibility of revolution. The Slavophils always contrasted to the European aristocratism a Slavic, a Russian democratism. The retinue-fealty spirit, the spirit of conquest in the West raised up the person, the self-willed person, striving upwards, with its hypertrophied sense of honour, and created the knighthood. The knightly-chivalry aspect is so characteristic to Western European history, and within it there is a necessity to search out the riddle of the intimate sides of this history. In the knightly-chivalry -- is the soul of European societal order, having matured during the Middle Ages, but even now not extinct. With the knightly-chivalry is connected the militancy and activeness of the European peoples. But here Khomyakov, just like all the Slavophils, reacted quite negatively towards the knightly-chivalry, he saw in it the sin of the European peoples, a downfall of the Catholic Church, in blessing the knight-chivalry. The knighthood exalted the person and his honour, the person was set higher than the commune. Khomyakov saw in this a betrayal of churchly sobornost', the absence of humility. I think, that Khomyakov did not understand the knightly chivalry, he did not have the feel of its mission. The spirit of knightly-humility is first of all the spirit of fidelity, and in it there lives the Church militant. In this knightly-chivalry there is an eternal principle, there is an element, without which the Kingdom of God would not compel. There is the image of the knight in Christ, the knight of the MostHoly Virgin Mary, and it is impossible for this image to be connected exclusively with the retinue-fealty principle, with the spirit of conquest. There is a mystique of knighthood, an eternal mystique. The knight-chivalry aspect was something organic within the European societal composite, it was profoundly of the people. In general it mustneeds be said, that the Middle Ages was an epoch organic and of the people within European history. The Slavophil attitude towards the Middle Ages was historically and religiously false. The knights were not conquering brigands, they were flesh from flesh and blood from blood of the Medieval people. The hierarchical idea of the Middle Ages was an idea organic and religious. Therefore also within the aristocracy there was a principle organic and religious. Khomyakov neither loved nor understood Catholicism, and therefore he did not understand the societal order and the culture, organically arising upon the soil of Catholicism. The entirety of the Catholic culture and societal order he ascribed to Kushitism and conquest by brigands.

Khomyakov wanted to overlook the creative role of geniuses, of great people, within the historical process. In this, he debased the personal principle and exalted the social community principle. He unjustly identified the creative role of the person, in pursuing its exclusive vocation, with individualism. The religious emphasis on the choral-group principle prevented him from appreciating the significance of the hero and the genius.

*   *   *

Khomyakov's philosophy of world history was only by way of a preparation for a philosophy of Russian history, with which the Slavophils were all the more concerned. The basic interest of Khomyakov -- was to justify the mission of Slavism and set at its head the Slavism of Russia. I do not intend to dwell at length upon the specific philosophic investigations of Khomyakov, by which he seeks to exalt Slavism to an unprecedented height, and therein to shew, that the Slavic language appears to be the most perfect expression of the verbal aspect, i.e. of the Iranian spirit, or likewise to demonstrate the essential closeness of the Slavs to the religion of the Word. The scientific value of these theories of Khomyakov are doubtful.[1] The attempts to derive the English from the Uglichian (Ulichian) tribe and regard them as Slavs -- is pathetic and ludicrous. It can be scarcely possible to admit as Slavs a people of such more greatly natural and scientifically grounded proclivities. I have already pointed out, that in Khomyakov there was an uncritical jumbling together of the scientific basis with the religious, a mixing of the naturalistic aspects with the religio-prophetic mission. Khomyakov makes an attempt first of all to provide a scientific-historical grounding to the great religious points of preference of the Russian people. The Russian people first received their culture via Christianity, they had no pre-Christian culture, there was not that inherited cultural past, which hindered Western Europe from

---

[1] For general bearings on this, vide Vatroslav Jagić, "History of Slavic Philology", where the teachings of the Slavophils is subjected to scrutiny from the side of philology.

becoming authentically Christian. In the West, the pagan ancient Rome continued to live on and leave its mark upon Christianity. We however received Christianity almost like children, still innocents, not corrupted nor gone senile. The seed of the Christian truth fell upon us as upon virgin soil. We began our history as Christians. Our age old paganism was not yet a culture, it was something barbaric and childish. With us there was neither a cultural tradition of paganism, nor a cultural decadence. Virginal Russia did not know a fruitful man of culture prior to the acceptance of the Christian culture into its bosom. In this was an advantageous point for Russia not only as regards Western Europe, but also as regards Byzantium, having its inheritance of Greek culture. But, according to Khomyakov's teaching, the Russians not only historically found themself in a propitious position; Khomyakov wants also to suggest, that the Russian soul in its nature -- is Christian. There is some sort of a mystery of the birth of the Russian soul as Christian, preferentially. And in this all the Slavophils believed.

Khomyakov, together with all the Slavophil school, posits his economic and social premises, in a way supportive of the Christian nature of the Russian soul. Conquest does not lay at the basis of the Russian societal aspect. And therefore the aristocracy has not assumed a form, in opposition to the people. This was a negative condition, propitious for the people, for the organic character of the Russian societal structure. The Russian people -- is preferably agrarian. The peaceful lifestyle of toilers on the soil, the organic connection with the earth, was set at the basis of Russian history. With the agrarian character of Russia is connected also this, that at the basis of Russian history and Russian sociability lies a communal principle. The spirit of the peaceful peasant commune, the obschina, and not a spirit of the military retinue, creates Russian history. The Russian people -- is an humble people, and therefore already a Christian people. Both the unique composition of the soul of the Russian people and its societal body, as it empirically formed within Russian history, created an exceptionally favourable condition for its inward acceptance of the truth of Christ. Russia is organically moreso a Christian land, than was Byzantium, more humble, more submissive to the law of love, more able to incorporate Christian societal truth. And therefore the idea of the Second Rome passed over to the Third Rome -- Russia. The Russian Church in its spirit is foreign to imperialism, to the idea of the pagan Rome. The Russian people does not love power nor does it strive to dominate, it is not captivated by worldly dominion, by a strong empire. It renounces power and entrusts to the tsar. Its chosen one, the burden of rule as an obedience. In the chapter following I shall speak about this teaching concerning society and the state, which results from such a conception of Russian history. Now however I shall mention certain critical points on the scientific-historical inconsistency of this outlook.

First off appears the question, whether the spirit of the Russian people and the vocation of the people can be posited so dependent upon societal and economic conditions, upon the empirical history. The spirit of the people is susceptible only to a mystical or artistic intuition. And its religious vocation is dependent upon propheticism. But it almost seems that the Slavophils fell into a sort of economic materialism. They so esteemed the Russian peasant commune, the obschina, they so bound up with it the entire future of Russia, the whole spiritual visage of the Russian people, as though precisely this -- that without the peasant commune neither the spirit of Russia could exist nor the vocation of Russia be realised. But actually the peasant commune is only a certain socio-economic form, historically fluid, a form empirically conditional, and not metaphysically absolute. It is impossible to see within the Russian agrarian peasant commune a perfect expression of the Christian community of love, a religious commune. The Christian community of love realises itself outside of the conditions of socio-economic forms and is not dependent upon them. A religious commune and an economic commune have nothing in common between them. It would be an inadmissible mixing together of the two different orders -- to assume that a Christian commune results in an agrarian commune. Spirit is not dependent upon economics, the religious societal order is not conditional upon the economic societal order. Sooner would be the reverse. The exaggerated significance, which Khomyakov and all the Slavophils ascribe to the Russian peasant commune, puts them in a position very indefensible and dangerous. History and social science have destroyed the idyllic conception of the Slavophils about the Russian peasant commune. Science has discovered, that the peasant commune is characteristic of all peoples at a certain stage of their historical developement and disappears in the stages following, that in the Russian peasant commune there is nothing especially original, that it was connected with the lower forms of a people's economic life and impedes the ultimate developement of the productive powers of the country. For the Slavophils, these inferences would be frightening, and shake their faith in Russia. But why should Russian messianism, the faith in the spirit of the people and its vocation, be posited dependent upon such a marshy ground?! The peasant commune for us has long since fallen apart, and life has resprouted amidst patriarchal societal forms. But our faith in the Russian people, in its uniqueness and its vocation, are nowise shaken by this. Herein thus is clearly apparent the twofold aspect of Khomyakov's philosophy of history, -- the jumbling together of the scientific and the religious, the empirical and the metaphysical. Science reveals in Russian history many features, in common with the history of every other people. The Slavophil history of Russia scientifically has been toppled. But this can nowise topple the Russian messianism. Vl. Solov'ev subscribed to an altogether different conception of Russian history, akin not to that of the Slavophils, but rather to that of his father, S. M. Solov'ev, and in this he no less confessed a faith in the great mission of Russia. Many features of the Russian way of life, with which the Slavophils were so delighted and to which they connected so much, ought to be cast aside as pertaining to Russian paganism, and not to Russian Christianity. In the Russian agrarian communal lifestyle there is a nuance of the age old Russian paganism, and there is many a feature, found in every pagan lifestyle. And it is impossible to jumble the Russian pagan lifestyle with Russian holy matters mixed up together all in one. With St. Sergei of Radonezh and with St. Seraphim of Sarov are connected hopes other than with the agrarian commune. It is possible even to take a Marxist view on the peasant commune whilst still believing in the religious vocation of Russia. Our narodnik populists adopted for themself the Slavophil view on the peasant commune, but they were materialists and positivists. One followed after the other. Russian messianism, such as was connected with the obschina peasant commune, was there in Hertsen, and with Hertsen it got further along, than it did with the Slavophils, standing as they were on religious a grounding. The fate of a Christian societal order in Russia, just like everywhere else in the world, is not dependent upon a particular economic lifestyle, upon particular social forms, upon the historically relative and conditional. The Russian people is Christian not because it had the peasant commune, but because its spirit within it had accepted Christ, and because that it had known the likes of Sts. Sergei of Radonezh, and Nil Sorgsky, and Seraphim of Sarov. The messianism, grounded upon the peasant commune, can be relegated to Hertsen and the populists. And it is not because the Russian people has Christian a vocation, from whence in its history it had not that militant retinue-fealty, nor knightly-chivalry. On the contrary, it was just that the element of the chivalrant knight did not take hold for the Russian people in its Christian calling in the world. And it was not already such a docile Russian people, as the Slavophils asserted; in it was a militant spirit. The Russian people created its own great state within the world, it made conquests in Siberia, and in the Caucasus, in the Crimea, in Poland, and many nationalities it added on to Great Russia. St. Sergei of Radonezh was a Christian knight, a saviour of Russia. And a sacred knighthood is still called to play a role in the destinies of Russia.

But it mustneeds be noted, that in Khomyakov there was not such an idealisation of ancient Rus', as is usually thought. On this question he resolutely engaged in polemics with Kireevsky, who saw in ancient Rus' almost a total realisation of Christianity. Khomyakov protests against this. He does not propose to turn backwards. He sees in ancient Rus' an high sort of developement, but the stage of developement involved he does not regard as high. He is very much aware of the sins of ancient Rus' and he expresses this sometimes very strongly. Thus in the article, "Concerning the Old and the New", he says: "Literacy! But upon *the transcript copy* with the oaths of the Russian nobility for the first of the Romanovs, in place of a signature of Prince Troekurov, along with two of the Rtischev nobles and many others I know of, there stands merely a cross with a notation -- through their ignorance of letters. -- The point of the matter! Still but within the span of the memory of many an old fellow I know of was preserved endless accounts about tocsin shouts; and the tocsin shout was the same thing that in the West is the *cri de guerre*, and incessantly in the capital city this shout brought out the partisans and kin and clients of the nobles, who on the smallest pretense took to the streets, ready for a fight or scuffle to the death or to bruises black and blue. -- True! And Prince Pozharsky was taken to trial for bribes; the old proverbial sayings are full of testimonies against the courts of former times; the ukaz-decrees of Mikhail Feodorovich and Aleksei Mikhailovich repeat the same song about bribes and concerning new measures of sheltering the accused from the authorities; torture was universally in use, and the weak never could win out over the strong. -- Enough already! With the slightest of failed harvests people perished from starvation by the thousands, they fled to Poland, they sold themselves off to the Tatars, they trafficked away the whole of life for themselves and future generations to the Crimeans, or to their Russian brethren, who hardly were better than Crimeans and Tatars. --

ALEKSEI STEPANOVICH KHOMYAKOV

A ruling power, in harmony of accord with the people! Not only in the remote extremities, but in Ryazan, in Kaluga and in Moscow itself the revolts of the people and the streltsi regiments were regular enough occurrences, and the tsar's might frequently hit an obstacle, things whatever put in the way by a motley throng of the streltsi, or some concession made over some vile court sedition. And then too there were no few oligarchs that tangled up matters and the fate of Russia and they stretched or trimmed down the truth for their own personal advantage. -- The Church is enlightened and free! But the destiny of the patriarch was always dependent upon the secular power, and how quick the secular power was wont to meddle; there was the Pskov archbishop, convicted in the killing and in the drowning of several tens of the Pskov people, was locked away in a monastery; and the Smolensk bishop strolls the courtyard of the patriarch and cleans his horses in punishment for this, that he lived sumptuously; the Stoglav [Hundred Chapters] Sobor remains an immortal memorial to ignorance, crudeness and paganism, and the ukaz-decrees against the robbery by the servants of the archbishops shows us pictured the morality of a clergy very debased and spiteful. What however was it there in the golden old times? A woesome sluggishness. And would we look to find the good and happiness before the Romanovs? Here we meet up with the wolfish head of Ivan the Terrible, the absurd disturbances of his youth, the immoral reign of Vasily, the blinding of Donskoy's grandson, then too the Mongol Yoke, the appanage system, the internecine strife, the degradation, the selling out of Russia to barbarians and the chaos of the filth and the bloodshed. Nothing good, nothing noble, nothing worthy of esteem or imitation was there in Russia. Everywhere and always there was illiteracy, injustice, robbery, riots, selfishness, oppression, poverty, disorder, ignorance and depravity. One's glance will not hit upon a single bright minute in the life of the people, nor upon a single consoling epoch, and having turned towards the present time, this gladdens one with the splendid picture, presented by our fatherland".[1] Then follows a listing of all the bright sides of ancient Rus'. But even in Western literature there is no such extreme and sharp a speaking about the dark sides. Characteristic likewise the aforementioned verse: "Say not, -- "That was the Past...". Khomyakov's attitude towards Peter the Great was less harsh, than the other Slavophils; he did not entirely repudiate the reforms of Peter. He

---

[1] A. S. Khomyakov, "Collected Works", Tome III, p. 12-13.

condemned only the inorganic character of these reforms, the coercive force imposed against the will of the people, but the necessity of the reform he did not deny. In this regard Khomyakov can be called a soberly moderate Slavophil, moreso a defender of culture. The brothers Kireevsky, and Konstantin Aksakov were rather moreso the extremists.

An innate deficiency of the Russian philosophy of history by Khomyakov and the whole of Slavophilism -- was the impossibility from this point of view to explain Russian imperialism, the aggressive, forcefully ongoing character of Russian historical power. The Slavophil psychology of the Russian people is unable to explain the formation of the enormous Russian state, vaster than all the empires of the world. Nor even can this psychology explain the fact, that the Russian historical power has become all less and less of the people, all the more devoted to the idol of the state, to a pagan imperialism. The core deficiency of Khomyakov's entire philosophy of history consists in this, that within it there is absent the idea of a religious-churchly developement. The Church for him is not a Divine-human process within history, for him it has no dynamics. Kushitism and Iranism remain but elements of the world, uncovered scientifically, ethnographically, linguistically. There is no mystique of history. There is no finality of history. Therefore also all the teachings about the national vocation of Russia -- are dubiously two-sided. And yet nonetheless, all the attempts of Khomyakov to construct a philosophy of history are very remarkable, and filled with valuable thoughts.

Chapter VI

The Teaching of Khomyakov Concerning Society and the State

The social philosophy of Khomyakov makes a distinction between society and the state. Slavophilism was not a state ideology, but societal instead. Khomyakov, like all the Slavophils, not only was not a statist, he was even an anti-statist. The idea of a living societal organism, and not some moribund state mechanism, lies at the basis of the Slavophil social philosophy. The hero of the Slavophil societal order -- is the people, and not the state. The very concept of the tsar for the Slavophils -- is not statist and is even anti-statist. The Slavophils not only did not worship the idol of state power, but with all their hearts they repudiated this idol, they did not love it and they were opposed to it. The Slavophils were peculiarly unique anarchists, and the anarchist motif in them was very strong. And in this they gave expression to the Russian national spirit, and not the state, not the formalistic, having but little inclination towards the political structure. The monarchism per se of the Slavophils -- is not statist, but anarchist rather. The Slavophils -- were adherents of autocracy, not because that the Russian people love political power and worship political might, but only because, this people does not love political power and it rejects political might. The higher, the religious vocation of the Russian people, its spiritual work demands being set free from political domination, from the burden of statecraft. The Russian people, according to the Slavophil faith, denies juridical guarantees, has no need of them, spurns every formalism as contrary to the hearts of the people. Formalism and juridical guarantees are necessary only in relationships of conquerors and conquered, but are unnecessary there where the state -- is organic, is of the people as regarding its source. From whence also derives the denial of a mechanical quantification, the principle of a majority of voices, a denial that social truth can be born of an arithmetical sum, i.e. mechanically. According to the teaching of Khomyakov, power initially belongs to the people, but the people does not love power nor desires to exercise power. The people understands power not as a right, but as an obligation, and herein the

Nicholas Berdyaev

Russian people, a people by nature non-dominating, refuses the temptation of a pagan imperialism, entrusts it to its chosen tsar to bear the burden of power, and it is for him to bear the weighty burden of governance and by this thus to free up the people for higher an activity. "When, -- says Khomyakov, -- after many a catastrophe and misfortune the Russian people in a common assemblage close Mikhail Romanov as their hereditary sovereign (such being the lofty origin of the imperial power in Russia), the people entrusted to their chosen one all the power, with which it was endowed, in all its aspects. In the capacity of chosen Sovereign he became the head of the people in matters churchly, the same also as in matters of civil governance".[1] The Slavophils had boundless a loathing towards the bureaucracy, separating the people from its chosen one -- the tsar. And the bureaucracy -- is not organic, it is something foreign to the Russian spirit, borrowed from the foreigners, and the bureaucracy -- is a malady of Russian life. Foreign to the bureaucracy is the consciousness of any higher calling of power and its origin from the people. Power -- is an obligation, a duty, a burden, an effort, and not a privilege, not a right. The Slavophils -- were opponents of a bureaucratic monarchism, of an imperialism comparable to Western absolutism, but they were however -- ardent adherents of a monarchism by the people, uniquely Russian, having nothing in common with bureaucratism, imperialism or state absolutism.

Autocracy is distinct from absolutism. This thought is particularly stressed and elaborated in detail by a faithful follower and investigator of Khomyakov, D. Kh., in his brochure entitled "Autocracy". "The whole core of the reforms of Peter, -- says D. Kh., -- boils down to this one thing -- *to a substitution of the Russian autocracy -- by absolutism.* Autocracy, originally signifying simply *monocratism,* is rendered from it instead into a Roman-Germanic *emperorship*".[2] "Within the bounds of the all-people concept the Tsar is fully sovereign; but his full-sovereignty (sole sovereignty) -- Autocracy -- has nothing in common with the Western Caesar sort. The Tsar is "the negative of absolutism", namely in that he is bound by the delimitations of the people's understanding and world-view, which serves as a frame, within the boundaries of which the ruling authority can and ought regard itself free. For example, the people has

---

[1] A. S. Khomyakov, "Collected Works", Tome II, p. 36.

[2] Vide D. Kh., "Autocracy", SPb [Sankt-Peterburg], 1907, p.11-12.

believed (and believes still) that the Tsar, when this seems to him needful, gives thought to the great realm, the country's own affairs together along with that of all the Earth".[1] "Autocracy has always regarded itself as delimited, and unlimited only conditionally, within the bounds of that delimitation, which obtains from the clearly perceived principles of "the people" and "faith". It has dwelt thus within the people and in the Church. "Absolutism" however would set itself higher than both of these. It would thus undermine these limitations, but on the other hand it would also fall under the law of delimitation imperceptibly into another and worse aspect -- that of a delimitation not organic, but instead external and from the outside, i.e. hence material and therefore actually oppressive".[2] "There obtain two types of peoples: the one, needful of a spiritual Autocracy but not tolerating it in the political sphere: this is the West of the Hellenic-Roman culture; the other type -- is the East with Russia at its head, standing firmly for an Autocracy in the civil sphere, but not tolerating it any power of interference in matters of spirit and almost even finding suchlike to be inconceivable. In the one instance there is a civil Autocracy but with a republic in the sphere of spirit; in the other case there is a spiritual Autocracy but a republic in the civil sphere".[3] This thought is very characteristic to all the Slavophils. For the Slavophils, the autocracy was necessary so as to have a spiritual liberation, and thus to be set free from the political. The civil authority mustneeds understand, that "*its proper existence is based on the non-desire of the people to hold power*".[4] The Russian people is not in love with the mundane matters of this world and therefore "it cannot manage without a political Autocracy but will not tolerate for itself a spiritual Autocracy".[5] The civil authority is merely "the bearer of the people's burden".[6] "The East stands for a state Autocracy,

---

[1] Vide D. Kh., "Autocracy", p. 12.

[2] Ibid., p. 15.

[3] Ibid., p. 34-35.

[4] Ibid., p. 38.

[5] Ibid., p. 43.

[6] Ibid., p. 48.

and therefore it is "comparatively" free from being swallowed up by interests of earthly well-being; but it does not permit of thoughts either about the possibility of a spiritual Autocracy, since for it the spiritual sphere is so dear, in that it does not find it possible to posit any sort of outward barriers in the way of that, which it esteems as absolutely important, as regards its own personal spirit. The West -- is just the opposite. It asserts the centre of gravity to be upon the mundane interests, leaving to "the other world" certainly a very lofty place in words, but only so and not in deeds. *The devotion to Autocracy is in the sense proportionally of a politically comparative indifference of the people to matters of this world in general, and consequently, to the strength of its interests within the higher sphere of spirit...* Insofar as a deliberate non-covetousness is a great force in the world, before which all wealth is as "dust and ashes", so likewise the Autocratic form of governance, beloved by the people and in full consciously so, is a source of national strength, since in the attainment to it is expressed the repudiation by the people of those political vices, which debilitates the people's spirit no less, than the chase after wealth spiritually weakens both the man and the people".[1] "The grandeur of Autocracy consists in the grandeur of the people, voluntarily having entrusted to it its fate, but nowise one way or the other does it mean, that it is a perfect form of governmental rule, since in itself it is neither bad nor good; rather, that it can be useful or harmful, despite whatever the intention".[2] I have indeed made many citations from the brochure of D. Kh., since he characterises quite well the outlook of Khomyakov on autocracy. And thus, autocracy is based upon the asceticism of the people, upon the abstaining from power, as something harmful for the soul of the people, as something subject to the temptations by the prince of this world. Autocracy is not an ideal of a powerful state, but rather only an indicator of the power of the people's spirit. Autocracy -- is an asceticism of the people, and not a sacred societal component, not a sacred corporeal body. The autocratic tsar is delimited by the mind of the people, by the lifestyle of the people and by the Orthodox Church, by the will of God. The ideal of autocracy -- is not statist, is not imperialist, nor power-loving. The Russian people therefore have created an autocracy, so

---

[1] Vide D. Kh., "Autocracy", p. 57.

[2] Ibid. p. 59.

that it should not have to desire the kingdom of this world and its effects, and so that its powers might be directed upon spiritual activity. The autocracy -- is not imperialism, not bureaucratism, not absolutism, nor a cult of power; the autocracy is connected with statelessness, with the anarchic spirit of the people, with its desire to live in accord with the truth of God, and not that of man. The Slavophil autocracy has nothing in common with the historical and empirical autocracy, with that absolutism, which triumphed in the Peterburg period of Russian history. And indeed, even in pre-Petrine Rus' such an autocracy was scarcely to be met with. The merit of D. Kh. Was in this, that he focuses especially upon this dichotomy between the Slavophil ideal and the empirical reality. And one can only be amazed, that D. Kh. Remained faithful to the Slavophil romanticism after all the historical tribulations of the last decades, and after the Russian Revolution [of 1905]. This -- is a Khomyakov somehow living frozen in time, living totally still in the decades of the 1830's and the 1840's; whereas, life has passed him by.

It is important to note, that in Khomyakov there is no mystical foundation to autocracy. A mystique of autocracy can sooner be found in Vl. Solov'ev with his teaching about the tsar, the high-priest and the prophet. But with Khomyakov thus there is no mystical conception of autocracy as some sort of sacred societal flesh. For him the autocracy does not possess an absolute significance. In it, Khomyakov did not see the revelation of a sacred societal construct, the City of God on earth, he saw in it only this, -- that the people was dealing with matters of this world in ascetic a manner. The ideology of autocracy was for Khomyakov first of all a matter national and historical. For the Russian people, corresponding to the spirit of Russian history, Khomyakov perceives the best sole form of statecraft. The autocratic monarchy -- is the statecraft of a stateless people. It is the people that desires the autocracy, and thus only from this, is it that Khomyakov desires the autocracy. Autocracy cannot be by force against the will of the people, as in Western absolutism, autocracy can only be the expression of the will of the people. The people itself creates the autocracy, and not the conquerors of the people. Khomyakov is an uniquely original protagonist for the power of the people and democracy. He writes regarding a Tyutchev article entitled "La question romaine": "For one thing ye upbraid him, for an assault upon the *souveraineté du peuple*. But in it actually is the *souveraineté suprême*. Otherwise, what about the year 1612?... I have the right to speak, namely because I am an anti-republican, an anti-constitutionalist, etc. The obedience itself of the people is *un acte de souveraineté*".[1] The initial fullness of power belongs to the people, but the people renounces for itself the power, it chooses for itself a tsar and entrusts him to bear the burden of power. Khomyakov is proud of the people's democratic origin of the tsar's power in Russia, he contrasts it to the origin of power in the West, arising from conquest and enslavement. But the people's power actualises itself not by a majority of voices, not by a mechanical numeric quantity, -- it tends to actualise itself organically, mysteriously, directly without intermediary. Thus it was in the year 1612. It was an act of the will of the people, the will of a Christian people, which had to actualise itself in accord with the Church, had to have churchly a sanctioning. From the Church comes the consecration of power, the anointing of authority. And the Orthodox Church consecrated that power, which by the will of the people was chosen to reign as the tsar. The Russian people has no need of formal guarantees, since it understands power as an obligation, and not as a right, as a weighty burden, and not as a privilege. The Russian people does not recognise authority as a political power, it recognises it only as a moral calling. When the authority begins to conceive of itself as a right and a privilege, when the people begins to sense it as something external to itself, as something compulsory and by force, then the authority degenerates. This tendency towards absolutism, towards imperialism on the Western model, started from the times of Peter and triumphed in the Peterburg-bureaucratic period. In accord with a certain aspect of the Slavophil teaching, most clearly formulated by Konstantin Aksakov, to the government ought to belong the fullness of authority and action, whereas to the people -- is the fullness of opinion, of mindset and freedom of spiritual life. The point of view of Khomyakov and all the classical Slavophils is spiritually revolutionary in regard to the historical actuality, in regard to the empirical Russian statecraft: the Slavophil autocracy was an ideal, nowise ever yet realised. This revolutionary idea was not sufficiently expressed by the Slavophils, and indeed could not be expressed under the conditions of those times; much was glossed over. But the Slavophils were never intellectual adherents of the empirical Russian absolutism and even less so were they among its practical minions.

---

[1] A. S. Khomyakov, "Collected Works", Tome VIII, p. 200.

ALEKSEI STEPANOVICH KHOMYAKOV

The First Rome and the Second Rome were states, they suffered the temptation of imperialism and they therefore fell. The Third Rome -- Russia -- is neither a state, nor desires imperialism. Russia is humble and therefore chosen of by God. All this would be fine, if there were not so radical a difference with the facts, with actuality, with the empirical aspect. Howsoever the ideology be arrayed, the fact remains, that Russia has created a mighty empire, -- an empire expansive and aggressive. The Russian historical power is motivated by the spirit of imperialism, by the pathos of a mighty earthly kingdom. The Slavophil ideology always was foreign to the Russian authority. This power was never humble, it was filled with arrogance and self-assertion. The Slavophils made their investigative work in private life, and how little the authority had in common with their ideals. The Slavophils regarded the bureaucratism and absolutism as entirely the result of the Peterburg period of Russian history, and they considered it a betrayal of age old Russian principles. But for too long has this betrayal continued and too obscure is its misunderstanding. The Slavophils protested against the historical reality in the name of ideal principles, and they all the time held the view, that these ideal principles are essentially the most real, the most genuine Russian principles. The Peterburg period of Russian history indeed with its swaying of power towards imperialism, absolutism and bureaucratism, and with the splitting away of authority from the life of the people, with the victory of mechanism over organism, is inexplicable from the Slavophil point of view. Evidently, in Russia there were principles, which the Slavophils either did not see or did not want to see. There was the temptation of the kingdom of this world and its prince. In Russia there was a Tatarism, which poisoned it. The Slavophils underestimated the strength of this Tatarism. In the Russian people there was much paganism, which the Slavophils confused with Christianity. The Slavophils insufficiently understood the historically relative character of all the forms of the state, and the impermissible absolutisation of these forms. Even if the Christian Church also acknowledges a sacred mission of authority as a principle, for contending against sinful chaos and anarchy, even then it does not recognise any particular form of authority as solely permissible and absolutely perfect. The forms of authority in their essence are fluid and fleet. The question about the forms of state -- is moreso an historical, than religious question. Forms excellent for one era can be ruinous for another. The Slavophils were proud of their historicism, but they insufficiently came to grips with history. Their conception of autocracy was idyllic-romantic, and not historical. That autocracy could be seen as a transitory historical form, is something that Russian messianism could thus only but little be bound up with, just as with the peasant commune. I tend to see the immortal service of the Slavophils to be in this, that they understood the power of authority to be an obligation, a duty, and not a right, and with this they tied in with an unique state-form ideal of Russia. The Slavophils did not desire, that Russia should enter upon the path of the struggles of political parties, the clash of special interests, the self-assertion of human passions. And in this there was a truth, towering over their state-form ideology. Within the Slavophil mentality prevails decisively the moral aspect over the juridical, the idea of obligation -- over the idea of rights. And in this, it is impossible not to see healthy principles. Although the Slavophil conception of autocracy was clearly repudiated and inconsistent with history, yet all the same the Slavophils caught sight of something within the coursings of the Russian societal aspect, something not discernable from the Western European societal order. In them lived the ideal of an organic Christian societal order, an ideal opposed to every sort of mechanism, to every formalism. We shall hence take a closer look at the Slavophil teaching about society.

*   *   *

Khomyakov, like all the other Slavophils, perceived society as an organism, rather than as a mechanism. There is an organic societal Sobornost', an organic collectivism, rather than mechanistic, beyond which lies concealed the churchly Sobornost'. Only a Christian sociality -- is organic in the genuine sense of the word; a societal order, having lost its faith, decays and is transformed into a mechanism. The Russian people -- is a people Christian and a society Russian -- a Christian society, and therefore a society which is organic, living by a single spirit of Sobornost'-communality. Khomyakov conceives of the societal order as a type of family and he constructs a patriarchal teaching concerning society. The family -- is the nucleus cell of the societal order, familial relationships -- are the ideal archetypes of societal relationships. All of the societal relationships assume a form modelled upon the relationships betwixt children and parents. The tsar is related to his people as a father is to his children. The relationships of the power of authority and the people -- are of patriarchal a sort, and only as patriarchal can they be acknowledged as good and sacred. This -- is a relationship based upon mutual love, and without the love they have sort of justification, they would become moribund and decay into despotism. The Russian people -- is preeminently familial and patriarchal, it loves not the state, but rather the family, and it desires to live in a large family, to relate to the tsar as to a father, and does not want to have to put up with a state mechanism. Khomyakov in his societal philosophy takes as his starting point the exceptional sense of family and the patriarchal aspect in the Slavic peoples. The Russian people, in his opinion, holds dear not a political freedom, but rather the freedom common to the familial lifestyle. Such a people hence can comprise only a patriarchal ideal of the societal order. In essence, Khomyakov desired that Russia as it were should cling to the stage of a pre-state and patriarchal lifestyle.

But K. Leont'ev quite justly says: "For us the state always was stronger, deeper, more worked out than not only the aristocracy, but also than the family itself. And I, frankly, do not understand those, who speak about the sense of family in our people... Almost all the foreign peoples, not only the Germans and the English, but also so many others: Little Russians, Greeks, Bulgarians, Serbs, and actually, both the rural and in general the provincial French, even the Turks, have quite more a sense of family than do we, who are Great Russian".[1] I think, that Leont'ev was correct, and not Khomyakov. There are no sort of grounds to speak about a special sense of family among the Russians. No one so readily becomes estranged from the family, as does a Russian, no one so readily takes to roaming and wandering. With Russians there is not such a nuclear family, not such a concern over family, as there is among the peoples of Western Europe. A prosaic, delimited sense of family is foreign to the Russian spirit, a structured sense of family is foreign. If Russian man is spiritually free from the state, then he is no less free also from the family. Spiritual freedom is characteristic for Russians, who are not wont to be reconciled with any form of an enslaving lifestyle. The Russian ideal of the societal order is not statist, nor familial-patriarchal, but instead religious. Khomyakov, just like all the Slavophils, did not understand, that the familial-patriarchal element is not a some sort of uniquely Christian

---

[1] K. Leont'ev, "The East, Russia and Slavdom", SPb., 1885, Tome I, p. 91.

element, derived of the New Testament, but rather that there is quite much in it of the pagan element, and of the Old Testament likewise. The sociology of Khomyakov stands neither on any high level of science, nor on any high level of religious awareness. Scientifically unbelievable is the thought, that the societal order developed out of the family, as its nuclear cell. There have existed forms of a societal order, prior to any family, and the family itself constantly has changed and passed through various stages of developement. Familial forms are quite more fluid, than Khomyakov thought. And religiously incredible is the thought, that the patriarchal family, whilst still set all entirely within the natural-kindred structure, should be the foretype of a Christian societal order. The patriarchal family -- is a societal order still bereft of grace, something natural, at its basis pre-Christian, of Old Testament a sort, and pagan. The Christian ideal of a religious societal order -- is not patriarchal, not delimited by family, but rather something altogether other, something new, -- the ideal of a new society based on love. Anything absolute can as little be found in the family, as in the peasant commune or the state; the absolute can only be sought for in love. And the patriarchal in out-living itself always degenerates into despotism.

The patriarchal family -- is the primitive cell of the Slavophil societal order. After it follows the patriarchal village peasant commune. The village peasant commune, the obschina -- is one of the whales in the Slavophil societal order. All the Slavophils were partisans for the obschina, they fought for it so strongly, as though world destinies were dependent on the fact of its existence. The over-estimation of the significance of the peasant commune as a fact of culture both material and economic, has within it an inner contradiction for the religious teaching about society. I have already pointed out, that the Slavophils unconsciously had tended herein towards an economic materialism, since they too closely constrict spirit via an aspect of economics. Sobornost', as a spiritual collectivism, -- cannot depend upon such economically derived facts, as the village obschina. Khomyakov was an adherent of the unique societal collectivism of the Slavophils, with a mutual responsibility of all for all. But he tended too much to chain down the idea of a Christian Sobornost' to temporal and changeable forms of social life. With him it tended to seem, that without the village peasant commune, Christianity itself would be impossible. *The idea of person, so very central to the religion of Christ, just like the idea of Sobornost' also, was stifled within the Slavophil societal philosophy.* The

ALEKSEI STEPANOVICH KHOMYAKOV

Russian village obschina stifled the person, forced it to remain at a lower cultural level, and therefore it had to be supplanted in the name of the higher forms of cultural life. The emergent person, freed of the racial elements, inevitably and rightly so rises up against the old patriarchal relationships. The Slavophil populist sort of social idyll has withered both in life, and under criticism. The fact of the developement of Capitalism in Russia and the Europeanisation of societal forms was positively inevitable. And it is impossible to counter this fact with a patriarchal reaction. Khomyakov himself would scarcely cleave to his societal ideal, if he were alive now, after the experience of the last decades; for this, he was too vitally alive a man. The struggle against the passionate adherents of capitalist developement cannot be led by means of the Slavophils. It is impossible already to hold back the person within a patriarchal setting, while inevitably it is being set free from it. Churchly Sobornost' however is an absolute, it is not dependent upon various times, as tend to depend societal orders, familial forms, patriarchal relationships, racial elements. The churchly ideas of Khomyakov remain in force even then, when nothing more remains of his societal ideas.

    According to Khomyakov's teaching, society, in distinction from the state, is first of all the zemschina, the people of the land, the soil. The voice of the people of the land is the voice of the land, the voice of the people. Only in Russia is there such a people of the land. In the West -- have prevailed classes and a stratified society. The Russian people of the soil is organic, it has not broken down into warring classes, into hostile interests. It still was thus believable back then for Khomyakov, in his time one could still believe in this. For the land and the people of the soil there is an organic will. The people of the soil, the zemschina -- is a consultative representation, with freedom of thought, and to its voice the authority ought to comply, and consult with it. From here derives the idea of the rural Duma, of the Zemsky Sobor or land assembly, as a consultative organ. The tsar rules together with the people of the land, serving as his adviser. The voice of the people through the zemschina ought to reach all the way to the tsar; no sort of partitions ought to wall off the tsar from the people, the power of authority from the people of the soil. That the bureaucracy has arisen between the tsar and the people of the land, -- is a grievous ill of Russian life. According to the Slavophil teaching, the voice of the Russian land cannot be heard or known from an arithmetical adding up of voices, this -- is a *sobornyi* voice of communality, and not some *sbornyi* voice of an assembly roll-call, it is organic, and not something mechanical. To the *sobornyi* voice of the communality of the land the tsar ought to comply, and rule in accord with it. The relationships between the land and the tsar are neither judicial nor formal, but instead patriarchal and organic. The Peterburg period of Russian history with its bureaucracy and absolutism negates the land, does not take it into account. In this is an evil of Russian life. Khomyakov reacts negatively towards the class structure, to the privileges of the nobility and the court ideology, to aristocraticism. He -- is a populist and democrat. Just like all the Slavophils, he was a good Russian nobleman, a good Russian landowner, and his populism itself had a gentry tinge. Khomyakov was a gentry democrat, and not a gentry aristocrat. The social ideology of Slavophilism was nowise aristocratic. Khomyakov reacted towards the Russian nobility with sharp criticism and censure, he saw in its visage a betrayal of the people's task, and the Western aristocracy he regarded as a radical evil. The ideal of Khomyakov -- was a populist-patriarchal monarchy with the village peasant commune and the rural Duma. This is first of all -- the ideal of a muzhik-peasant Christian kingdom, via the soul of an enlightened nobleman. In the Slavophil ideology of Khomyakov there are present all the features of the Russian national populism in general. For him, the people consisted first of all of the common people, of the peasant, and from this people the educated classes had to learn, had to live according to its truth. The people had not betrayed the Russian spirit, -- only the educated and privileged classes had betrayed it. The nobility and educated Russian society had to return to the people and be healed by it. To live in common with the life of the people was possible only upon a common ground with the faith of the people. In this, the Slavophil populism was infinitely higher than the Westerniser populism, which wanted to unite with the people on materialistic grounds. But the idealisation of the life of the people as a fact escaped the Slavophils. Khomyakov repudiated the principles of a spiritual aristocracy.

Khomyakov adhered to a conservative teaching about the power of authority. But he was a fervent adherent of every freedom, -- freedom of conscience, freedom of thought, freedom of the press. Likewise known is the active participation of Khomyakov in preparation for the emancipation of the peasants. He pushed for the idea of the emancipation of the peasants with the land together with their preserving of the peasant commune. To the Slavophils belongs a visible place in the struggle against serfdom.

ALEKSEI STEPANOVICH KHOMYAKOV

In this, there was a realistic side to the Slavophil politics, which was appreciated even by the Westernisers. The social ideology of Khomyakov -- was an hodgepodge of conservatism with liberalism and democratism. In the teaching about the power of authority he was a romantic conservative, he denied the right of participation of the people and society to hold power, to be in politics. But he was a liberal, insofar as he demanded every sort of freedom for the Zemschina, for the people, and he was a democrat, insofar as he defended the interests of the peasantry and as such asserted the idea of the people's authority. In Khomyakov's ideas on society and the state the romantic motifs were interspersed together with realistic motifs. He conformed his romantic ideal to the realism of life, and this gave his realism a romantic tinge. The Slavophil teaching about society and the state ultimately became subject to decline and decay. In the generations subsequent upon that of the Slavophils, with the nationalists and the reactionaries there remained only the conservative side of the Slavophil teaching. The emancipative side vanished altogether. The idea of state absolutism gained out over the romantic anarchism of the Slavophils. And an ugly realism won out, resigned to the fact of reality, and the old romanticism was powerless to oppose it.

* * *

Although the societal and state ideology of the Slavophils did not hold up under criticism, and was repudiated in life, yet it mustneeds be all acknowledged, that the Slavophils succeeded in pointing out the unique within the Russian societal order. Just as with Russian thought aspiring towards a religious philosophy, so also the Russian will, in creating societal ideals, aspired towards a religious societal order. The thirst for a religious, a sacred ordering of society is unconsciously present both in Russian socialism, and in Russian anarchism. In the name of this sacred thirst, Russians tend to spurn juridical formalism, they do not love the abstract self-serving politics and lack the capacity for it. Russians view politics not so much the struggle for the right to rule, as rather a struggle for truth, for service. Certain features of the Slavophil psychology are present in all genuine Russians. And if this Slavophil psychology be absent from our historical power of authority and bureaucracy, then it is because these latter are moreso German than they are Russian, denationalised, split off from the people. There is an healthy and eternal grain of truth in the

Slavophil dislike for politics and abstract statecraft, in a spiritual resistance to the raging of political passions, and selfish interests. A just societal order ought not to be constructed based on the self-assertion of the human will, not upon its struggle for power and dominion. And indeed the societal order ought not to be based upon the authority of man, but rather upon the authority of God! This imperative was bequeathed to us by the Slavophils. Eternally and unconditionally of value was the Slavophil denial of the power of authority as some sort of right, some sort of privilege. The right to the power of authority belongs to no one: neither to a monarch, nor to some portion of the people, nor to all the people; no man possesses the right to power. For the Slavophil consciousness, therefore, equally all unacceptable are an absolute monarchy, or a constitutional monarchy, or a democratic republic, or a socialist republic. The Western European monarchies were based upon the rights and privileges of conquerors, and are therefore godless and unjust. To the tsar belongs not the right and privilege to power, but rather the obligation and burden of power. This Slavophil idea is deeper and broader than their ideal of autocracy as a form historically relative. The Slavophil understanding of the power of authority can in principle inspire also other historical forms of power of authority. If to the injustice of absolutism there corresponds the truth of autocracy, then to the injustice of the constitutional monarchy and the republic there corresponds their own truth, for which the power of authority would be as a service, and not a right. The idea of a religious societal order remains in force, although the patriarchal order, with which the Slavophils tended to connect so much, has decayed and collapsed. It would indeed be impossible to tie in the idea of a theocratic, just, God-based societal order with the relative and out-moded forms of a social and state order, with the fluidly empirical.

    A central question about the relationship of the Church and the state was however not resolved by Khomyakov, although he did more than the other Slavophils for the teaching about the Church. Khomyakov resolutely and with indignation repudiates the charge of Caesaropapism made against the Russian Church. But the denial of Caesaropapism was based moreso on principle by Khomyakov, than from the reality of Russian life. Khomyakov on principle repudiated the state's hold on the Church through Caesaropapism. Yet factually however there was a tendency towards Caesaropapism, which he tended to fudge over, and he was wont to recognise the captivity of the Church only but as a sin of Russian life.

ALEKSEI STEPANOVICH KHOMYAKOV

For Khomyakov, however, the Russian state was the state of Holy Rus'. He would not allow for a separation of Church and state, he did not want a secularised state. The power of authority in Russia ought thus to be a Christian, an Orthodox power. Khomyakov, just like all the Slavophils, proceeded from this assumption, that the Russian people -- is Christian, and therefore can create only a Christian power of authority and a Christian state. This is namely, because that the state power in Russia originates from the people, namely because that it is a Christian people and cannot be neutral. The state and the Church in Russia are connected inseparably not through Caesaropapism, but through the people: in the Christian consciousness of the people, the state is inseparable from the Church. The Russian people, as a Christian people, cannot be reconciled with a godless power of authority, with a non-Christian state. The people would not permit a separation of the state from the Church. A state power, not consecrated by the Church, is something the people would neither recognise nor submit to. Khomyakov demands submission to a state power, consecrated by the Church, and he rebels against state power, separated from the Church. The Russian people wants only to live in a Christian state, and the Russian people too much the anarchist, to want to live in some other sort of state. And here Khomyakov guessed at some sort of truth about Russia, -- the impossibility for Russia of an irreligious, churchless state path, the thirst for a religious sanctioning of power, a power that is from God, and not from man. But all the Slavophil teaching about a Christian state, however, about a power of authority consecrated by the Church, is to no effect. A Christian state in any case ought to be a state of Christians. Scarcely can it be recognised, that the modern Russian state is a state of Christians, and it is impossible therefore also to say, that it is a Christian state. The betrayal of Christianity by the people and by society, the falling away from faith, makes it impossible to be a Christian state, and transforms it into hypocrisy. The Russian historical power of authority -- is non-Christian, it does not serve Christian truth, and its split from the people is fatal. And indeed there never was nor can there be a Christian state; the state -- is not the City of God. Khomyakov tended to confuse the half-pagan Russian city with the Coming City of Christ. One can dispute over the forms of division of Church and state, over the time periods of this separation, but this division itself is providentially inevitable, and it is needful for the world destiny of the Church. This would thus represent a division between Christianity and paganism, between the New and the Old Testament, between grace and law, between freedom and necessity.

With Khomyakov, just as with everything during the period of the Slavophil generation, there was not the premonition of the growing power of the spirit of the Anti-Christ in society and the state; in Khomyakov there was too much of the idyllic. He did not yet comprehend, that every state power is pervaded by the spirit of the Anti-Christ, by the spirit of human self-deification. There is an aspect of human power-wielding and human self-deification both in state absolutism, and in social democracy. All is not so grand, as it seemed to the Slavophils. In statecraft, in the nature of the power of authority there are revealed the satanic depths. The Slavophils guessed accurately at much, but their consciousness was limited. There is much in the societal spirit of Slavophilism that we acknowledge by way of a legacy, but their state ideology has been repudiated by life. At this point, we shall turn now to the teaching of Khomyakov concerning nationality and the national vocation.

Chapter VII

The Teaching of Khomyakov
On Nationalness and the National Vocation

Khomyakov's Slavophil teaching involves also first of all a national self-awareness. Everything he wrote, was a teaching about nationality and the national vocation, the national calling. His whole teaching was but a grounding and justification of the national mission of Russia. With Khomyakov, there are no specific tracts on the national problem, since all his treatises were devoted to either this or that side of the problem. When the question is addressed, as to what the Slavophils thought on nationality and the national vocation, then first some preliminary issues on principle mustneeds be resolved: 1) was Slavophilism a *messianism* or was it a *missionism*, 2) was it a *nationalism* or was it *populism*. The concepts of *messianism* and *missionism* often get mixed up and substituted for each other, although between them there exists a substantial difference. Messianism derives from *Messiah*, missionism -- from *mission*. Messianism is far more pretentious and attractive than missionism. It is easy to admit, that each nation has its own special mission, its own vocation in the world, corresponding to the uniquely individual within it. But the messianic consciousness makes pretension to an exclusive calling, to a vocation religious and universal in its significance, and it sees within a given people the bearer of a messianic spirit. The given people -- is a chosen people of God, in it lives the Messiah. Every messianism is rooted in the ancient Jewish messianism. Thus, the Polish messianists of the early XIX Century believed, that the Polish people is Christ amongst the peoples, that the perishing of Poland was a crucifixion anew of the Messiah, that this is a chosen and exceptional people, called to be the herald of a new Christian era. Their most consequential messianist was Towiansky.[1] The modern French, the English, the Germans -- are almost all

---

[1] Vide: Canonico, "André Towiansky", 1897. The messianic consciousness of Towiansky was more radical and more mystical than the

nationalists, they all believe in the cultural calling, the mission of their people, but with messianism they have nothing in common. The messianic consciousness is not a nationalistic consciousness, it is always a consciousness universal and religious, permeated by faith in the Messiah. Upon a messianic people lies the seal of God's chosenness. Missionism is possible even upon a basis of positivism, messianism however is always mystical. Within messianism there is a prophetic spirit, a prophetic presentiment. The messianic consciousness mystically imbibes the spirit of ancient Jewish prophecy. And here arises the question: was Slavophilism of suchlike a messianism? The Slavophilism of Khomyakov and Slavophilism in general was not the partisan, the radical form of a messianic consciousness in the prophetically Jewish, religiously-mystical sense of the word. The Slavophil consciousness presents itself as a sort of admixture of messianism with missionism, on the one hand -- a teaching about the exclusive calling of the Russian people, allowing for only a prophetic mystical justification, and on the other -- a teaching about the cultural calling of the Russian people, allowing for a scientific positivist justification. I have more than once already pointed to this twofold aspect in Khomyakov's mindset and teaching. Khomyakov in his teaching on the national vocation constantly mixes up the religio-mystical perspective with the scientifico-historical perspective. His teaching therefore cannot be termed a pure messianism. The Slavophil idea of the Christian nature of the Russian people and Holy Rus', embodying this nature, includes in it an element of messianism. But this idea was mixed up with a positivist nationalism, grounded upon ethnographic and historical advantages. The Jewish messianism saw in its people the chosen people of God, from which was to come forth the Messiah, but it had nothing in common with a positivist nationalism. The messianic consciousness is always universal a consciousness, it is opposed to every provincialism and exclusive nationalism. It is thus impossible to term the Jewish messianism a nationalism, just as it would be impossible to term the Roman Empire a nation. The messianic consciousness posits a task, oriented towards a coming future event; the nationalistic consciousness in contrast is readily transformed into the worship of something factual, empirical, and tends to fall into an idolisation of the past. The Slavophil national consciousness is

---

consciousness of the Slavophils, and it was bound up with the onset of a new religious epoch.

complex and multi-faceted, within it are intertwined elements both religious and positivistic, messianic and nationalistic, Christian and pagan. As regards Khomyakov, we have seen this throughout the entirety of the whole book. And in this chapter we have merely to restate it in summation.

A second preliminary question: is Slavophilism a national type consciousness or a populist consciousness, is the basic position of the Slavophil teaching -- the idea of a nation or the idea of the people? The people -- is a concept quite complex and unclear, especially with us in Russia. The word "narod" (народ, i.e. "the people") can be employed in a sense identical with the word "natsiya" (нация, i.e. "the nation"). The Russian people is also the Russian nation. But the people tends to signify likewise a part of the nation; the word "narod" (the people) is employed likewise in social a nuance as the common people, the peasants, the workers, the democratic segments of society. Russian populism has always employed the word "narod" (the people) in the sense of the common people, the peasantry, the oppressed classes of society. In this sense, the people is a social format. The nation however is a reality on mystical a basis. To the nation is applicable no sort of social-class categories. The Russian people as a nation, as an integrally whole organism is a reality intelligible, supra-empirical, mystical. It is clear, that the riddle of Russia and its fate in the world can depend only upon the people as a nation, as a mystical organism, and not the people as a social grouping, such as the peasantry or some other democratic segment of society. Russian messianism is a consciousness which is national, and not populist. The people as a nation is affirmed only religiously. The people as a social grouping, as with the common people, tends to have positivist a basis. Facing the Russian consciousness stands the enigma of the world vocation of the Russian people, of this mysterious reality, comprised not merely of the Russian peasantry or the Russian working class. And if in the grasping of the spirit of the Russian people a special significance is had by the common people, the muzhik-peasants, this has nothing at all to do with social-class principles, but rather because, that the common people up til now has best preserved the spiritual visage of Russia and its faith together with the greatest Russian geniuses and saints. In the camp of our atheistic and materialistic intelligentsia this idea of the people as a nation, as a living organism, has disintegrated, has crumbled, has splintered off into social classes and groups. For this type of consciousness, Russia with its enigma has ceased to exist, and only the peasants and workers exist, only the social groups. For them, the national consciousness has been lost.

What however did Khomyakov teach, concerning the people and the nation, in the context of his Slavophil teaching? The Slavophilism of Khomyakov was, certainly, first of all an affirmation of the national consciousness, the affirmation of the Russian people as a living organism, as a reality, ascendant over the social classes all within an integrally whole nation. In this was a great merit of the Slavophils. But in Slavophilism also there were aspects regarding the people in the particularised sense of the word, there was a revering of the common people, the affirmation of the Russian people as muzhik-peasants predominantly. With Khomyakov we find the populism grounded upon a religious basis, just as with Hertsen the populism was grounded upon the basis of positivism. With Khomyakov the national consciousness was intermixed with the populist consciousness. In this incessant association with the common people, with the peasantry, in a copying of it, he sees as the task of the educated elements of Russian society. Hence the need to wear the people's garb, to coalesce with the people in lifestyle, in rituals and customs. But the populism of Khomyakov had altogether a different source, than with the populism of Hertsen and the subsequent populists. Khomyakov was a populist, because that within the people, in the peasantry, had most been preserved the Christian faith and the national Russian way of life. The Russian nobility, and our cultural educated society, had betrayed the spirit of Russia, had lost its faith and had begun to live not as Russians, but as Europeans, to live in a national sense only impersonally, fecklessly, and denationalised. The Slavophils idealised the common people and revered it not on the strength of its social attributes, but on the strength of attributes national and religious. What captivated Khomyakov was not a social democratism, economic and political, but rather a democratism national and religious. He sensed his own blood relationship with the people, with the peasantry, a bonding national and religious, rather than economic and political. The good Russian gentry landowner could not merge himself with the peasantry, he could merge only in faith and in the national manner. Khomyakov loved the common people as kindred and nigh close to him; this was more healthy an attitude, than with the subsequent narodniki-populists, who created an idol of the people, whilst inwardly alienated from them. Khomyakov was not the typical nobleman, in him there was not that stiffness. He understood, that to be united with the people is impossible on the basis of a worshipping of it and its economic interests, and only on the basis of an oneness of faith and a national oneness, in belonging to the selfsame one mother -- Russia. In this was the healthy grain of truth in Slavophilism. But in the teaching of Khomyakov the concepts of nation and the people are insufficiently delineated critically, and therefore in a jumbling together of the national and messianic consciousness is the aspect of the populist consciousness and an idealisation of the peasantry. If the Slavophil teaching of Khomyakov be detached from the elements of populism and from the quasi-scientific historical basis of the national developement, then what results is a teaching about the nation as a mystical organism. The concept of nation is definable not through some social aspect, nor through the state aspect, nor through racial aspects. Nation -- is rationally indefinable. And in this, the idea of nation has analogy with the idea of the Church.

In the extensive eight volumes of his collected works, Khomyakov attempted to sketch out the image of the Russian people, to trace out the uniqueness of its character, like none other. In verse and in prose, in his theology and in his journalistic works, in his philosophy and in his history he sang the praise of his people, the kindred people of his native land. He lived and he wrote under the inexpressible charm of Russia, of the Russian people, of Russian history. Khomyakov -- was first of all a Russian right down to the marrow of his bones, a Russian in his merits and in his failings, he was a Russian by element and a Russian consciously. To live fully and morally meant for him to live a Russian life, to live together with Russia and the Russian people. To live otherwise seemed to him an abstraction, ghostly, almost a non-existence. He was aware, better than most of the other Slavophils, of the sins of Russian history and the defects of the Russian character; he was sharply self-critical, of an inclination towards a national repentance. Khomyakov was never awed by the mere fact, the empirical, he always called for something higher. But he believed in the great truth of the discernable character of the Russian people, he loved the ideal image of his people. And these feelings of Khomyakov stayed sacred with him forever. One could clearly see the sins of the Russian peasantry, its darkness, its unruliness and wildness. Yet all the same, the ideal image of the Russian wanderer from among the people remains characteristic for the ideal essence of our people; just like as how regarding the ideal essence of the Russian Church there forever remains characteristic the ideal image of the Russian starets-elder, having risen up over the failings of the Russian hierarchy. With all his being, Khomyakov not only perceived, but he also experienced the spiritual integral wholeness of the Russian people as a primal basis of its unique character. He sensed the unique humility of the Russian people, a thing unknowable with the European peoples. And Khomyakov believed implicitly, that only such a people is called to realise a Christian social order, to manifest to the world an Orthodox society, the societal truth in Christ. This was neither accomplished nor could be accomplished by Orthodox Byzantium, because of its character. The Russian people, having assimilated in itself the truth of Christ, desires that Rus' should be Holy Rus', rather than some mighty empire. The Russian people thirsts for a land made holy, for a land of the saints and the sanctified, rather than for a land of the mighty and the powerful. In Khomyakov, just as also in the other Slavophils, there can be found the seeds of the religious idea of a new and holy earth, though the idea was yet then insufficiently revealed, insufficiently yet conceived as the Coming City of Christ. Khomyakov calls Rus' holy not because it is holy, but because it lives an ideal of holiness, because that the Russian ideal is the ideal of the holy foremost of all.

     The views of Khomyakov on the national character and the vocation of the Russian people is best of all characterised by his verses. And in the verses is well reflected the twofold aspect of his perception of Russia, which assumes here at some points an image of humility foremost of all, and at other points an image militant and strong. In the verse, "Ostrov" ("Island"), Khomyakov prophesies:

> And to another land humble,
> Full of faith and wonders,
> God doth bestow a fate universal,
> Both thunder of earth and voice of heaven.

God's chosen people can be only a people humble.

> God endureth not a people proud;
> He be not with those who say:
> "We be the salt of the earth, we be the pillars of things holy,
> We be God's sword, we be God's shield and buckler".

....

ALEKSEI STEPANOVICH KHOMYAKOV

> He doth be against those, who of wicked pride
> In humble words know not joy,
> In popular adulation are smitten,
> Of themself do idols fashion.
> He doth be with those, who of spirit and freedom
> Up to Him do incense lift;
> He doth be with those, who summon all peoples
> To the spiritual world, to the temple of the Lord.

In the verse, "Russia", he makes the appeal not to give credance the falsity of flatterers.

> Believe it not, hearken not, be not proud!
> ....
> With all this power, with all this glory,
> With all this dust be not proud.

And further on:

> And here be that, for which thou art humbled,
> That in the feeling of a childlike simplicity,
> Within the quiet of the heart is treasured,
> The Voice of the Creator thou hast received, --
> Thee did He give thine calling,
> Thee did He give bright allotment:
> To preserve for the world the worth
> Of sacrifices lofty and deeds pure;
> To preserve of tribes holy the brotherhood
> With love in the vital vein,
> And fiery faith the riches,
> And truth, and unbloody justice.
> Thine all this, in what spirit doth make holy,
> In what for heart be heard the voice of heaven,
> In what the life of days to come conceiveth,
> Beginnings of glory and wonders!...
> O, be mindful thine high allotment,

Nicholas Berdyaev

> The past in heart do resurrect,
> And in its hidden depths
> Examine thou the spirit of life!
> Attend to it -- and all peoples
> Having embraced with thine love,
> Bespeak them the mystery of freedom,
> The radiance of faith open forth to them!
> And becomest then thou in glory wondrous
> Foremost of all the sons of earth,
> Like that azure vault of sky
> Transparent veil of the Most-High!

Khomyakov denounces the sins of Russia in his famed verse, -- "Russia":

> In courts brimming with black injustice
> And by yoke of slavery branded;
> By godless blandishment, by falsity rot making,
> And sloth deadly and disgraceful,
> And every abomination filled.
> O, unworthy chosen,
> Thou art chosen! Haste thou to wash
> Thineself with tearful waters of repentance,
> That the thundering chastisement redoubled
> Fall not upon thine head.

And in "Russia Repentant" he says:

> Go! Thee the peoples do summon.
> And, having made thine material feast,
> Bestow them the gift of holy freedom,
> Bestow the life the thought, bestow the world life!
> Go! Bright be thine path:
> In soul with love, in right hand with thunder,
> Threatening, and beauteous -- Angel of God
> With fire-flashing brow!

ALEKSEI STEPANOVICH KHOMYAKOV

His endless love for Russia quite lyrically flows forth in Khomyakov's verse, -- "The Clef Brook":

> In thy bosom, O my Russia,
> Is likewise a tranquil, sparkling brook;
> It likewise pours forth with waters vital,
> Hidden, unknown, yet mighty.
> Not disturbed by people's passions
> Be its crystalline depths,
> As ere the cold powers foreign
> Froze not its flow.
> And it streams forth ne'er drying,
> Like the mysteries of life unseen,
> But pure, and to the world foreign, and known
> But to God yes to Him holy!

In another verse is proclaimed the idea of a Russian messianism:

> That by sufferings -- be freedom
> And grace acquired,
> That readied the peoples be
> The call of truth to heed;
> That the voice of its prophet
> Might pervade deep for people their spirit,
> Like the ray deep distant from the East
> Doth warm the moist and fecund field!

Russia is humble and for its humbleness it is chosen. And here to this humble land speaks Khomyakov:

> ...Proudly over the expanse
> To the vault of the blue sky,
> The Slavic eagles fly
> With far-flung and bold the cry,
> But their mighty head they bow
> Before their foremost elder -- the Northern eagle.

Nicholas Berdyaev

In the verses of Khomyakov is reflected the twofold aspect of the Slavophil messianism: the Russian people is humble, yet this humble people recognises itself as singularly foremost in the world. The Slavophil consciousness lashes out at the sins of Russia, but it likewise summons Russia to the carrying out of an audacious and proud task. Russia should relate to the world the mystery of freedom, unknown to the peoples of the West. With humble repentance in its sins, and self-abasement, the national humility for Khomyakov alternates with "the thunder of victory resounding". Khomyakov seeks to assure, that the Russian people is not warlike, but he himself, a typical Russian man, was full of a martial spirit, and this was captivatingly an aspect in him. He repudiated the temptation of imperialism, but at the same time he desired the dominion of Russia not only over the Slavs, but over the world as well. This antinomy of the messianic consciousness was inevitable, was in essence contradictory, but this contradiction is not a negation of its truth. It is impossible rationalistically to surmount the contradictions of the Slavophil mindset, -- they must be accepted and passed over. The most humble people -- is however the most proud people. With this, one gets nowhere. With a messianic consciousness nothing can be gainsaid except for self-smugness and a reverence for empty facts.

The central position of Khomyakov is further confirmed by this, that the famed Missive to the Serbs, and signed by all the eminent Slavophils, was composed by Khomyakov. And in Slavophil politics the role of its leader devolved upon Khomyakov, -- by him were coined the watch-words, and to him they entrusted the expressing of the Slavophil attitude towards the Slavs of the Balkan Peninsula. Khomyakov warmly greeted the idea of an All-Slav brotherhood, and he was a promulgator of the idea of Pan-Slavism. All his life he dreamt of the coming together of all the Orthodox Slavdom, with Orthodox Russia at its head. Not only Russia, but to all the Slavic world was adjudged the fulfilling of a great mission. He disregarded only Poland, as a Catholic land, towards which he had not such brotherly feelings. The Slavophils did not have a brotherly and Christian attitude towards the Polish, albeit fellow Slavs and Christians, and this attitude deepened and intensified the historical hostility.

Khomyakov begins his Missive to the Serbs in Christian a manner with repentance, with a denunciation of the sins of Russia. "The foremost and greatest danger, accompanying every glory and every success, consists in pride. For a man, just as for a people, there are possible three forms of pride: spiritual pride, mental pride, and the pride of outward successes and glories. In all three forms it can be the reason for causing the downfall of a man or the ruin of a people, and we meet with all three both in history and in the modern world".[1] Spiritual a pride he sees most recently among the modern Greeks, and intellectual a pride -- amongst the Western peoples. The pride of outward successes and glory is however the sin of Russia. "Having turned to you, our brethren, in full candour of love, we cannot hide either our own guilt. The Russian land, after many also grievous tribulations through incursions from the East and from the West, by the mercy of God has been freed of its enemies, and has spread out afar across the earthly orb, in all an expanse from the Baltic Sea to the Pacific Ocean, and rendered the vastest of modern states. Power begat pride; and when the influence of Western Enlightenment distorted the very structure of the Old-Russian life, we became forgetful of giving thanks to God, and forgetful of humility, without which neither man nor people can receive of Him mercy. True so to speak and occasionally, during times of great societal threats, in actual fact we became humbled in soul; but not such was the general disposition of our spirit. That material power, by which we were set apart amongst the other peoples, was made the object of our constant praise, and its increase -- the sole object of our efforts. To increase the army, to enlarge the revenue, to expand its sphere, sometimes not without injustice, -- such was our striving; to introduce courts and justice, to hold in check the rapaciousness of the strong, to defend the weak and the helpless, to cleanse morals, to exalt the spirit -- seemed to us useless. About spiritual an improving we gave no thought; we corrupted the people's morality; upon the very sciences over which obviously we concerned ourselves, we viewed not as the developement of our God-given reason, but solely as a means to the increase of the external power of the state, and never did we ponder this, that only spiritual power can be a reliant source even of powers material. How inconstant was our course, how God-opposed our developement, one can already conclude from this, that in the time of our blindness we turned into slaves upon their own land more than twenty millions of our free brethren, and we made societal corruption the chief source of societal profit. Such were the fruits of our pride. The war -- a just war, having been undertaken by us against the Turks for easing the lot of our Eastern brethren, -- served us as punishment:

---

[1] A. S. Khomyakov, "Collected Works", Tome I, p. 379.

God foreordained it not for impure hands to accomplish such pure a deed. The union of the two mightiest powers in Europe, England and France, and the betrayal of the Austria that we had saved, and the hostile mood of almost all the other peoples, forced us to conclude an humiliating peace: our boundaries were constricted, our military dominion over the Black Sea abolished. *We give thanks to God, for having smitten us unto correction* (italics mine -- N. B.). Now have we learned the vanity of our self-deception; now we emancipate our enslaved brethren, we strive to bring justice into the courts and to lessen the depravity of morals amongst the people. God grant, that the deed of our repentance and correction not stop short, that the good start may bear good fruit in our spiritual cleansing and that we realise forever, that love, truth and humility alone only can suffice a people, the same also as for a man, trough the mercy of God amidst the good will of people. Without doubt, the pride of material powers is at its very basis more disgraceful, than the pride intellectual and the pride spiritual; it turns all the strivings of man towards ends extremely unworthy, but on the other hand it be not so deeply rooted in the soul and the easier still corrected, since that its lie be detected with the first failures and misfortunes of life. The calamitous war has brought us to our senses; we firmly hope, that successes also not lead us astray into our former errors".[1] These remarkable words, deeply instructive even in our own time, clearly show, how far removed Khomyakov was from any sort of coarse and pagan idolatry n facing the facts of national life. Herein is a radical and religious condemnation of the official-chambers Russia with its revering of power and outward success. The Russian people -- is an humble people, a people of Christ, but the Russian arrogance of power is a very low form of pride. Yet still, for the sins of the power of authority, all the people are responsible, the whole society, all of Russia. And Khomyakov does not seek to hide away the sins of Russia from his brother Slavs, he wants to prevent them from their own mistakes, he wants a sincere unity. The national self-flagellation with Khomyakov went so far, that he thanked God for the smiting, which Russia suffered in the Crimean War. In this smiting he saw the righteous wrath of God. What would he have said about the smiting in the Russo-Japanese War? What would he have said about the arrogant and violent politics of recent years, about the cult of outward prospering, about the conceit and the self-adoration of our nationalists?

---

[1] A. S. Khomyakov, "Collected Works", Tome I, p. 381-382.

ALEKSEI STEPANOVICH KHOMYAKOV

In his Missive to the Serbs, Khomyakov expresses a whole series of warm wishes, which he addresses also towards Russia, since in Russia his programme had not been realised. "Let there be for all a full freedom in the Faith and in its confession! Let no one suffer oppression or persecution in the matter of knowing and worshipping God! No one, even though (from which God deliver us) he stray from the path of a true Serb! Let him be for all of you yet a brother, even though a wretch and blind! But let him not be a legislator, nor a governor, nor a judge, nor member of a general assembly: since his conscience is at variance from yours".[1] Herein is expressed, in common to all the spirit of Slavophilism, the thirst for freedom of conscience together with a thirst for a religious, a Christian, a non-secular societal order. Society for the Slavophils -- is an Orthodox Christian society, and it has to live within the covenant of Christ, in conscience with Christ; but coercion over a variant conscience there ought not to be, since this coercion is contrary to the spirit of Christ. With one of a different belief there cannot be an Orthodox Christian society, with such an one it is impossible to build a Christian societal order, but his freedom of conscience ought still to be respected. "Do not use the new wealth on empty sparkles, trifles and luxury! Let the rich use the surfeit of their wealth to help the destitute or on something to the general benefit and general enlightenment. Let there be with the land of Serbia that holy luxury, wherein there be neither need nor deprivation for a work-loving man! Then wealth and glitter will adorn the temple of God. But in your private dwellings there ought to be simplicity, the same also in all your domestic affairs. The pomposity of a private man is always a theft and to the harming of society".[2] Society for the Slavophils ought thus not to be bourgeois, -- it ought to be of the people. Capitalistic profits and the capitalistic cult of luxury are impermissible in a Christian society and contrary to the democratic spirit of Slavophilism. "In the law and criminal courts let there be mercy, for remember, that in each private transgression there is a greater or less guilt of society, little having guarded its members from the initial temptation, or not having concerned itself over the Christian upbringing in the early years. *Do not condemn the transgressor to death. He already cannot defend himself, and for a manly people it is*

---

[1] A. S. Khomyakov, "Collected Works", Tome I, p. 386.

[2] Ibid., p. 401.

Nicholas Berdyaev

shameful to kill the defenseless, and for a Christian it is sinful to deprive a man of the possibility to repent. In the Russian land, from of old for us the death penalty was abolished, and now for us all it is something opposed and in the general course of the criminal courts it is not allowed. Such a showing of mercy is to the glory of the Orthodox Slavonic peoples. From the Tatars and indeed the learned Germans we displayed fierceness in punishments, but soon its traces also vanished (italics mine -- N.B.)".[1] Khomyakov was a resolute opponent of the death penalty and in this he expressed the Russian national spirit. The spirit of the Russian people is opposed to the death penalty and cruelty of punishment. But the ruling authorities, in taking their path with executions, -- are not Russian in spirit, not of the people, and this -- has become some sort of a German-Tatar authority. Khomyakov and the Slavophils did not say it outright, nor were they able to say it outright, that our historical ruling powers are a foreign and alien power, but they nonetheless thought this, and all their teachings led to this conclusion. This power was never led by Slavic politics, and the ideals of Slavophilism are foreign to it.

More than once already in this book I have indicated, that Khomyakov is innocent of a total denial of the West. Western Europe was for him all the same "a land of holy miracles", he all the same saw in the West the Aryan genius. We know already, that he was not merely fond of England, but that he was an Anglophile. The fate of world history, in his opinion, should be decided in Moscow and London. He highly valued German culture and recognised its important significance. Peterburg however was for him more foreign and distasteful, than some of the cities of Europe. London, certainly, was closer to his heart than was Peterburg. Bureaucratic Peterburg seemed to him a distortion of the image of Russia, a betrayal of the spirit of the Russian people. The failing of Khomyakov was not in this, that he denied the West (he did not deny the West, and his criticism of the West often was correct), -- his failing was in this, that he related towards Catholicism with a lack of love, i.e. towards an entire half of the Christian world, and he nurtured also an antipathy towards the Romance peoples, i.e. the living bearers of Catholicism in the West. Khomyakov always gave preference to Germany over the Romance lands. I think, that in this he committed a great mistake in regard to the ideals of Russia and Slavdom. Germany -- is the bearer of the ideals of

---

[1] A. S. Khomyakov, "Collected Works", Tome I, p. 402.

ALEKSEI STEPANOVICH KHOMYAKOV

Pan-Germanism, which is deeply hostile to the ideals of Pan-Slavdom. Germany aspires to a world-historical effort of Germanising the Slavs, to engraft onto them its culture. Germany -- is one of the historical dangers for Russia and Slavdom, similar in ways to Pan-Mongolism. With the Romance lands for us there is nothing similar. Catholicism is organically closer to Orthodoxy, than is Protestantism, and the Romance peoples are organically closer to the Russians and the Slavs, than are the Germanic peoples. The worldwide Slavic-Orthodox politics ought to be a politics of drawing closer with the Catholic and Romance lands and peoples. We have already suffered enough from our historical ruling powers having become Germanised, Teutonicised, and in our religious life and spiritual culture there has crept in unnoticed a Protestant rationalism. Dostoevsky also shared the same basic mistake of Khomyakov and the Slavophils, wanting in an union with Protestant Germany to divide up the Catholic world. But Catholicism cannot be an inward danger for Russia. The historical fright at Polonisation ought not to blind us; Poland has long since ceased to be a danger for Russia, and it already long since time to make our attitude towards Poland properly correspond to the spirit of the Russian people. Germanism -- is quite moreso the real danger. Only a passive, moribund Orthodoxy, forever seeking protection under the ruling powers, can be afraid of Catholicism; an active and living Orthodoxy cannot fear it, and can be seek for an active reunification in an OEcumenical Christianity. And the idea of Slavdom ought finally to be freed of Byzantium. The deadening effects of Byzantium has left an heavy burden upon the Russian people, it muddles the national self-consciousness and hinders the realisation of the national calling. Khomyakov was conscious of the profound difference of Slavdom from Byzantium, and he understood, that Byzantium namely was most alien an ideal for a Christian societal order. In its legacy to Russia, Byzantium bequeathed a false relationship of Church and state. But the Russian thirst for the City of Christ is opposed to this legacy. And it was thus necessary for the still more radical Slavophils to sunder off the idea of Russia and Slavdom apart from Byzantium.

In the consciousness of Khomyakov, the Christian messianism had not yet been freed from the elements of a pagan nationalism. This pagan nationalism triumphed victorious among the offshoots of Slavophilism. The problem of Russia, of the Russian self-consciousness and Russian messianism, is the problem of East and West, hence universal a problem. This problem has been bequeathed to us courtesy of the Slavophils. But the admixture of a pagan nationalism within Slavophilism obscures this universal problem, has closed Russia in upon itself, into its own self-sufficiency, and deprives it of its universal significance. "Russia for the Russians", this -- is a pagan nationalism. "Russia or the world", this -- is Christian a messianism. Pagan nationalism lacks the ability to differentiate in Russia the Christian East from the non-Christian East, a danger not only for Russia, but also for all the Christian world; it does not distinguish the "Russia of Xerxes" from the "Russia of Christ". The Russian and the Christian messianism, universal in its nature and its task, ought to be decidedly distinct both from the Western imperialistic nationalism, which has infected our ruling authorities, and from the Eastern fanatic-pagan nationalism, which breathes forth in our elemental nationalist circles. Neither the one, nor the other, is able to solve the riddle of Russia. The enigma of Russia will be divined only in a Christian and universal messianism. Russia is needful not for its own national-egoistic flourishing, but for the salvation of the world. Khomyakov had presentiment of this, when he perceived the mission of Russia to consist of this, that it relate to the world "the mystery of freedom", "warm with the breath of freedom", "give the gift of holy freedom". Khomyakov had in view the freedom of Christ, which the West betrays all more and more. This freedom does not hold sway even with us, and it is impossible to measure it quantitatively. But the spiritually perceptive catch sight within the Russian Orthodox East of the "holy freedom", the freedom of the saints. It manifests itself at a decisive hour of history, and with it will be connected the appearance of the City of Christ.

Chapter VIII

The Significance of Khomyakov.
The Fate of Slavophilism

The fate of Slavophilism is sad. Up to the present time the Slavophils have not received their just due. The Slavophil teaching was subjected to abuse both by its enemies, as well as by its unsought friends and followers. The greatest phenomenon in the history of our self-consciousness was either ignored, or cast in disreputable a light. Slavophilism -- is complex a matter, within it are combined manifold elements, sometimes vert contradictory, despite the outward construct and organicity of the Slavophil teaching; from the very beginning it was fraught with various possibilities, and from it issued differing paths: the path of freedom and the path of necessity, the path of developement and the path of reaction, the path of mystical hopes and the path of positivist-naturalistic pretensions. In Slavophilism there was both a Russian Christianity, and a Russian paganism, a Christian messianism and a pagan nationalism, a theocratic-anarchist denial of every form of state together with an absolutisation of historically relative forms of state, freedom from every external form and slavery to a conditional mode of life. All these contradictions in fatal a form found expression in the ultimate fate of Slavophilism. Slavophilism began to decay into its various elements, and then went off into various paths. I have attempted to shed light upon the most central and most imposing figure of Slavophilism. In Khomyakov it was possible to embody everything positive, and everything negative in Slavophilism, all its antitheses. Attempting an estimation of Khomyakov in summation, one mustneeds look likewise into his fate and his legacy. "*Khomyakov and us*" -- here is the core theme of this concluding chapter of my book. In what ways do we have still a blood connection with Khomyakov and in what have we parted paths from him? This implies also to examine the fate of Slavophilism, such as has happened with it betwixt the period separating Khomyakov from us. In all the chapters of this book there has partially been mentioned, about what there was in Khomyakov eternally and enduringly of value, and what there was in him of the out-moded and no longer alive for us. It is necessary now to lead up to a summation.

From the Slavophilism of Khomyakov there extend several lines. Direct and like-minded disciples of A. S. Khomyakov -- were A. Koshelev and Yu. Samarin. And Ivan Aksakov appears ultimately as a representative of the classical, the Old Slavophilism, not yet in decay. This resulted in the journalistic and societal activity of Yu. Samarin, A. Koshelev, I. Aksakov. These -- were the liberal Slavophils, actively undertaking the defense of every freedom, but faithful to the truth of Orthodoxy and the historical mode of the Russian state. The liberative activity of the Slavophils, faithful to the best things bequeathed from the people's self-consciousness -- was a practical fruit of Slavophilism. The Slavophils emancipated the peasants with land, they struggled for the freedom of conscience and freedom of the word, they denounced what was ulcerous within our churchly structure and its wrongful relationship to the state, they fought for the interests of oppressed Slavs and they proclaimed the ideals of Pan-Slavism. Together with this, they led the struggle against the waves of nihilism, of materialism and unbelief, that had come crashing down upon us. They wanted to avert the fatal process of the disintegration of Russian society into hostile forces, they wanted to stem the growth of the mutual hatred. They believed still, that there was possible an organic connection of the ruling powers with the people, that Russia could avoid the political struggle for power and the economic struggle of classes, that our people, as a Christian people, is endowed with an organic oneness, that within it there beats a single heart. The Old Slavophils recognised the intelligentsia as the expression of the spirit and mindset of the people, as an organ of national self-consciousness and they denied that there was any specific "intelligentsia", as afterwards became defined for us. The fatal course of Russian life, in which hatred and discord won out over oneness and love, wrecked all the hopes of the Slavophils and fractured Slavophilism.

In the epoch, so foreign to anything mystical and so little religious, as the decades of the 1860's, the 1870's and 1880's tended to be, Slavophilism also gradually took on the hue of nationalism and positivism, and the messianism was reborn into nationalism. In Danilevsky, the author of "Russia and Europe", there is clearly evident a nationalistic degeneration of Slavophilism. Danilevsky in his personal life, actually, was Orthodox in the customary sense of this word, but in his nationalistic concepts there is nothing religious or Christian; he entirely bases the great pre-eminence of

ALEKSEI STEPANOVICH KHOMYAKOV

Russia upon the naturalistic, the positivist-scientific. A naturalistic nationalism is always reactionary, and exclusive in its self-affirmation. Pagan nationalism triumphs over the Christian messianism, power takes precedence over truth. Danilevsky was not faithful to the ideals bequeathed by the Old Slavophils. He -- is already the new man, poisoned by naturalism and the cult of power, he -- is a Darwinist in reverse. It is impossible to consider him an herald of the Russian national self-consciousness, of the spirit of the Russian people, for he -- is a nationalist in the Western sense of this word. Danilevsky himself was nevertheless pure a thinker, whereas those who in practice followed upon him, have attained to an egoistic savagery and demonic darkness. The most recent nationalists have lost the last semblance of any spiritual connection with the Old Slavophils, and from them Khomyakov would have recoiled in horror. The reactionary nationalism assumes an acridly anti-Christian, pagan hue, it is indicative of nothing save that sustained of egoism and greed, and this reactionary nationalism to quite great a degree has fallen under the grip of the spirit of this age, it renders itself subject to the powers of naturalistic positivism and utilitarianism, moreso than it itself is able to realise. The people of this spirit have perverted Orthodoxy into a positivist-naturalist institution and relate to it as an aspect of power.

But the genuine Nemesis of the Slavophils, in the expression of Solov'ev, was Katkov. Katkov has nothing in common with the Slavophils and it is impossible in any sense of the word to call him a Slavophil. Katkov -- is a conservative and nationalist of the shrill Western type. He is as foreign as anyone to the religious hopes of Russia, in him there are no traces of an unique Russian mysticism. Katkov was entirely predisposed to the pagan cult of power. His pathos -- is in state absolutism and state positivism. Katkov -- is a statist first of all; in contrast the Slavophils -- were anti-statists, anarchists of an unique sort; they have no love for the ruling power and they view imperialism and absolutism as demonic a temptation. The Slavophils would consider Katkov as alien to them and alien to the Russian people; he would have presented himself to them as such by the liberal initiation of his activity and as such he would seem in his reactionary ends. I. Aksakov was a resolute opponent of the Katkovites. Katkov served not Russia, not the Russian people and its mysteried destiny, but rather the state and the ruling power as abstract principles. He is as much a foreigner, as much alien, as is our Teutonic bureaucracy. And nonetheless still often for the sins of Katkov the onus happened to fall upon the Slavophils, since the Katkovites have no love for Slavophilism. This point of confusion mustneeds be clarified. But it must also be realised, that in Slavophilism there were admissible mistakes, which gave cause to connect Katkovism with them.

On the sidelines off from the main pathways stands the imposing figure of Konstantin Leont'ev, one of the most gifted and original among Russian people. It is impossible to term K. Leont'ev in any exact sense of the word a Slavophil, but he certainly has aspects in common with the Slavophils; the Slavophil leaven fermented within him, but the results received were not those anticipated by the Old Slavophils. Leont'ev -- was a Nietzschean within Slavophilism, a Nietzschean before Nietzsche, an aesthete, a foolish romantic, revering power as beauty. This was a singer of the aesthetic beauties of Byzantine statecraft and Byzantine monasticism, mutually fond both of a severe asceticism and of a pagan blossoming of diversely complex life, and he hated the democratic dullness and philistine insipidness, he detested the bourgeois sense of well-being and the ideals of universal happiness. But to Leont'ev was foreign the optimism of the Old Slavophils, their non-tragic aspect, their old Russian good-naturedness. Leont'ev sensed already the tragic course of Russian life. In him already was an apocalyptic sense of terror. In K. Leont'ev the integral wholeness of Khomyakov's Slavophilism disintegrated, the old became deathly stiffened and the new, the terrible, almost painful, was born. In Leont'ev there appeared both a mystical trembling and an aesthetic demonism, neither which the Old Slavophilism knew. No one was more complex, than K. Leont'ev: into him had been poured monstrous contradictions. The age old opposition of Christianity and paganism raged within the blood of Leont'ev, to his very end this insurmountable demonism all his life accompanied this monastic-obedient, seeking to surrender all his will and all his life over to the startsi-elders. Leont'ev did not believe in the exclusive beauty of the good; in the name of beauty evil also was necessary. He became intoxicated with Christian prophecies concerning the triumph of evil in the world. In Russian Orthodoxy this was the appearance of something new: a Christian aesthete and romantic, fierce and dark. Suchlike a phenomenon was more familiar to Western Catholicism. We can thus recollect in France the remarkable figure of Barbey d'Aurevilly. Leont'ev was a Russian Orthodox form of Joseph de Maistre, but lacking his organic wholeness. Not only in the person of Leont'ev, but also in his ideology there were mixed together incompatible opposites. A naturalistic nationalism and statecraft positivism were combined in him with a dark apocalyptic mysticism, the reverencing of a pagan beauty of life together with a Christian asceticism, the ideals of imperialism with the ideals of the startsi-elders. In Leont'ev everything was murky and jagged, the contradictions of Slavophilism were laid bare in him. Here on the one side he is the naturalist-positivist, there elsewhere he is the mystic and romantic. Leont'ev already was not typical of life, in him the vital vigour had already fractured, and in this he is the new sort of man, a modernist, despite his reactionism. In the naturalism of Leont'ev there decomposes and dies off the weak side of Slavophilism; within the mysticism of Leont'ev is born the new, the apocalyptic. Leont'ev was dangerous for Slavophilism, and the more circumspect Slavophilism could not compare with him. The appearance of Leont'ev demands dynamism from the Slavophil consciousness. The dark elements of the Russian societal order could make use of the reactionism of Leont'ev, but they lack the wherewithal to understand his genius.[1]

Within the history of the Slavophil mentality, a revolutionary fact was the appearance of Dostoevsky. After Dostoevsky the feel of life had become different, than it had been before him. With Dostoevsky came the catastrophically tragic life sensation and it brought an end to the felicitous mode of life. Dostoevsky was, certainly, spiritually connected with the Slavophils and he himself was a Slavophil, but he is so very distinct from

---

[1] *translator note*: By way of further perspective on K. Leont'ev, our present "Khomyakov" text was originally published in 1912. Already back in the year 1905, Berdyaev penned an insightful article on Leont'ev, entitled: "K. Leont'ev -- Philosopher of a Reactionary Romanticism", (Klepinina № 120), well worth reading via the Internet.

Berdyaev was later in exile to publish in 1926 his book on Leont'ev, entitled [in Russian] "КОНСТАНТИН ЛЕОНТЬЕВ: Очерк из истории русской религиозной мысли", Paris, IMKA/YMCA Press, (Klepinina № 22).

The English translation of this 1926 work, by George Reavey, was published in 1940 by publisher Geoffrey Bles, London, under the title, "LEONTIEV" (Klepinina № 22b). In Berdyaev's "Preface" in the English edition (this "Preface" is absent from recent Russian reprints), Berdyaev mentions that, "It is some eighteen years since I wrote this book", i.e. that Berdyaev had already written it back in 1905-1906...

the Old Slavophils, he is so very new in spirit. In Dostoevsky the Slavophil consciousness developed in revolutionary a direction. In him, there sharply prevail religio-mystical elements over the positivist-naturalistic elements. In "The Brothers Karamazov" there weaves a prophetic spirit. Not in vain was the religious consciousness of Dostoevsky received by him as an ancestral legacy; it passed through great suffering, through terrible temptations, searchings and doubts. Khomyakov's bright outlook and assuredness in life cannot be found in Dostoevsky. Dostoevsky discovered suchlike a knowledge of evil, as did not exist for Khomyakov. The sense of the spirit of the Anti-Christ is so characteristic of this new consciousness in an Orthodox and Slavophil. With the awareness of the impending danger of the spirit of the Anti-Christ is connected an awareness of the two cities, -- the Coming City of Christ and the city of the enemy of Christ. With Dostoevsky there is aspiration for the New Earth and there is the frightening terror of times apocalyptic. Dostoevsky lives in a different cosmic atmosphere, from that in which lived Khomyakov and the Slavophils, he belongs to a new religious epoch. For this newly commenced epoch, which can only be called apocalyptic, oriented towards the end, towards finality, to the eschatological themes concerning the end, there is characteristic a catastrophism, an aspiration towards the City of Christ and terror afront the city of the Anti-Christ. Dostoevsky is wholly within the apocalypse, wholly pervaded by eschatological themes, quite foreign to Khomyakov. Between Khomyakov and Dostoevsky there lies the disintegration of the patriarchal way of life, the wreck of the Slavophil lifestyle hopes, the appearance within Russian life of fatal symptoms of the spirit of the Anti-Christ, the disenchantment as to the good will of the ruling power and its all the greater rift from the people. If the worse elements within Slavophilism degenerated into a reactionary mode of life, into social-class and national greed, then the best elements in Slavophilism may be considered to have developed on the side of the prophetic and mystical. The times of separation have ensued. Many themes, unclear yet in the years of the 1830's and 1840's, have deepened and become relevant as regards Russian messianism. Russian messianism has entered into a new stage. Dostoevsky already says concerning this, that Russian man -- is an all-man, universal a man, and that the vocation of Russia -- is worldwide. Messianism that is thus conscious of its universal nature.

We see in Vl. Solov'ev a creative developement of the consciousness of the Slavophils and of Dostoevsky. Vl. Solov'ev -- is a

ALEKSEI STEPANOVICH KHOMYAKOV

Slavophil as regards his sources, from the Slavophils he received his themes, his religious trend, his faith in the vocation of Russia. But he developes the Slavophil consciousness on the side of a Christian universalism, and in him the pagan nationalism finally is overcome. Hence, with Vl. Solov'ev there is a radical change in attitude towards the Catholic West. In his attitude towards Catholicism Solov'ev is closer to Chaadayev, than to Khomyakov; in Solov'ev these two antipodes, opposite poles, both religiously thought out, align. Solov'ev recognises the truth of Catholicism, he thirsts for the reunion of the Churches and the sharing of Russia in Western culture. He confesses the ideals of an universal Christianity and he sees the mission of Russia to comprise the uniting into a single truth of Christ the truths of the East and the truths of the West. He stands firmly upon the grounds of a religio-mystical basis for messianism in contrast to the historico-ethnographical basis of nationalism. He calls for self-criticism, and not for self-smugness, he denounces the pagan egoism of the heirs of Slavophilism. After Dostoevsky and Solov'ev, Russian messianism ultimately has entered into an epoch of universal a consciousness; to return to the nationalism of the Slavophils is religiously impossible, or possible only in the format of reaction. The truth of Khomyakov passed through Dostoevsky and Solov'ev and has now reached us in creative and transfigurative a guise. Danilevsky, the Katkovites, the savagery of the nationalistic and class greed, the pagan self-smugness, the servility before empirical facts, the toadyism of the ruling authority -- all this remains on the sidelines, does not enter into the history of the religious and national self-consciousness of the Russian people. With Dostoevsky and Solov'ev there has appeared in the Russian consciousness a prophetic spirit. The Russian searchings for the City ultimately have become conscious, the religious awareness becomes oriented forwards, towards the end-times, towards completion. Christianity is conceived of not only a guarding of things holy, as the priesthood, but also as prophecy, as creative developement. Solov'ev already the possibility of dogmatic developement, he understood the Church as a Divine-human process upon the earth, he perceived, that history moves towards God-manhood. N. F. Fedorov in his "Philosophy of the Common Task" preaches an active attitude towards nature and he proclaims the madly bold and audacious idea of the resuscitation of the dead by the efforts of mankind. There has breathed a new spirit. This new spirit is completely foreign to the Western rationalistic streak of our thought, it is genetically connected with

Slavophilism, but it likewise surmounts the one-sidedness and limitedness of Slavophilism.

Remarkably symptomatic of the new religious searchings and disquiet mustneeds be considered the Peterburg religio-philosophic gatherings of 1903-1904.[1] At these gatherings, where the intelligentsia, seeking faith, met with hierarchs of the Church, new themes were sharply presented -- the theme concerning the relationship of Christianity to culture and still more to the point, though unknown to the Slavophils, the theme about the possibility of a new revelation. The positive results of these gatherings were not overly remarkable: the intelligentsia, with rare exceptions, were religiously ungrounded and inept, and their merit was in the positing of questions, not in their resolution; the representatives of the Church guarded things holy, but with the conservatism and inertia inherent to them, they were not sensitive to new religious themes. Yet all still these gatherings, at which inspired words were pronounced, signified the onset of a new religious epoch. These gatherings in the given instance are of interest for us, in that they all connect back to Slavophilism, and not with Westernism, although these connections as such were not then perceived. These gatherings disclosed, how convoluted and lengthy was the pathway trodden by our religious and national consciousness from Khomyakov up til us. Our grandfathers -- the Slavophils -- seem to us to have passed though only the good times. Everything has become so acute since those times, so much has been lived through. We live now exactly like right after an earthquake and we have no confidence in the firmness of the ground under our feet. Between us and Khomyakov there lies the experiencing of a revolution [1905], the shattered remnants of a patriarchal lifestyle, the survived experience of socialism and anarchism, Nietzscheanism and decadentism, and all in an extreme and ultimate form. And our religiosity is no longer a matter of lifestyle, but instead mystical. Modern people, in knowing the times and the seasons, cannot but be mystics. The quite especial interest in mysticism, unknown to Slavophil times, is characteristic for our era, at the summits of its religious consciousness. Yet

---

[1] *translator note*: For an account on the personages and the sessions of these Peterburg Religio-Philosophic Gatherings, vide chapter entitled: "The Encounter and Meeting", in the book of Fr. Aleksandr Men', "*Russian Religious Philosophy: 1989-1990 Lectures*", frsj Publications, 2015, p. 69-84.

at the same time we ought to feel a deep, a trans-temporal bond with Khomyakov: we live by that same holiness of Church, not shaken by the passage of decades, and against which the gates of Hell will not prevail, as Khomyakov also lived, and we desire to be faithful the same to this holiness and the same to be strengthened by it, as he was. To lose every connection with Khomyakov would mean to become groundless, wisked about by the wind. And there is blowing up a strong wind, quickly whipping up into a storm, and Khomyakov's strength and firmness is needful, so as not to be carried along and scattered off into the distance. We have inherited from Khomyakov the religio-Christian current, a national consciousness, the positing of the problem of East and West, connected with the tasks of Russia, the free and freedom-loving theologising, a Russian philosophy, warring against the spirit of non-being. We have clearly enough discovered the tremendous significance of Khomyakov for theology, for philosophy, for national self-consciousness. Everywhere he has tended to set the foundations for a national tradition in Russian spiritual culture. The illegitimate offspring of the Slavophils ought not to hinder us from recognising the legitimate offspring. The official chamber-cabinet conservatism, the savage nationalism -- is among the illegitimate offspring of Slavophilism, just as another of its illegitimate offspring can be considered the Russian populism, seeing in the obschina peasant commune some sort of salvation of the world, but with a grounding for its ideals not religious, but instead materialistic. But both the materialist-populists, and the materialist-nationalists, are alike foreign to what is holy for the Slavophils. And from this holy concern comes another path that reaches us.

Facing the Russian self-consciousness stands the task of overcoming both Slavophilism and Westernism. The epoch of the dispute between Slavophilism and Westernism has drawn to a close, and there ensuing a new epoch of a mature national self-consciousness. A mature national self-consciousness would tend to perceive everything true in Slavophilism, everything sacred in Eastern Orthodoxy, but it would possess a different attitude towards the truth of Western culture and Catholicism. A mature national self-consciousness would first of all affirm within the national flesh and blood the universal principles of Christ's truth and the all-human aspect of the mission of Russia. But the creative national self-consciousness demands further investigation into the history of our national self-consciousness in the XIX Century, a going deeper into the figures of our national religious thinkers. It is important to determine the significance of these thinkers for the fate of Russia, and to perceive the connection of these thoughts with that fate. It is time to make use of the riches, accumulated from our past. It is necessary to connect our future with our past. The deeper we get into the fate of our national religious thought, the clearer then it will become for us, what Sobornost' actually is within out thought, and what the supra-individual reason alive within it comprises. A collective reason shows itself to be an organ of our national self-consciousness, and there is a truth not just only human within this self-consciousness. There are judgements of God that have to be divined, but the history of these enigmatic judgements cannot be conceived of by those, who cannot believe in God nor allow that there are mysteries in the fate of Russia. The history of Russian thought, always religious in essence, filled with the utmost agitation, has yet to be written. One mustneeds cleanse one's self-consciousness, orient it towards the supreme meaning of life, in order to approach this task. Such a cleansing and orientation is only now beginning among us, and now is the proper moment to address an appreciation of our past. Our Westerniser thought has done nothing by way of an investigation of Slavophilism nor for its understanding. The depths of Slavophilism have remained inaccessible for this superficial approach in thought, torn asunder as it is from the national and religious spirit. The currents of spirit and thought, holding sway among us during the decades of the 1860's and the 1870's, and preserving still its grip over the consciousness of wide circles of the intelligentsia even during the XX Century, has ripped away from them even the tasks, posited by the Slavophils. This tradition of Russian spiritual culture among the broad circles has been perverted. And this tradition has been continued only by such people as Dostoevsky, Vl. Solov'ev and others like them. Now has begun a time to renew and strengthen the impaired tradition, since without a tradition it is impossible to have any sort of a national culture. Tradition is not stagnation and inertia, tradition -- is dynamic, and it calls for creativity. It is necessary to conjoin tradition with the prophetic spirit. The tradition of a national culture ought constantly to cleanse itself of the dirty weeds of reactionary stagnation; a true tradition is a power dynamic and creative. With Khomyakov one can unite oneself statically, -- wherein would begin a further degeneration of Slavophilism, or one can unite oneself dynamically, -- therein to continue the creative developement of

ALEKSEI STEPANOVICH KHOMYAKOV

Slavophilism. We call thus for a dynamic attitude -- towards the truth of Slavophilism.

The Slavophils did not express all the features of the Russian and Slavic character. Thus, the Russo-Slavic revolt and rebelliousness, -- very profound religious national traits, -- are scantily reflected in Slavophilism. And as regards all this, revolt and rebelliousness are no less characteristic for us, than is humility and submissiveness. Russians do not have their own city, they seek for the Coming City, in the nature of the Russian people is an eternal wanderlust. Gogol, Dostoevsky, L. Tolstoy -- are wanderers. The wanderer type -- is a type beloved by the Russian people. In the wanderer is expressed in vivid an image the search for the City. In the Slavophils the spirit of a Russian rootedness prevailed over the spirit of the Russian wandering. The wanderer goes about the land, but the element inspiring him is stronger than the element of the land. Khomyakov was not a wanderer. Of the Slavophil generation from among the people of the decades of the 1830's and 1840's, Gogol alone had that agitated and searching spirit, akin to our own times. O Certainly, the Slavophils also thirsted for the truth of Christ about the land, concerning the City of Christ, but for the triumph of this truth they demanded not so much the wandering, as rather the rootedness, not so much the inspired soaring flight, as rather growth upon the land. But the great truth of the Russians is in this, that they cannot be reconciled with this earthly city, with a city, set up by the prince of this world; rather, it is that they seek for the Heavenly Jerusalem, come down to earth. With this, the Russians are radically distinct from the peoples of the West, finely organised and satisfied, having their own city. The Catholic West has believed, that it possesses its own city, and this City -- is the Church; in the hierarchical structure of the Church with the pope at the top this City of God has already been realised, and the thousand year reign of Christ has already ensued. The atheistic West believes, that this City has been realised in the bourgeois state or is to be realised in a socialistic state. Orthodox Russia has not imagined, that the Church is already the City, for the Orthodox consciousness distinguishes the Church from the City. And for Khomyakov the Church never was the City. In the Orthodox Church there is no chiliasm, whether it be true or false a sort. But the chiliastic searching remains. In Slavophilism, the chiliastic yearning was weakened not by a false teaching about the Church, but by a false teaching about nationality, in which Christianity was jumbled up together with paganism. In the best aspects of modern Russian art is felt the Slavic spirit of agitation, revolt and wandering. And from this art one can judge, how much has changed since the time of the Slavophils.

In summary, we have to say, that Slavophilism has both degenerated and has developed, that such a twofold judgement upon it is connected with a differentiation of various aspects of Slavophilism. The aspects of the pagan-nationalistic, inertia lifestyle, class greed, the positivist statecraft all degenerated and decayed. But creatively there has developed the truth of Slavophilism, i.e. of elements genuinely churchly, Christian-mystical, national-messianic. There is an immortal truth in the churchly and national consciousness of the Slavophils, and thus truth can be smothered neither by a reactionary-pagan nationalism, nor by an atheistic internationalism. But the societal sentiment and societal consciousness for us have become so muddled and fouled, that it is impossible to sit in judgement on Slavophilism, which at first glance is unclear and confusing. We have not yet a genuine national intelligentsia -- reflecting the mindset of the people, upon which can be grounded the destiny of Russia. The Westerniser consciousness does not see facing it the enigma of Russia, for this -- is a riddle of the Slavophil consciousness. The Slavophils, and not the Westernisers, were the ones to worry themself over the enigma, of what the Creator had intended concerning Russia and what sort of path He had prepared for it. There had been a "Westerniser" who had plagued himself over this, -- Chaadayev, both foe and friend of the Slavophils, but the Westernism of Chaadayev had nothing in common with the further trend of Westernism. Our Westernism always was deeply provincial, in it there was so much of a provincial imitation of fads from the capital. Together with this, the Westernism was juvenile and immature, in it there is sensed a thought level from grade school courses. The Westernisers never had a true universalism, which all the sooner could be found with the Slavophils or with Chaadayev. And this is understandable. An authentic universalism is present only for the religious consciousness. The Russian Westerniser consciousness in the majority of instances is either irreligious or anti-religious, atheistic and materialistic. This tends to become apparent in the juvenile provincialism of the Russian Westernisers, since the consciousness of the Western peoples all told is not necessarily atheistic, and there exist there both a religious consciousness and a religious truth. The great Western culture is first of all however a Catholic culture. In the land of holy wonders there are the great cemeteries, into which the Russian Westernisers go not nor chance to revere. Therein be the graves not only of Marx and Spenser, but also the graves of Dante and Jacob Boehme. But in order to go and thus revere the graves of Dante and Jacob Boehme requires a greater maturity and a greater universalism, than which our Westernisers possess. In paying respects afront the great tombs of the West we should want to be greater Westernisers than the whole of our present Westernisers, we should want to become more cultured and more universal Westernisers. And this means, that we should not want to be mere Westernisers, since that in Europe there are no Westernisers, since Westernism -- is a provincial phenomenon.

Russia, East and West -- here is a worldwide theme to be worked at, facing our generation and the generations to come. In this theme, highlighted for us by the Slavophils, all the threads merge together. Russia stands at the centre of two currents within world history -- the Eastern and the Western. Only Russia can resolve for European culture the question about the East. But there exist two Easts -- the Christian East and the non-Christian East. Russia itself is a Christian East-West, and its truth is first of all the truth of Orthodoxy. But in the flesh and blood of Russia, into its mode of life there have entered in elements of the non-Christian East, and poisoned it. The Christian world vocation of Russia can be fulfilled only by conquering within itself the extreme and non-Christian East, only by having cleansed itself, i.e. by having become conscious of itself ultimately as a Christian East-West, and not as an anti-Christian East. The extreme non-Christian East -- is Pan-Mongolism, and this is a sort of Pan-Mongolism, which eternally threatens us both from without and from within; it is likewise chaos and inertia. A rather more refined and tempting opponent of Christian mankind is Indian Buddhism, which imperceptibly impairs the Christian will and obscures the Christian revelation about the concept of person. I have in view the modern Buddhism, which is making the rounds of Christian Europe. In the old Brahmanism there was an eternal truth of a primordial, pre-Christian revelation, and India possessed its own positive mission. But after the Christian revelation the role of India has changed, just like the role of Israel has changed. In Buddhism there is a spirit of non-being, dangerous for Christian Europe and for Russia. Khomyakov understood this. Russia is great and has a vocation only insofar as it preserves the Christian truth. If Russia has a world role, then this mission is in the uniting of East and West into a single Christian mankind.

Nicholas Berdyaev

If a great and original culture be possible in Russia, this can only be as a culture religiously synthetic, and not analytically differentiated. And everything, such as has been great in the spiritual life of Russia, has namely been so. The religiously synthetic spirit has left its imprint upon Russian literature, and upon Russian philosophy, and upon the Russian searchings for integrally whole truth in everything and everywhere. Our national spirit denies politics as an abstract and self-sufficing principle. And in nothing do we love abstract and self-sufficing principles. The Slavophils had intuition of this tendency of our national spirit and by it thus accomplished an exploit of the national self-consciousness.

Addenda

The Slavophilism of the Ruling Powers

(1915 -202)[1]

I.

The appointment of the Moscow Gubernia Marshall of the Nobility, A. D. Samarin, as OberProkurator of the Holy Synod -- is the most interesting and remarkable of all the appointments of recent times. In the person of A. D. Samarin, Slavophilism for the first time is receiving power and receives it within the churchly sphere, which always has stood at the centre of Slavophil interests. Slavophilism up to the present has been unauthorised, and the conservative character of its basic principles has not saved this current of thought from the eternal suspicions on the part of the ruling authorities. Many of the ideas of the Slavophils were irresponsible and in experience not accurate. We tend to remember, that the theological writings of A. S. Khomyakov were prohibited by the religious censor and appeared abroad in the French language. And Khomyakov was not only the greatest theologian of the Slavophil school, but he contributed also to an utmost degree, to the uplifting of the churchly awareness in the East, within Orthodoxy. And now it avails the OberProkurator Samarin to

---

[1] SLAVYANOPHIL'STVO Y VLASTI. Article was originally published in newspaper "Birzhevye vedomosti", 3 aug. 1915, № 15003.

trans. note: our *Padenie* Russian source notes (p. 1093) correctly that the 1978 Klepinina Bibliographie was mistaken in considering this article as identical (pp. 31, 83) with the 15th Chapter of Berdyaev's book, "The Fate of Russia", entitled "Slavophilism and the Slavic Idea".

Padenie (p. 1093) *ed. note*: "A. D. Samarin was appointed as OberProkurator of the Holy Synod in July 1915, but through the opposition of G. Rasputin in September the same year he was removed". (*trans. note*: this present Berdyaev article appeared in the interim, 3 August 1915).

transfer over into life many of the ideas of Khomyakov, which seemed so dangerous to all the former OberProkurators. The uncle of the current OberProkurator, Yu. Samarin, wrote: "Khomyakov himself represented an original, a phenomenon almost unprecedented among us *of fullest a freedom in religious awareness*".[1] This "fullest freedom in the religious consciousness" of Khomyakov was something that never could be understood, nor accepted by the official churchly circles, those situated in authority. "Fullest freedom: always indeed and to all seemed dangerous and treasonous. At the very same time as the Slavophils were asserting churchly life to be in "fullest freedom" and saw in freedom to be the very essence of the Church, the churchly authorities were asserting churchly life to be instead in fullest necessity and saw the very essence of the Church to be in coercion. The Slavophil and Khomyakov conception of the Church had many points coinciding with the genuine churchly life amongst the Russian people, but not in a single point did it intersect with the official churchly authorities.

The first point of intersection of the Slavophil Orthodoxy with the official Orthodoxy is now in the new OberProkurator of the Synod, -- A. D. Samarin.

The appointment of Mr. Samarin -- is very responsible a fact for the old Slavophilism, a great putting to the test of its suitability for life, its sacrificing of idea. A. D. Samarin -- is not simply some bureaucrat, who can foppishly adapt to whatever and be obligated to nothing. And perchance, never yet has a Russian minister come to power being so intense and devoted to his ideas. Samarin comes to power from a perspective most responsible to Slavophilism. Behind him stand very definite churchly ideals, those of his spiritual and by-blood fathers and forefathers. His very name already is terribly imposing. Upon him gaze familial portraits, and they connect him with familial traditions. How bound up or devoted to any sort of intellectual or familial traditions was Mr. Sabler? He indulged to the fullest in bureaucratic liberties, a license for endless connivance and officious fawning. But A. D. Samarin -- is no bureaucrat. His "legitimacy" -- is societal, and not some "legitimacy" based upon official rank. He aspires to be the bearer of the ideals of the people's

---

[1] Vide: Yu. Samarin, "Preface to the 1st Edition of the Theological Collected Works of Khomyakov" (in Tome II of the "Collected Works of Khomyakov", or in the "Collected Works of Yu. Samarin, Tome VI).

conservatism. We are not accustomed to anything like this, that the intellectual and societal conservatism of the people should be in power. The traditional bureaucratic "legitimacy" has never been of suchlike a conservatism. It was bereft of conservative ideas, the like of which evidently Mr. Samarin does have. A. D. Samarin -- is the first Synod OberProkurator driving from the Moscow, rather than Petrograd Orthodoxy, i.e. in essence the first moreso Orthodox, moreso churchly, moreso nationally Russian an OberProkurator. In this -- is the significant meaning of his appointment. I do not know, how Mr. Samarin will be in his efforts, but as such he has to be on the basis of his position, his person, and his connections with the past. The Petrograd, the state-bureaucratic Orthodoxy has always indeed differed from the age old Moscow Orthodoxy, an Orthodoxy quite more closely tied in with the startsi-elders and the monasteries, with the people's sanctities and with the religious life of the Russian Land.

A. D. Samarin, evidently, is strongly a Moscow Orthodox type of churchman. He can be a representative empowering the Moscow Orthodox circles, genuine believers and intellectuals, those circles, which not so very long ago were in sharp opposition to the Synod and the official churchly authorities on the question of the "Imyaslavtsi/Name-Praisers"[1] and on certain other major questions of churchly life. In these rightist Orthodox circles and enjoying the greatest reknown are a brother of the new

---

[1] *trans. note*: The Imyaslavtsi, apparently grew out of the Hesychiast practice of mystical repetition of the "Jesus Prayer" among the monks of Holy Mount Athos. In 1912-13 this practice was declared "heretical" by the official churchly authorities in Russia, and "477 monks were forcibly removed from Athos and dispersed among various monasteries in Russia" (*Padenie note № 2, p.1093*). Among the expression of outrage in public opinion at the brutal roughing up of old Russian monks by the Russian government, in August 1913 Berdyaev penned his fiery famous article, "Quenchers of the Spirit" ("Gasiteli Dukha" Kl. № 172, in the gazette "Russkaya molva", № 232), -- the publication of which caused Berdyaev to be officially charged with "blasphemy" which after a trial would have resulted in perpetual banishment to Siberia, except that WWI and the 1917 Revolutions intervened, with the Bolsheviks subsequently in 1922 banishing Berdyaev instead to the West. Another irony of fate...

OberProkurator, by the name of F. D. Samarin, and also M. A. Novoselov, V. A. Kushevnikov, P. B. Mansurov.[1] The intellectual conservatism and strong churchliness of these people has set them in opposition to the dubious Synod politics, which have ravaged churchly life and caused its demoralisation. A lack of success by A. D. Samarin in power would to a certain degree be also misfortunate for these Moscow Orthodox circles, an intellectual crisis for them. All Orthodox Russia looks to A. D. Samarin at present, all the genuinely churchly Russia, which has been repressed under the OberProkurator leadership, hemming in always the "fullest freedom" in churchly life, such as when the persecution against the "Imyaslavtsi" occurred. How will the Slavophil traditions of A. D. Samarin tie in with the sphere of churchly ideals?

II.

The Slavophils were in resolute an intellectual opposition to the bureaucratic Synod structure, although under the conditions of those times they could not fully express it. In the bureaucratisation of the churchly structure, which in their opinion began with Peter the Great, they saw an enormous evil. The Sobornost'/Communality[2] within the Church -- in this indeed was the pathos, the feeling of something unique, for the old and classical Slavophilism. They loved to set the conciliar-catholic spirit of the East in contrast to Western Catholicism. In the Sobornost' of the churchly

---

[1] The group publishes a religio-philosophic selection of books under the editorship of M. A. Novoselov and organises religious talks.

[2] *trans. note*: "Sobornost'" derives from the Slavonic word for "catholic" ["sobornyi"] in the liturgically used Nicene Creed: -- "I believe... in one, holy, catholic and apostolic Church" ["Veruiu... vo edinu svyatuiu *cobornuiu* i apostol'skuiu tserkov'"]. In contrast to the Romanist understanding of "catholicity" as "universality *of* the Church", an external mark, the Orthodox nuance of "sobornost'/catholicity" reflects rather an "universality or wholeness *within* the Church", an inner non-static dynamic Divine-human process, evidenced in the Epiklesis during the Liturgy, and similar invokings of the Holy Spirit and of Christ [Mt. 18: 20] at spiritual and churchly gatherings, and Sobors/Councils. Hence, Sobornost' at times is translated as "conciliarity", "catholicity", "communality" and suchlike...

people they saw a lofty sanctioning for a churchly lifestyle, and this conciliar-catholic Sobornost' they conceived of as non-juridical, not something external, but inward and free. In this sanctioning by the people of the Church Khomyakov considered to be a sign of veracity for a Council to be OEcumenical.

But in the Synodal arrangement from the Peterburg period of Russian history, the people of the Church ceased to play any sort of role whatsoever, and the idea of Sobornost' was completely distorted. The Synodal arrangement is non-conciliar not only from that inward point of view, upon which Khomyakov stood and which cannot be expressed juridically, but non-conciliar also from the external and canonical point of view. This arrangement was an expression of the servility of the Church to the state. The feeling of the Slavophils regarding the Church was beautifully expressed by Yu. Samarin in the following words: "*I admit, I yield, I submit* -- means consequently, *I do not believe*. The Church lays claim only to faith and anything less does not suffice; in other words, it accepts into its bosom only the *free*. Whosoever offers it a slave-like grudging acceptance, does not have faith in it, and that one is not truly in the Church nor of the Church". And still further on he says: "The Church is not a doctrine, nor a system nor an institution. *The Church* is a living organism, an organism of truth and of love, or more precisely, *truth and love as an organism*". But the official Synodal arrangement has asserted the Church as an "institution" and has demanded, that the Church "should be offered slave-like an acceptance, irregardless of any faith in it". Is it possible then to esteem one's churchly authorities as an adequate expression of the Church, as "a living organism of truth and love"? The Slavophils quite well understood, that their ideal conception of the Church nowise at all corresponded to the churchly actuality or to the churchly ordering of things in fact. Their harsh criticism of the Western Church with certain transpositions can be turned also on the Eastern Church. If it be regarded poor an affair, when the Church becomes in effect the state and is in everything comparable to it, then it is no less poor an affair, when the Church is subordinated to the state and becomes its tool, its foil. The conception of the Orthodox Church by Khomyakov, Samarin and the other Slavophils was an ideal construct, an expression of the OEcumenico-Universal Church of Christ as above all the historical embodiments, and their conception is to their great credit. The teaching of Khomyakov concerning the Church represents an utmost point of ecclesial consciousness in the East, but it is far remote from the churchly activity of the East.

I shall provide certain characteristic places in Khomyakov as reflect the characteristics of the churchly views of the Slavophils, very bold and free and inevitably clashing with churchly actuality and churchly authority. "The Church is not authority, just as God is not authority, just as Christ is not authority: since an authority is something external to us. Not authority, I say, but truth rather and at the same time within the life of the Christian, his inner life".[1] "Every act of believing, every meaningful act of faith is an act of freedom and indispensably issues forth from a preliminary free investigating".[2] The Church "knows brotherhood, but it does not know subjection".[3] "The oneness of the Church was free; more precisely, the unity was of freedom itself, structurally an expression of its inner accord. When this new oneness was sundered, churchly freedom had to be sacrificed for instead the attainment of an unity artificial and capricious, an external token or sign having to replace the spiritual sensing of truth".[4] "The clergy, in its *Christian* actuality, is indispensably a free clergy".[5] "Christianity is naught other, than freedom in Christ... I admit of the Church as moreso free, than do the Protestants... It is extremely wrong to think, that the Church demands compulsory unity or compulsory obedience; on the contrary, it abhors both the one and the other: wherefore *in deeds of faith compulsory unity is a lie, and compulsory obedience is death*".[6] "No sort of external token, no sort of external sign should restrict the freedom of the Christian conscience: the Lord Himself teaches us

---

[1] *Padenie note (p.1093)*: A. S. Khomyakov, "Collected Works", Moscow, 1900, Tom II, p. 54. (alternately, A. S. Khomyakov, "Works" in 2 volumes, Moscow, 1994, Tom 2, pp. 43-44. In following this latter source pagination will be indicated within ( ) brackets).

[2] *Padenie note (p.1093)*: Ibid, p. 43 (35).

[3] *Padenie note (p.1093)*: Ibid., p. 69 (55).

[4] *Padenie note (p.1093)*: Ibid., p. 72 (57).

[5] *Padenie note (p.1093)*: Ibid., p. 181 (141).

[6] *Padenie note (p.1093)*: Ibid., p. 192 (150).

this".¹ "The oneness (of the Church) is naught other, than the consent of the personally free".² "Neither hierarchical power, nor the significance of the clergy as a class can serve as a guarantee for truth; the knowledge of truth obtains only by mutual love".³

"It would have been better, if we had less of an official and political religion, and if the government could be persuaded that the Christian truth has no need of constant protection, and that excessive solicitude over it tends to impair, and not strengthen it".⁴ "In that the members of the Church are we ourself -- the bearers of its greatness and majesty, we -- the sole ones in all the wayward world the keepers of the truth of Christ. And keeping silent, when we are obligated to proclaim the word of God, we bring upon ourself judgement, as being craven and heedless slaves... Howsoever lofty a man might stand upon the societal ladder, be he even prince or ruler for us, if he be not of the Church, then in the area of faith he can only be as a learner for us, but hence not the equal for us".⁵ And thus Khomyakov proclaims not only the freedom of the people of the Church and of each member of the Church, but also the authority of the people of the Church in the matter of teaching. That Khomyakov was opposed to Caesaropapism, is evident from the following words: "We think, that in being free, the sovereign just like every man, can fall into error, and if, though may God grant it not to occur, if some like misfortune were to befall, despite the perpetual prayers of the sons of the Church, thereupon also this emperor should not lose any of his rights of obedience from his subjects on matters secular: but the Church should bear no sort of detriment in its majesty and in its plenitude: since never must it betray its true and its sole Head. In suchlike a presupposed instance the

---

¹ *Padenie note (p.1093)*: A. S. Khomyakov, "Collected Works", Tom II, p. 231 (181).

² *Padenie note (p.1093)*: Ibid., p. 235 (183).

³ *Padenie note (p.1093)*: Ibid., p. 363 (279).

⁴ *Padenie note (p.1093)*: Ibid., p. 364 (280).

⁵ *Padenie note (p.1094)*: Ibid., p. 86 (68-69).

Christian thus astray would become lesser in its bosom -- and only so".[1] If a Slavophil were empowered and wanted seriously to carry out in life the churchly ideas of Khomyakov, then there would have to happen an enormous and radical turnabout. Khomyakov's ideas bear heavily upon his spirit of freedom. Khomyakov was a teacher of the Church for the Slavophil camp. Samarin was his student and follower, as were all the Slavophils of the time of its flourishing, they were inspired by Khomyakov's churchly ideals, unlike the later times of decline. But the inevitable course of life shows, that to be a Slavophil in 1915 signifies something altogether different, than to be a Slavophil in the year 1840.

The old Slavophilism at present is in a period of decline and decay. It is still possible as a closet an antiquarian interest, as a non-vital mindset of a not large number of people standing off afar from the prevailing currents of life. But it is almost impossible to empower. An active attentiveness to life demands a new creative religious energy or it will lead to a betrayal of the old, the good ideals. It is too late for Slavophilism to have come to power. And every delay in history gets fiercely punished. The children and grandchildren of Khomyakov and Samarin no longer still possess this freshness in the affirming of churchly freedom. Too strong in them is the fear of facing the disintegration of a fond lifestyle.

III.

The position of the new OberProkurator of the Synod is difficult, in that the Slavophil traditions obligate him to a diminishing of the OberProkurator authority, i.e. to a self-limitation and self-denial. And this always becomes very difficult for a man, standing in power. Yet what is needed is a directing of his power towards a lessening of the power of the OberProkurator upon the Church. This task demands enormous energy, will-power and self-assertion. It is necessary to overcome the terrible power of inertia in our churchly governance, to win out over the Synodal bureaucratic routine, to set on new rails all the colossal mechanism, so accustomed as it is to grovelling and toadyism. And for this within our episcopate there has to be, finally, awakened the feeling of churchly worthliness, that of being proud of the Church, which has nothing in

---

[1] *Padenie note (p.1094)*: A. S. Khomyakov, "Collected Works", Tom II, p. 37-38 (31).

common with human or personal pride. A. D. Samarin, if he be the Slavophil, has to make an attempt at the emancipation of churchly life, setting free the positive religious energy of the people of the Church. He has to apply all his efforts to this, -- the restoration of Sobornost' in churchly life. The Sobornost' of churchly life -- is a dogma of the Slavophils. But the Slavophils have yet another dogma -- freedom of conscience. Freedom of conscience for all the Slavophils was something sacred, they contrasted it against the obligatory within Catholicism.

We have seen, how the pathos for freedom pervaded the churchly ideas of Khomyakov. Khomyakov, and all the Slavophils together with him did not admit of obligation and coercion in matters of faith. A. D. Samarin has thus first of all and most of all has to be a defender of freedom of conscience, calling to mind the words of his uncle, that the Church "doth accept into its bosom only the *free*. Whoso offers it a slave-like grudging acceptance, is not in the Church nor of the Church".

But one should not overstate the role, which the OberProkurator of the Synod can play. His role -- is moreso negative, than positive, he is called not so much to do good, as rather not to do evil. The OberProkurator cannot be termed a churchly activist, he is only an intermediary between the Church and the state, he directs the affairs of the Church, insofar as they concern the state, and the affairs of the state, insofar as they concern the Church. But the OberProkurator is not a participant of the Holy Synod and churchly a power does not belong to him. Our OberProkurators often in fact have run the Church and had greater an influence, than the metropolitans and bishops, but this was only a factual expression of the correlation between the Church and the state, and nowise an expression of the principal position of the OberProkurator within the Church. But the OberProkurator of the Holy Synod, one such as who esteems the freedom and independence of the Church, at a minimum has to reduce the grip of the civil authorities over churchly life, the coercion in matters of faith. The persecution of sectarians has tended to be justified for us as necessary an activity by the state, and not the Church. The OberProkurator, as the intermediary between the Church and the state, can take a stand on this, that the Church is not interested in having privileged a position from the state for its faithful sons, and that the protective services of the state authority are degrading for the dignity of the Church. A church of persecutors cannot flourish. A church of the persecuted has always flourished more. A. D. Samarin, as a Slavophil and a conservative, certainly, cannot be a proponent for the separation of the Church from the state, he still believes in "the Christian state". But he can and he ought to preserve the sacredness of freedom of conscience, which for us has been proclaimed, but not fulfilled.

IV.

It is difficult to believe, that our churchly life can be revived by those measures, which usually among us would be regarded as of renewal and progressive: the convening of a local Sobor-Council, the restoration of the parish, the return to a conciliar structure, in accord with the canons, or a reconstituting of the Patriarchate. The outward reforms, which irreligious and non-churchly people often demand, can be wished for, but in themself as such they will not renew the churchly-religious life. Church life has stagnated not because, that for so long a time it was directed and run by Pobedonostsev, and that the living spirit within it was smothered by the bureaucratic structure, and that the Church had become subjugated to the state. The reverse is true: Pobedonostsev directed and ran churchly life, the Church was oppressed by the state, because the religious energy had weakened, because the living spirit within the Church had diminished. The Church in disarray is the result of a decline in religious life, a religious crisis within the Russian people. It is impossible to renew the parish by external measures. The factual absence of the parish is but an expression of the weakness of churchly life among the people. A genuine churchly renewal is possible and can occur only from within, inwardly, from a gaining of spirit. Sobornost' in the Church is a manifestation of spirit, and not an external, juridical expression of form. From the outside there can be attained only a negative emancipation, a liberation from lies and coercion. But the positive values of churchly life are not reached by such a path.

The grievous symptom of the decline of religious energy in our churchly life happens to be seen in this, that in this threatening and extraordinary hour of Russian and world history, the Church has proven to be so inactive. The churchly forces are not mobilising for the defense of the country, for the repelling of the enemy. Our monasteries have done shamefully little for the help of the wounded. Our clergy have least of all participated in the patriotic upsurge and exertion of all the forces of the nation.

ALEKSEI STEPANOVICH KHOMYAKOV

One can say, that this is not the business of the Church to be bothered with. But we are mindful of the times of St. Sergei Radinezh and the role, which the Church then played in the saving of Russia. The Church has been one of the defining forces within Russian history. And now Russia anew is undergoing difficult days of responsibility. But in the Church is not felt historical an energy. The religious energy has as it were departed to different a place and in concealment it acts within all the great, the heroic, the sacrificial and spiritually precious, that now happens within life.

Slavophilism cannot still renew churchly life: it is too late. In late an hour of history has appeared a Slavophil OberProkurator. The old schema was already powerless over the infinite complexity of life. The ideals of pre-Petrine Rus' could be a beautiful dream of idealistically minded a clutch of literary landowners of the 1840's, set not upon actual deeds, and remote from the vital struggle. But it is impossible already to look upon A. D. Samarin as such an idealistic dreamer, remote from life. He has been very involved with life and in the affairs of "this world" in his capacity of Marshall of the Nobility and a visible representative of an united nobility. Within this thicket of life, in this struggle for the interests of an outmoded nobility, in the eternal resistance to the growth of new life there will have to have faded the ideals of Khomyakov and Yu. Samarin. The old gentry, though quite pure and intelligent, cannot still renew churchly life or any sort of life. The final beautiful and majestic gesture of the nobility can be only a gesture of historical self-denial and sacrifice. But not such has been the activity on behalf of the nobility by the new OberProkurator. In the quite energetic image of A. D. Samarin is sensed a final spark of a dying lifestyle. This -- is a final showing forth of old Russia, which has had to give way to the new Russia in all the spheres of life. A. D. Samarin, certainly, is better than Mr. Sabler, he is more churchly, more intellectual, and moreso societal a man. And he can prove more progressive in the life of the Church namely upon the strength of his conservativeness. But it would be mistaken to place any sort of special hopes on him. In religious life, just as with life in general, it is necessary most of all to rely upon oneself, upon the people of the Church, upon their religious energy. The Slavophils proceeded upon the assumption, that the entirety of the Russian people and society -- is Orthodox. And upon this conviction rested all their organic system. But now it is impossible still to sincerely construct one's civil state activity upon the principle, that all the whole Russian people is Orthodox and that the Russian state is truly Christian. And it is possible beforehand to say, that it will not be easy for the new, intellectually so overwhelmed OberProkurator to authoritatively establish an attitude towards the Church not as towards an "institution", but rather as to "a living organism of truth and love". Religious renewal is possible only upon the basis of a creative experience and creative ideas, which cannot be from a Slavophil of the old type.

Translator Comments

"*Khomyakov and us*". What a charming and indeed challenging series of ironies, intriguing paradoxes, deceptive mirages beggaring a dispelling clarity, that this book presents us. And which impels the translator to venture some few further words and thoughts. For students of the history of Russian intellectual thought, the name of A. S. Khomyakov betokens a core founding figure among the Slavophils, in contrast to the opposing camp of the Westernisers. Both camps germinated together and were initially co-terminous within the stifling reign of Nicholas I in the first half of the XIX Century. As a stereotype, the "Slavyanophils" have come to be viewed as reactionary "conservatives" looking back to "the good old days of Muscovite Rus'" and the innately chaotic Russian Eastern way of doing things. In contrast, the Westernisers were the "progressives", of various hues, looking to the West, Western Europe, as a panacea to "progress" Russia economically and societally out of its backwardness. And yet, matters are not so simple as might seem to superficial a glance, viewed with biased stereotypes, which we shall touch upon in our comments.

In recent times, there is a fairly voluminous literature in English on the Orthodox Church and Eastern Christian thought, and readers quite likely will have encountered the term "Sobornost'", which traces its coinage as a concept back to the theological ponderings of Khomyakov. Sobornost' is typically translated as "catholicity", "conciliarity", "communality" and suchlike, having become a slogan-word in discourse. Consider the irony of a non-professor lay theologian of so significant a concept in Russian religious thought! The irony that the theological writings of this staunchly conservative "supporter" of the autocracy had to get published abroad in French because of religious censorship! And hence the ultimate "*Khomyakov and us*" question: is Sobornost', buttressed upon "freedom" and "love", truly and validly an aspect of the Orthodox Church, or was it merely the muddled-headed musing on the part of yet another dreamy Russian poet-philosopher?

But first, the bibliographic textual details. Berdyaev early on in his text lists a number of then current books on Khomyakov, along with Khomyakov's 8 volume "Collected Works", from which he generous quotes. Berdyaev relates critically and even negatively at times, piercing through stereotypical views. And as Berdyaev notes, even Khomyakov's "Collected Works" tend to be problematic, since they are fragmentary and scattered, mere drafts, the dabblings of a man of many interests such as leisure affords, free of the demands of scribbling for a few paltry pennies...

Berdyaev's present book, "Aleksei Stepanovich Khomyakov", was originally published in 1912, in Moscow by the Izdatel'stvo/Publisher "Put'"[1] (i.e. "The Way"), 256 pages. In the T. Klepinina 1978 YMCA Press "Berdiaev Bibliographie" our present Berdyaev "Khomyakov" book is assigned as *Kl. № 6*.

Translation was made using the 1996 Russian reprint of Berdyaev's "Khomyakov", by the Tomsk (Russia) Izdatel'stvo "Vodolei", 160 p. Also at hand is the 1997 Volume 5 of Berdyaev's "Collected Works" by the Paris IMKA-YMCA Press. This latter tome actually comprises within it three of Berdyaev's books: "Khomyakov" (p. 9-202), the 1923 "Dostoevsky" (Kl. № 18), and the 1926 "Leont'ev" (Kl. № 22). Other more recent Russian reprints have also become available.

In our present English edition, we have also appended to Berdyaev's original 1912 text, by way of addendum, his 1915 article, "Slavophilism and the Ruling Powers" (Kl. № 202). This was done for several reasons. First of all, by way of ironic example, to demonstrate that the Slavophil inspired concept of Sobornost' was not regarded as something artificial and alien to Orthodox ecclesiology, howsoever novel the concept. But secondly, as regards Berdyaev himself. Berdyaev's "Khomyakov" was published in 1912; in 1913 Berdyaev penned his fiery "Gasiteli Dukha" article ("Quenchers of the Spirit", Kl. № 172). This resulted in Berdyaev being charged with blasphemy against the Holy Synod, with likely a fate of his perpetual banishment to Siberia, save for the outbreak of WWI and eventually his instead banishment to the West under Lenin. Yet in 1914 and thereafter we find Berdyaev continuing to write on churchly issues and

---

[1] To dispel some possible confusion: the reknown later 1924-1940 Paris IMKA Press "Journal Put'" (with Berdyaev as "editeur") likely chose its name in memory of this earlier publishing effort in Moscow. The Izdatel'stvo Put' was a collaborative effort, sponsored by the wealthy patroness of the arts Margarita Morozova, publishing a number of titles by significant figures in Russian religious thought, among them P. Florensky, S. Bulgakov and N. Berdyaev.

ALEKSEI STEPANOVICH KHOMYAKOV

in public a voice, ultimately neither silenced nor giving up on the Church under this setback -- to his credit! The *Padenie* Russian language source containing this article is a massive tome of Berdyaev 1914-1923 articles recently published in 2007 under the title, "Padenie svyaschennogo russkogo tsarstva" ["The Downfall of the Holy Russian Tsardom"], publisher "Astrel'", Moskva, 1180 p.

Rather striking, for the modern reader, is Berdyaev's strong contrast of the placidly tranquil Russia of Khomyakov's time, from that of the 1912 Russia, -- when "the very ground underfoot quakes and burns, amidst infernal rumblings". And for us, even moreso, save that we have become already numb... The Russia of Khomyakov's "classical Slavophil" generation was that of the reign of Nicholas I, an era of societal and intellectual stagnation and inertia, and backwardness. Just prior to this, Russia's prominent role in post-Napoleonic Europe had provided direct Western intellectual and cultural exposure primarily to impressionable idealistic elements of the Russian gentry. The subsequent failed Decembrist Revolt early in the reign of Nicholas I fueled the tsar's paranoia, which congealed and froze Russia for a generation. Berdyaev elsewhere describes this as a "muzhik-peasant kingdom". Common sense would suggest, that an ideology so strongly (on the surface) supportive to the autocratic regime as with the Slavophils, would find warm support and embrace on the part of the ruling authorities. Yet on the contrary, as our text succinctly shows, Khomyakov is viewed as a "dangerous man" by the tsar's functionaries, and the sovereign himself replies to Khomyakov in an air of mild bemusement. Along with this is the churchly frowning against permitting any printing on religious thought by this firm advocate of Orthodoxy. When one can count on friends in high places like this, -- who needs enemies?

There is perhaps a paradoxical irony to be gleaned from all this: in the perspective of a black-souled reactionism, an authentic conservatism is more "revolutionary" a force ultimately, than is a leftist revolutionary front lusting to seize power. A people, a "narod", and what cohesively comprises it, is more unitary a threat, than is its disintegration into a competing array of vengeful victim classes. Yet with any inspired idea and ideal, always with time there transpires a prostituting of what is holy, a defiling and distortion by its subsequent epigonal practitioners. And thus also with the spirit of the "classical Slavophilism" of Khomyakov and his generation, at the hands of the opportunist Katkov and eventually the Slavophilism of

Nicholas Berdyaev

Danilevsky -- another vulgar nationalism transplanted from the West and given Russian a name. One need but remember the psychology underlying the rise of Fascism under Hitler, wherein the "inferiority complex" induced by the WWI-defeat became sublimated (a Nietzschean term) into its virulent opposite of a "superiority complex". Consider, for a moment, the officially adopted slogan of Slavophilism: "Orthodoxy, Autocracy, Nationality", as it is typically translated and perceived. Yet there is an ironic flaw linguistically in the third term, "Narodnost'". In Russian there are two terms typically translated as "nation": "*natsiya*", a Western loan-word specifically meaning "*nation*", and "*narod*" specifically meaning "*the people*" and hence by inference "the nation". The Russian Narodniki (Populists) of the 1860's and thereafter were typically leftist revolutionaries, having a sense of their own alienation from "the people" and sought to be of service to them. And it is interesting to note, from a close reading of our text, that Khomyakov grounded the Russian autocracy upon this historical event, -- the Russian people coming together in peaceful accord at the 1613 Zemsky Sobor and choosing Mikhail Romanov (and his progeny) as tsar, to "assume the burden of rule". Within this lies buried the inference, that what the Russian people had in their prerogative to give, they had also the prerogative to remove. As it did in 1917, though not in peaceful accord, but amidst the tragedy and horror of civil war. And actually yes, Khomyakov with his profound thoughts was indeed a "dangerous man", moreso than appears on the surface.

In his comments, Berdyaev secretly displays a bit of critical envy towards the lifestyle afforded Khomyakov, that solidly grounded landowner and man of the soil, an adept at many pursuits and interests, insightful in many an area. This indeed was the goal of a well-rounded classical education, in such leisure as life might afford, -- in contrast to our present age of discipline-narrow specialists. Khomyakov's widely scattered attention have left us drafts fragmentary and unpolished, unfinished results, and with much now outdated. Hounds and the hunt nowadays might be considered a bit much, but who of us would not like to steal time off for fishing, rather than writing or reading these present lines, eh? The pace of time flows differently in the countryside lifestyle, more attuned to the slower tempo in nature; the perception of life and the real also differs, for one having grown up organically on the "clean dirt" of the soil. Yet for us also much of that lies in the past, with Dostoevsky's ant-hill city bustle having intruded its effect ever outwards, into our life.

ALEKSEI STEPANOVICH KHOMYAKOV

Berdyaev's account of A. S. Khomyakov's family history is both charming and instructive to an understanding of Khomyakov. Perhaps an oversight, but Berdyaev fails to mention an event from the dawn of Russian history, that closely parallels the tale, of how old Kirill Khomyakov sent out his obschina peasant emissaries to find a worthy bearer to continue ownership in the Khomyakov family name. This echoes almost exactly the template from the ancient Russian Letopisi-Chronicles leading up to the Baptism of Rus' in the year 988. Prince St. Vladimir had dispatched his emissaries to find a worthy new religious faith for his people: the teetotaler Moslems eschewed vodka, the Jews had lost their kingdom, Latin Catholicism was too gloomy an affair, but at Hagia Sophia in Tsargrad-Constantinople the Russian emissaries "knew not whether they were already in heaven or on earth". Hence, to jest slightly concerning a most solemn event, Prince St. Vladimir told his people "to go jump in the river" (Dnepr) with Byzantine clergy standing at the ready to perform the Rite of Holy Baptism. And even far earlier in the Letopisi-Chronicles, there is the legendary account of the Russian people peaceably "inviting" the Varangians (Varyagi) to assume the burden of rule over them-- a process over generations by which the Nordic Varangians, coursing the Eastern trade waterways to Tsargrad, gradually became assimilated and Slavicised, as we see with the Scandinavian name "Helga" transformed into "Olga", by way of example. There is apparent this same peaceful non-conquest "invitation to assume the burden of rule" in Khomyakov's account about the choosing by the Russian people of Mikhail Romanov as tsar constituting the basis of the Russian autocracy (implanting an Anglophile "poison-pill" into this justification). A. S. Khomyakov seems to have inherited old Kirill Khomyakov's respect for the wisdom of the peasant obschina and one's relationship towards the soil. My own father, a farmer now reposed, once wisely expressed it thus: "God has entrusted to us but a temporary good use of this land, the true ownership of which is His". This accords with the Gospel parable of good and wicked servants with the talents given them by God.

Which leads us to a discussion of the significance of Khomyakov's mother, Maria Alekseevna, to his personal formation. She was a strong and practical woman, taking family and estate affairs in hand and setting them right after her husband had squandered a fortune at gambling, so typical a vice of the Russian gentry. She inculcated a firm religious and moral code in the upbringing of her sons, quite moreso than typical. Khomyakov's observance of church services and religious fasts while in the military is evidence of this. So also is Khomyakov's reservedness towards women in terms of proper conduct, as well as his strong emotional control even in times of personal tragedy -- men don't cry, nor do they act like women, and they are expected to be respectfully chivalrous towards women. In Russian literature too, in writers like Dostoevsky, in the Russian psyche, the motif of a woman's solid love and faith provides the path to salvation from a man's prodigally lost wanderings. Khomyakov saw an example of this in his own parental household.

And then too, from Khomyakov's youth -- might not his negative attitude towards Roman Catholicism and the Romance peoples derive from that incident with his Latin tutor, the prelate abbe Boivin? It is not difficult to imagine the visceral revulsion, perhaps further justified by the foppish person of this prelate, in the youthful soul of Khomyakov festering over a lifetime against anything reminiscent of the visage of this foreigner, this Roman prelate. Where in the first place did this "juvenile schismatic" Khomyakov even learn the boastful concept of "papal infallibility" -- which for the credulous is the claim that the Pope is infallible in everything he says. And suddenly, eureka, the clever young Khomyakov discovers a Latin grammatical error in a papal bull (decree) to puncture this myth. And then, instead of deftly evading the issue with some jesuitical non-reply, the vengeful prelate resorts to the brute force of "parental punishment". No wonder that the chastised but unrepentant youth continues to nurture a last-word on this incident, in the spirit of "Fiat iustitia, et pereat mundus!". And yes, Berdyaev is correct that Khomyakov was unjust and blind to everything religiously real in Roman Catholicism, quite apart from the matter of papal pretensions.

But Berdyaev, on the other hand, was also unjust in his criticism of Khomyakov's Germanophile bias. The menacing imperialistic Germany of Berdyaev's time did not then exist during Khomyakov's time. The unification of Germany occurred only after Khomyakov's death in 1860, in the 1860-70's under Bismarck and Prussia. Prior to this, Germany as such represented moreso a Protestant and cultural force, in philosophy that of Kant and Hegelianism. Kant's "categorical moral imperative" in a sense leads to Hegel's absolute reason, bereft of a substrate, i.e. ungrounded and left suspended up in the air. And indeed, to his credit Khomyakov provided a religious substrate to the Hegelian idealism, with a "concrete idealism" deriving from "the integral wholeness of life", and therein validating the dignity of the human person, signified by Christ. It is boastful arrogance to preach the moral imperatives of an absolute Universal Reason and "inalienable rights" to barbaric cultures, for which their own sort of "universal reason" dictates quite otherwise. "Inalienable rights" -- based on what? If there is no actual substrate, then this becomes an intellectually self-deluded rationalist slogan. Upon what rests the inviolability of the dignity of the human person, the "inalienable rights"? Berdyaev himself was strongly under the influence of German philosophy in his early years. He was among those who worked their way from Marxist materialism into philosophic idealism; subsequently, in attempting to break free from Neo-Kantianism Berdyaev worked himself into some convoluted positions -- evident in some of his 1900-1906 articles contained in his 1907 book, "Sub specie aeternitatis".

Ironies. The typical gloss on the Slavophils is that they were fervent anti-Westerners, anti-progress, xenophobic. Khomyakov's proclaiming of Europe as "the land of holy wonders" -- exposes the lie to this shallow calumny of Slavophilism. Unlike many of the Westernisers, and especially the Westerniser "street", like children mouthing impressive sounding big words, parroting the pretty ideas to sound grown up, -- the Slavophils in contrast engaged the West on deeper a level, critically, and creatively reworked Western motifs into forms more commensurate with the national psyche. It devolves essentially into a question, of "whether one size actually does fit all", in cultural and socio-economic forms. In our own day, we see this in the tension between resurgent national identities against the forces of a depersonalising globalism. As Berdyaev noted, the sin underlying the conservatism of the Slavophils was that they were too content in having "their own city", living in memory of the glory days of the past, rather than in search for the adventive City to Come. Their "city" was too much grounded in static a consciousness, and stasis is an aspect proper to a corpse, rather than the vital dynamism of a living organism -- if Russia be viewed as such. In a sense, the conservatism of the Slavophils lacked sufficiently a sense of "catholicity" at inherently historical a depth. A vitally coherent and authentic conservatism embraces within its soul all the generations, preserving what was truly most precious from the legacy of the past, whilst creatively re-engaging and reworking it in the present, as our legacy to the future. Just like biologically, so also spiritually and culturally, we do not beget ourself, we share a genetic linkage with others, extending both into the past and into the future. The narcissist immersion in our throw-away culture is bourgeois to the extreme. Religiously, it is the expression of those who prefer to be step-sons rather than the sons and daughters of the MostHigh, which Christ adjures us to be via the "Our Father".

And yet this critique of the Slavophils is not entirely fair. As Berdyaev notes, they were too much their "own men", yet powerless to ever survive employ in the suffocating bureaucracy. Their ideas on freedom leaked out "between the lines", samizdat' style. And in especially some of Khomyakov's poems, we see that he could be extremely critical of the historical failings and sins of Russia, with a call to deep repentance for such. This call for a collective consciousness of repentance is a trait which carries over into Berdyaev's own writings, something oddly difficult to explain to our present culture. And even with the Germans, Khomyakov was wont to mock them as "those learned schmerzens, who don't know how to distinguish a dog's biting end from its tail end"...

It is interesting to observe a process of mutual revulsion and attraction within Berdyaev towards the Slavophilism of Khomyakov. There is the sweet lifestyle of well-off men of leisure, afforded by the injustice of serfdom, men dabbling in many a thing with dreamy speculations bereft of practicality and bringing nothing into proper completion. But Berdyaev is imperceptibly drawn towards Khomyakov. And indeed, in Khomyakov's thought there is much of Berdyaev's own philosophy in embryonic form. Many of Khomyakov's motifs resonate within Berdyaev's soul, which were there already before engaging Khomyakov. Such was an authentically originated Russian national philosophy, not merely parroting Western thought, and providing the formative roots of that "Russian philosopher", Vladimir Solov'ev. The radical perception of the inner essence of the Church, of Christ and grounded upon Christ, as comprising utmost love and freedom, words we meet with again and again in Berdyaev's quotes from Khomyakov, a love and freedom resonating as words uttered in intense conviction, not hollow sloganeering. It is a speaking on the basis of our spiritual birthright of being a member of the living organism which is the Church in Christ, a direct witnessing, in contrast to the all too typical objectively polite religious discourse uttered nowadays, as it were, from the outside church doorsteps vista. It is from the vantage point of a "believer", rather than of a nominal Christian. A Christianity bereft of Christ, of the presence of Christ, is an abomination. And an awareness of the Presence of Christ is implicitly a consciousness of the utmost Holiness of God. This emphasis on the Church as freedom and love underlies the "spiritual aristocratism", a perspective common to both Berdyaev and Khomyakov, deriving ultimately from Christ's "Sermon on the Mount". Christ bids us to be sons and daughters of the MostHigh, i.e. "Our Father", so radically significant a concept. A true suchlike son or daughter, conscious of the noble lineage of their ancestry is zealous and jealous for the repute and good name of one's forefathers, is riven to the core over one's own failings in this regard, in seeking the "rightful glorification" (i.e. pravoslavlenie) in Christ of "Our Father". It involves likewise a pervasive sense of being "at home" in the House of "God Our Father". "For Holy is the Lord Our God" (Яко свят Госпoд Бог наш). In familial matters, a spiritually sober and mature son or daughter acts out of a sense of love and freedom, quite differently a spirit from that of a contractual hired-hand, a mercenary whose first interest is generally themselves and their own benefit or gain. To bear the name of "Christian" is no trivial matter, it is the most august dignity in all the world, the validation of the assertion of the "inalienable rights" to the dignity of the human person, created in "the image of God". Is a non-narcissic love of God possible? This is perhaps dangerous a question. To love God first of all for God's sake, not mine. But this is perhaps suggested in the dynamic of Christ's dual summation of the Law of God -- to love the Lord Our God with all our heart, soul, mind, and thence to love our neighbour like unto ourself (which presupposes likewise a proper love of self). How authentic can our love for God be, if it be nothing more than fear of eternal perdition and the mercenary's narcissic intent of assuring a salvation-ticket to Heaven? Our modern world seems largely to have become sold on the devil's "better deal of a bird in the hand", relegating the Church into a mausoleum museum of the past... functionally where not actually.

    Another core Berdyaev motif in embryonic a form in Khomyakov is that of creativity. Khomyakov contrasts two conflicting dynamics, that of the Kushite and that of the Iranian. Which presents another irony, shocking at first glance -- the "Iranian"? But Khomyakov is not speaking about modern Iran, an Islamic theocracy so prominent upon the world stage. Rather, Khomyakov's Iran is the ancient Persia, that age old Eastern threat and rival to Rome, a Zoroastrian "fire-worshipper" culture which Khomyakov links in its spiritual dynamics to the uniqueness of Judaism and Christianity. The mere mention of Zarathustra (with its variant form "Zerdushta") brings to mind, of course, Friedrich Nietzsche's famous tome,

"Also Spracht Zarathustra". And there are parallels to the Zarathustra motif in both Khomyakov and Nietzsche. Nietzsche's Zarathustra dwells a solitary atop the heights of self-realisation, far from the maddening herd (including that herd of Nietzscheans) while Khomyakov's decisively herdlike Kushite element is given over to superstition and magicism. Who stumbled first upon the Zarathustra motif, Khomyakov or Nietzsche? Was there some common source, some significant book of research or scholarly round of discussion at the time that so caught the fancy of both these thinkers? It poses an interesting question.

Khomyakov posits two distinctly contrast and conflicting cultural types: the Kushite and the Iranian. The exertion of human energies in Kushite a culture results in massive but mute architectural works and strivings. The primary medium with which it is concerned and involved, is materiality, along with a concurrent concentration upon the natural laws governing necessity. At a primitive subliminal level of sub-consciousness, these laws of natural necessity are viewed with superstitious a regard, with a magical mindset approach, howsoever sophisticated. Freud was of course a later figure than Khomyakov, but Freud's book on "Totemism and Taboo" deals with this magicism in the psychology of the primitive mind. Man becomes immersed in an idolatrous fetish relationship with the world of things, with the magical allure governing necessity in the world of things, defined in toto and controlled by magical incantations of power, albeit modernly by scientific and mathematical formulae. Man thus views himself as a thing in a world of things, as an object, wherein both himself as a person and other persons are rendered and treated in an idolatrous-sort process of psychological objectification, where things exist to be used, abused, and then discarded in our modern "throw-away" society, whilst garnering the "mana-power" of these devoured things. In primitive societies man had no consciousness of himself subjectively unique as a person, he is immersed in the magical interplay of "necessary" natural forces. But in our modern world the consciousness of oneself and others as persons has become submerged and likewise disappears. Everything obtains in magical fetish a manner. Man defines himself and is governed by the magical allures of money, of possessions, of eroticism and the like, to which he consents to become enslaved, leaving no residue remaining, having virtually already become ossified into a living corpse, a mere walking tombstone, an obituary in the making, and little else. This "existential posture" of self-objectification is what both Hegel and Sartre term as a relationship of "bad faith". It is also what characterises the bourgeois approach to life. This Kushite ossification of life shatters and decomposes the integrally whole organic unity of life and of reality, projecting a falsified image, a mirage as it were within consciousness, a surface phenomenology where everything at depth disappears and is rendered moot. Man is cut adrift from any stable mooring, any durable and enduring values, and becomes a will o the wisp plaything at the mercy of a maelstrom of chaotic cosmic forces under the guise of necessity. "Nihil vere, nihil sancti", to quote Hannibal, all is relative, and all we can do is to play out our odds in the game of life, until ultimately we lose. The ultimate meaning of life thus consists in its meaninglessness, and in the interim we indulge in "role-playing" as professor or politician or parent, "living the role". Yet beneathe this mask (Latin *persona*") is there to be perceived any "substrate" (Greek "ὑπόστασις")? There may indeed exist a rationally concocted gnosseology, magically invoked of mental incantations, hanging all suspended up in the air, yet what is needed is a "concrete ontologism", grounded upon being. These above thoughts, of course, mix many disparate threads into a seemingly incongruous whole, of what comprises the Kushite psyche.

Although not specifically addressed as such by Berdyaev or Khomyakov, a significant difference of the Kushite psyche, differentiating it from Khomyakov's Iranian, -- is its idolatrous manner of worship. Idolatry is one of the major historical religious prohibitions within Judaism and Christianity. Idolatry involves the fashioning of some "graven image" (not necessarily physical) and worshipping it instead of the authentic God. The manner of worship is one motivated by a superstitious fear of powerful hostile forces, which must be supplicated and placated by magical means. Even in Christianity there are those who are motivated primarily by a fear of death and hell-fire, seeking to gain their ticket to Heaven amidst the frown of an angry God. The idol substituting for the authentic God need not be the "golden calf" wrought in the boredom of ancient Israel, -- a symbol modernly suggestive of the money-worship in capitalism, but just as likely the apposite worship of a jealous proletariat. The idol, worshipped in place of the authentic god, can take many forms -- the apotheosis of the state in the image of Caesar, the apotheosis of progress and human reason, the apotheosis of a lifestyle, and a narcissic self-centred egoism. It might even assume the form of an apotheosis of the "Church" as a self-perpetuating institution but marginally aligned in name with Christ

(Dostoevsky's "Grand Inquisitor"), as also in Khomyakov's view of Roman Catholicism. Berdyaev quite correctly criticised Khomyakov for his unjust bias against western Catholicism and the culture of the Latin peoples, taking to task the "mystical deaf-ear" of Khomyakov and the Slavophils toward the spiritual dynamics and significance of the Sacraments. And yes, the Slavophils were at fault, the same as with Rome's papal pretensions, as being too "this-worldly" with their "City", contrary as such to the prayed imperative of "Thy Kingdom come" in the "Our Father". Indicative of such a magic minded view is the derivation of our saying in English, -- "hocus-pocus". It is what results with a semi-literate and carelessly muttered mangling of the Latin words of Consecration of the Holy Elements, "Hoc est Corpus Meum". Nor should Protestantism escape censure for idolatrous a mindset with its exclusive reliance on "Sola Scriptura" -- the translation of which at times are flawed, unmoored from the insights of a living Holy Tradition of which it is but part; moreover having lost sight of the centrality within Scripture of Christ's direct words and teachings within the Gospel. Protestantism, especially of the fundamentalist sort, at times produces a spectacle of befuddled sophisticates with an array of "Biblical quotations for every occasion", yet another sort of credulous magical incantation "hocus-pocus". And in Orthodox Christianity, just as with Western Catholicism and Protestantism, the legalistic mindset can reflect idolatrous an approach, revering the "Law of God" in place of and higher than the Lord God. There is novo-Pharisaical delight of knowing and living by all the Church's rules, with attention to God but optional. And hence the jesuitical question: is the Lord God truly and absolutely free "to do whatsoever He doth will", or must God also suffer constraint in necessary accordance to His Law? The Lord God as Author of His Law is the more primal reality. And in a certain sense, the Law of God, the Zakon Bozhii, is but another iconic or symbolic signification of that deeper reality behind it.

Because of its troubled history over the Iconoclast Controversy, the Orthodox Church has taken great pains to clarify proper an understanding of the veneration of holy images, which of course in "hocus-pocus" a fashion can degenerate into another sort of superstitious idolatry among the simple-minded or poorly taught. The "*ikon-obraz*" is typically a visual "*image*" symbolic of some actual greater reality, and serves psychologically as a mnemonic stimulus of attentiveness to that veiled reality. The "icon" religiously represents a "window or aperture through to the spiritual world", in which there exists a real presence of that which is "imaged". In philosophic a context, in our externalistic world of phenomena, of which we are so vividly conscious of the unknowable "not-me" aspect of that which is apart from me on the phenomenological plane, the concrete intuitive dynamic in engaging the symbolic image involves a penetrating through to the deeper noumenal reality, the subterranean spiritual substrate. The emphasis upon "spirit" as one of the essential motifs in the philosophy of Berdyaev witnesses to a perception of the concept of the "icon" as "symbol". In simple and even mundane a sense, consider (in pre-Internet days) taking up a treasured photo of some awhile distant "beloved", or of a dear departed pious grandmother, and in a gesture of tearful love we bestow a kiss to the image. The tears of love are for the "imaged", the bonds of love for whom not even death can ultimately sever, -- as we intone from our heart (for the reposed) "Memory eternal", -- with conviction. Only a blockhead of a positivist would declare that this is nothing more than narcissic auto-suggestion. For us, however, their image evokes for us their presence, howsoever dimly. The same dynamic transpires also with religious icons, some of which more directly manifest the living presence, and hence become "wonder-working" icons. And in profound a sense, the symbolic realism of the icon is not limited to the visual, but also the other sense as well. Thus, in the Orthodox Liturgy at its best, all five human senses come into play: the transporting visual splendour and the auditory beauty of churchly song, the fragrance of the clouds of incense, the "taste ye and see" in the communing of the Sacred Elements, and the tactile sense of finding oneself "elbow to elbow" with fellow believers. All which helps to concentrate our attention to the prayerful task at hand. Pews represent a Western innovation and are optional, -- without them can be packed together "more believers per square inch"...

The most cogent, the strongest argument in support of the symbolic nature underlying religious veneration of holy icons, begins at the very beginning, in the Biblical Book of Genesis with the Creation account regarding humankind. In Gen. 1: 26 the Lord God bespeaks His intent: "Let Us make mankind in our own *image* and *likeness*". And therefore, in Gen. 1: 27 "God created mankind in His image... male and female He created them". First, we might note that although God creates with the ultimate intent that "mankind should be in the image and likeness of God", God however creates man only in the "image of God" (imagio dei), and absent at this point is the "God-likeness". This already would seem prophetically to hint at the fore-ordained Soteriology of Christ the Son of God. One might suggest that God held back on this aspect of "God-likeness", in assigning to us the religious vocation and task to bring ourself into conformity to "God-likeness", in evidence of our filial love for God through Christ. And secondly, that the creation of man involves also the creation of woman, that the path in striving towards this "God-likeness" and salvation for a man can obtain through the guiding gentle hand and love by true a woman, a motif we earlier suggested to be found in both Russian and world literature. Of course, the demonically opposite is also possible. In our sermons, with a bit of levity we used to jest about how the Lord God, in creating woman by taking a rib out of Adam as he slept, resulted in God's having given Adam a "good ribbing" [Engl. idiom] forever since, and in God's happy laugh at us fellas, leaving us eternally befuddled by women. Which, truth be told, is true. But the important point here is this, that the human person, created in the "image of God", is the foremost example of a virtual icon, worthy of veneration. Living as we do on the peripheral plane of life, it is difficult to perceive and actually do. It is only great saints, gifted with the spiritual charism of "perspicacity" (prozorlivost'") that see clearly in this regard.

There is truth to the Gospel adage, that a tree is known of its fruits, good or bad. And this applies also to what Khomyakov terms as Kushite religions and Kushite influences within Christianity. The mute stones speak, only with difficulty. And Khomyakov's classification represents an over-simplification, where nothing is ever totally black or white. As Berdyaev points out, Khomyakov was unaware of the research insights of Erwin Rhode and others into the gradual consciousness of the immortality of the soul in the mystery religions of antiquity, which can be seen as God's providential preparing pagan a soil for the acceptance of Christianity. But Khomyakov's critical point remains valid, even in context of Christianity with elements degenerating into superstitious magicism, and which is to be found there also in Orthodoxy, which Khomyakov is loathe to criticise, as already a "dangerous man" quite wary of censorship. As regards our recently referenced human person created in the "image of God", the Kushite effect further obscures and darkens this imagio dei within man, in effect deadens and ossifies it into something stone-like, something corpse-like. In the various Neo-Platonic systems, and the ancient Gnostic systems of salvation (for a price), and in pantheism, in Buddhism, in various systems of philosophic idealism, as well as in materialism -- there lies concealed a latent psychological "death-wish", a veiled suicidal proclivity. Emanation in the Neo-Platonist systems of Origen and Plotinos, pantheism and Buddhism with the sought for absorption of the individual into the universality of the all, or the nothingness of Nirvana -- are all inherently expressive of this. And as Berdyaev likewise notes, this is also a trait in German mysticism and in German philosophy. And so also the many depersonalising mass movements and ideologies of our time. Spiritually, this is a denial of God by way of a denial of man, a denial of the eternal validity of the unrepeatably unique human person. Even Khomyakov's "organicity" suffers from this weakness, as does also Vl. Solov'ev's "All-Unity". The concrete human person becomes submerged and dissolves away into the cosmic darkness. Khomyakov attempts to supply a corrective via his concept of a "concrete idealism of an integral wholeness", and Vl. Solov'ev does likewise through his "Lectures on Godmanhood". But it is difficult to discern clearly the operative Chalcedon "hypostatic union" dynamics within this tome, which in much is more suggestive of German philosophy. The Genesis account of man created in the "image of God" serves as solid a foundation to any otherwise vapid assertion of "inalienable rights". Chalcedon likewise serves as solid a foundation for the concept of God-manhood, that since within Christ the awesome power and might of the Divine nature does not annihilate and absorb nor become commingled with Christ's also Human nature, but instead respects and preserves its inviolability, so also with the inviolability of the human person in the face of whatever the collective totalitarian totality. On profound a religious level, violence against the human person, and likewise the latent suicidal impulse of self-annihilation, can be viewed as an act of blasphemy against God imaged within the human person. Conversely, the autonomy of the human person is limited in turn by the autonomy of other human persons. Sin against our neighbour is sinful precisely because it is an outrage committed against God as imaged in our fellow man. This is all so very obvious, and yet all so conveniently overlooked. It is interesting to note, moreover, that Khomyakov includes the serpent fetish amongst the "death cult" of Kushite proclivities, thus anticipating Freud with the serpent phthalic symbol.

      The fluidity and plasticity possible with freedom ceases to exist when being has become congealed, ossified, frozen into place, petrified into stone. Stone is external to us, cold to the touch, as is likewise a corpse. In contrast to this Kushite superstitious sort of worship of some lifeless cold object, some idol, some golden calf in whatever the form, Khomyakov discerns a different religious psyche, than that of a death cult. In this regard, we might note the great significance of somewhat later a figure in Russian thought -- N. F. Fedorov, who while over-emphasising the physical avenue, sought for a creatively active cooperation with God in working towards the Universal Resurrection, via a conscious and concerted effort towards the "resuscitation" of our forefathers. Khomyakov's alternate to the Kushite, with the Iranian, perhaps derives from the Zoroastrian fascination with fire, its formless dynamism, akin to the verbal plasticity of form within the human person. Moreover, typically at graves we find burning "eternal flames" and lighted candles, the warmth of the flickering formless fire a symbol of faith against the coldness of death. In embryonic and symbolic a form within Neo-Platonism is expressed the significance of the Logos/Verbum/Word. The opening words of St. John's Gospel express a Neo-Platonist creation account: "In the Beginning was the Word (Logos/Verbum), and the Word was with God and was God". This verbal ability was the beginning of the inward self-consciousness of man, a source of light akin to that of fire. Yet, in a sense, we might suggest that German philosophy especially introduced motifs absent in the philosophy of antiquity, -- specifically that of "will" and voluntarism. Philosophers and theologians over the span of many centuries have penned elaborate treatises about what God is, all which have proven so unconvincing in the long run. Perhaps was this not from addressing the wrong question, by posing the lesser question, -- the "*What*" of God, rather the "*Who*"of God? It is significant, that in the Gospel passage of Mt. 16: 15-16, Christ is asking not "*what*", but rather "And *Whom* say ye that I am?", -- with St. Peter then famously answering, -- "Thou art the Christ, the Son of the *Living* God". And further, Christ teaches: "God is not the God of the dead, but of the living" (Mt. 22: 32). This is an important aspect within a personalist and existentialist religious philosophy, and it represents in part perhaps the gist of Khomyakov's Iranian intuition.

There is the greatest of ironies regarding Khomyakov and Ecumenism, the modern Ecumenical Movement. Both Khomyakov and Vl. Solov'ev are considered progenitors among the Orthodox on the push for ecumenical an awareness, which took on greater an urgency in the direct contact with the West by the Russian diaspora in the 1920's and thereafter. Yet Khomyakov was sharply polemical in his religious writings, and viewed only the Orthodox Church as real. And Vl. Solov'ev likewise is said to have regretted his hasty attempt to bridge the re-union of churches. Yet Khomyakov's short pamphlet, "The Church is One", has served as a symbolic rallying cry for the Ecumenical Movement. Contrary to how it might appear to the casual observer, the Orthodox Church is not monolithic in its views and opinions, just as similarly neither Roman Catholicism nor Protestantism are monolithic. In each there exists a broad spectrum from left to right on virtually everything. In Orthodoxy, there are those who are avidly pro-ecumenical, ranging to the opposite extreme of a religiously xenophobic anti-ecumenism, while the broad middle portion remain disengaged, viewing the ecumenical stuff as keeping certain folk from getting into otherwise greater mischief. There are serious ecumenical contacts that go unnoticed. But in the Ecumenical Movement generally there is much foppishness, a frivolous shallowness, a feckless jesuitical insincerity. Among the Orthodox over the years we have seen a periodic swooning over this or that impending Great Council to be convened, prelude to an Eighth OEcumenical Council after a thousand year hiatus, which will put everything right towards re-uniting the churches. However, any authentic and true re-union of churches can transpire *only if* the Lord God so wills it to occur, and *only if* it be done through the workings of the Holy Spirit. Absent this, politically effected attempts at re-union have always had the devil to pay.

But for those of us who are Orthodox, some thorny considerations. Given that the Church *is* and can authentically *only* be "One", -- then what of those numerous non-Orthodox who term themself "Christian"? Are they "Christian", and if not, then what? A facile answer might be that they are "heterodox Christians", deficient in the fullness of the faith, thus already admitting that they are "Christian", contrary to the accepted Oneness of the Church of Christ. On very profound a level, to assume and take upon oneself and bear the name of "Christian" is to bear the verymost august and tremulous of responsibilities, frightful to answer for afront the Dread Judgement Seat of God. Not something to be assumed or be taken lightly. In Utrenie/Matins, when served separately, there is the small ektenie-litany, where we pray "for all the brethren and all Christians" (за вся христианы). And please note, that "*for*" is far different a matter than "*with*" all Christians, a completely separate issue. In this "for all Christians", are we praying for those non-Orthodox who call themself "Christian"? A formulaic dynamic for the Oneness of the Church can be seen in the Gospel passage from Jn. 17: 21 -- "That all might be one, as Thou Father art in Me, and I in Thee, that they thus may be One in Us...". What is this indicating? Between the Father and the Son there is the unity of oneness, and yet there is the uniqueness of each Person, Father and Son, -- which reflects an antinomic mystery. To deny the actual uniqueness between the Divine Persons would be the heretical outlook of Modalism, Sabellianism. This antinomic "uniqueness in oneness" in the gospel passage addresses also the "they all" of the seemingly dis-united state of Christendom. Perhaps the current state of affairs is in accord with the will of God to forestall even greater evils, such as might be evoked in the papal pretensions of Dostoevsky's "Grand Inquisitor" or even the Protestant trends of rationalising away of the actual existence of Christ. With a chill we remember presentiments of the Anti-Christ in Vl. Solov'ev's famous tale. And yet Christ speaks of "other sheep, not of this fold" -- which would seem to assert the validity of non-Orthodox as "Christians", and the imperative that they "must hear My Voice, so that there be one fold, and one Shepherd" (Jn. 10: 16). All which signifies attentiveness foremost to the Voice of Christ. Ecumenism is not a matter of simply being nice to each other. It involves, or it should, spiritual sobriety and seriousness.

Which brings us to the final matter -- Sobornost". Is Sobornost' validly an aspect of the Church, or is it merely a rosy theory dreamt up by idle Russian laymen too satiated upon the German philosophy of the time? There is a churchly element that would subscribe to this latter view, and be content to discard and be rid of the Slavophil concept of Sobornost', along with Vl. Solov'ev and the rest of the Russian religio-philosophic movement, as not "authentically Orthodox". We sometimes wonder, whether Christ Himself was "sufficiently Orthodox" enough for them... We provided an example of the tacit blessing of the concept of Sobornost' by the pre-revolutionary Russian Church, with our addendum of Berdyaev's 1915 article, "Slavophilism and the Ruling Powers". This 1915 event was sabotaged by Rasputin. Rasputinism, the manipulation and lust for wielding power, is a sickness within portions of the churchly organism to be found at all times and in all churches, not only the Orthodox. Extremely troubling, while writing these comments, was Berdyaev's valid criticism of the Slavophils, that they projected an ideal of Orthodoxy, while failing to address its ills, which they did tenaciously with other churches. As Orthodox, we face the same dilemma of conscience. The Slavophils were men without any sort of power, either in the Church or the Russian state. Thus in a sense, their silence to openly address these obvious ills represented a more powerful denunciation, than if they had made some heroic gesture at the wrong time and in the wrong place, as had the Decembrists. At the core of this matter is the example of Christ's silence before Caiaphas (Mt. 26: 62-63, 65), where Christ's silence and refusal of acknowledgement is more cutting and damning than any vehement words of denunciation. The Slavophils refused to defile themself by stooping to the level of those responsible for rot in the Church. Berdyaev learned this the hard way in 1913. There is a motif of "passive resistance" threading its way in Christ's Sermon on the Mount. There are times to openly speak, and there are to judiciously remain silent, and the discerning of such times is a matter of wrestling with one's own conscience. There is a Rasputinite aspect to Dostoevsky's "Grand Inquisitor", who has *improved* matters in Christ's long absence, and there is also Dostoevsky's Shigalev... But there is a famous saying by the Russian great national Saint, Pr. Aleksandr Nevsky -- "*Not in power is God, but in truth!*" ("Не в силе Бог, а в правде"). And Christ Himself cautions us: "*Judge not by appearances*, judge rather righteous a judgement" (Jn. 7: 24).

    What is Sobornost'? Where in Khomyakov's fragmented theological writings does the concept initially arise? The sad irony with Berdyaev's book on Khomyakov, our present text, fails to reveal it, this initial intuition. At one point (p. 140), Berdyaev tells us that Sobornost' cannot be grounded upon the transient and already vanished societal aspects inherent in the peasant obschina of Khomyakov's time. But then upon what grounding? Neither our texts extensive Khomyakov quotes, nor Berdyaev, provides an answer. Nor are we competent at depth to delve into the further permutations by Vl. Solov'ev and Pr. S. Trubetskoy on this subject. The occasion that gave rise to the concept of Sobornost' for Khomyakov may have been his defense of the 1848 Missive of the Eastern Patriarchs, issued in response against papal pretensions. The issue involves one's definition and meaning of the "catholicity" of the Church. For Rome, catholicity implies "universality", Rome's claim to universal dominion over the Church. The Orthodox Church perceives catholicity differently, based on its legacy of the Seven OEcumenical Councils and historically centred "local" (mestnoe) churches, autocephalous patriarchates. For the Orthodox East, the pre-schism Roman Church is viewed merely as the "*primus inter pares*", "*the first merely in dignity among equals*" -- a Latin formulaic title assumed by the "foremost in dignity citizen" Caesar Augustus. For Khomyakov, the true catholicity of the Church is manifest in an authentic universality, which preserves rather than abolishes the integrity of its "equal" component members. And it is an universality everywhere locally situated, of equal members freely gathered together by mutual love, rather than by external force. Yet even if this were the occasion, it still does not serve as justification, a solid basis. We hence must attempt to do so.

We would suggest that the archetype of Sobornost', most profoundly, consists in the dynamics of the MostHoly Trinity. This indeed is an example of catholicity as an "unity within diversity". Three Divine Persons Who are and Who remain One God -- is an ineffable mystery. Each Divine Person is most authentically whatever comprises "person" in its most mysterious depths. Each Divine Person in the Holy Trinity is uniquely and unrepeatably so, not some mere function or aspect of the "Godness", which would be a semi-Modalist heretical view. We are given to know the Father in knowing the Son (Jn. 14: 9), but we no more know the "Person" in its fullness than we know the (noumenal) fullness of person in our fellow man, -- only what is manifest and revealed to us. The Three Divine Persons of the Holy Trinity abide in eternal an accord, an eternal harmony. What binds Them together in this accord and harmony? Certainly not some natural force of necessity akin to magnetism, which would imply that the omnipotent God is not free, is not omnipotent. Hence God is free. God is love, and it is this love at its most authentic that unifies together the Divine Persons of the Holy Trinity. In personalist a perspective, love at its most real is "freely given, freely received", wherein the "I" as person is rendered into a "we" as persons, each unique, yet freely not forcibly through love gathered into community, into a communality. True community involves the freedom of "we" as subjects, rather than "us" as objects. Eternity differs from our fallen state in time, of course. Eternity is often thought of as timelessness, and ancient Greek thought perceived perfection as the stasis embodied in the idol form of a statue, not subject to death and decay like a living man. Although a statue may reflect stasis, indeed even as a "symbolic image", it however is not alive. The eternal God, moreover, is not some idolatrous statue or object, but rather, the "Living God" (Mt. 16: 16). The MostHoly Trinity is termed by the Orthodox as "zhivotvoraschii" ("life-creating" or "life-originating"). There is a dynamism of life within the Holy Trinity, just as there is a dynamism of life within love, if it be not a dead love. Indeed. One might argue that in the Genesis Creation account, when the Lord God says, "Let Us make man in Our Own image", that the "Us" spoken herein is not merely use of the pseudo-plural majestic "We" as typically interpreted, rather that it involves a dynamic mystical interaction of the Triune Divine Persons.

But apart from such theoretical considerations, which serve by way of justification of the concept of Sobornost', there remains another source more readily apparent for a direct experiencing of Sobornost', with consequent the consciousness of such, providing an inspiration to the concept. This direct conscious experiencing of Sobornost' occurs within the Orthodox Divine Liturgy, for such of those who are actively and prayerfully participating in it. The Liturgy is not something monotonously static in tone throughout, when properly served. Rather, it builds in intensity with a series of steps, plateaus, until it reaches its heightened climax at the Epiklesis, followed by the anti-climax with the Communion by the people, a mystical moment and manifestation of the realisation, -- "God is with us!" (Съ нами Богъ!). In a sense, it is an apocalyptic moment, when eternity erupts forth and time collapses. At a point in the Holy Liturgy, when Christ's words of the Consecration have already been spoken over the Holy Gifts, there occurs the Epiklesis, invoking the Descent (*Nizhkhozhdenie*) of the Holy Spirit, transforming the consecrated bread and wine into the "real presence" Body and Blood of Christ, which is followed by the thrice uttered "Amen" on behalf of the people. That the laypeople present do not now generally utter their direct "Amen" reflects apparently a process over long centuries tied in with the evolution of the iconostasis from something initially quite simple into something far more substantial, but initially similar in effect to the altar railing that formerly existed in the Roman Catholic Church.

In the Roman Church, apparently, a priest is able to consecrate the holy gifts by himself, alone. Not so in the Orthodox Church, where the people, the laypeople, are never "optional". This is in witness to the Christ-invoking command by Our Lord: "Where two or three be gathered in My Name, there I am in the midst of them" (Mt. 18: 20). Further indicative of this is that our word, "liturgy", derives from the Greek word "leit-ourgos", meaning literally "work of the people". Hence, the people ought not to be "optional". The psychological pretensions of clericalism have historically long been a problem in both the West and the East. There arose the idiom of "the religious", in contrast to the laypeople, as in effect being lesser a sort of "Christian". The Roman Church in the 1960's and the 1970's saw an exodus of their best and brightest from among "the religious", to better witness to Christ in the "world". Among them was my now reposed wife. In Russia, the Orthodox Church with its married priests (the "white clergy", in contrast to the "black clergy" monks and bishops) over long centuries evolved into a semi-hereditary class between that of the peasants and that of the nobility. Large clergy families living in conditions of crushing poverty had their share of dysfunction and trauma, while held to an higher standard of smiling away problems, helping to render seminaries into hotbeds of revolutionary atheism in tsarist Russia. And although not Orthodox, we might also consider our notorious fellow Nietzsche, who grew up in a clergy family, the son of a Lutheran minister -- has anyone delved into this in interpreting Nietzsche's thought? Berdyaev in our current text makes passing mention of the pressing problem of the needed restoration of the parish, enigmatically, but he does not elaborate further.

  At its best, the basic unit in the catholicity or sobornost' of the Church, in a communality of "I's' becoming existentially a "we", -- is the family. Too often, and tragically, this is not the case. At its best, the parish can be experienced like the extended family of old, and the parish is the most local (mestnoe) liturgical manifestation of the universal Catholicity, Sobornost', of the Church. Mindful of the "primus inter pares" Orthodox formulation that we have already mentioned, the priest is not separate but indeed part of his people, at the altar the "first among equals" eldest brother who has been gifted with the spiritual charism of sacramental Ordination. A true priest is conscious of his people as brethren, as kindred in Christ. For parishioners to regard the priest as merely an hired-hand -- is a Protestant aberration too common in our Western mindset. And conversely, for a priest to view his current parish as but a stepping-stone to another, a more lucrative "living" (an old British idiom), shews him to be a mercenary at heart, the proverbial "Judas-priest". Contrary to the current Roman practice, and indicative symbolically of the sobornost' communality of the Orthodox priest with his people, is this quaint fact. In liturgical prayer the priest faces together in common with the people in the same sacred direction, in front of the prestol' (altar table); the sacred direction is that of the East, from whence is the rising of the sun, symbolic of the Rising of Christ the Son of God in His Paschal Resurrection. The priest turns and faces the people when blessing the people, and in the presenting of spiritual illumination with the Holy Gospel and sermon. At times, when turning and blessing the people with one's gaze briefly sweeping across faces attentively and intensely at prayer, one is both humbled and struck with awe, not knowing whether one is beholding angelic or human visages. There are such moments. The priest sets the liturgical tempo -- as monotonously wooden, mere muttered words, or as something intense, as though our life depended upon it. Which of course, it does. All this must sound like radically revolutionary a conservatism, which of course it is. But it is implicit from the religious perspective of the Slavophils.

Orthodox in the typical Liturgy confess the Nicene-Constantinople Creed from the year 381, in its original form, without the later Western inclusion of the "filioque" clause. It is the same Creed used also, but with this "filioque" added, by Roman Catholicism and some of the Protestant faith-confessions. Our word "Creed" derives from the Latin word "credo", meaning "I believe". Idiomatically, the Creed has also become known as the "Symbol of Faith"; curious, is it not, the choice of word as "*symbol*". In the Creed, the relevant phrase regarding the Church is this: "I believe... in one, holy, catholic and apostolic church". It is sad to note that most commentators typically fail to address how each of these four characteristics is mutually interdependent, each upon the other. The Church per se cannot be truly catholic (as earthly a phenomenon) if it fails to be truly one and holy and apostolic (as eternal a reality, no such defects can be attributed to the Church). When the Creed was translated from the Greek into the Church Slavonic language, the word crafted to render the (adjective) "catholic/καθολικὴν" became "sobornnyiu/соборную" -- which in noun form becomes our "sobornost'", "catholicity". What subtle nuance of inspired insight provided us the present word "sobornyi", rather than some other word? That is a matter for philological research to answer. Although, we would humbly suggest that the Holy Spirit was involved. We likewise detect a religiously grounded nuance similarly in the rendering of the Greek word "ὀρθοδοξία/orthodoxia" into the Slavic "православие/pravoslavie", meaning literally "rightful doxology" ("doxa" in NT times meant "praise/glory"). In pre-Christian antiquity, the Greek word "doxa" signified "belief/doctrine". Hence, in Russian there results two different words: "Pravoslavie" signifies the Christian religious "Orthodoxy", in contrast to the word "ортодокс/ortodoks" signifying "correct beliefs", usually with the pejorative negative connotation of zealotry ("правоверие/pravoverie" would be the word for "correct belief"). Neophyte Orthodox here in English speaking America typically are confused on this, and think that their Orthodox Church is all about having the "right beliefs", in contrast to all the "heretics" out there...

Nicholas Berdyaev

On p. 140 of our text, Berdyaev contrasts the almost similarly spelled words, "*sbornyi*" and "*sobornyi*", as regards the Church. *Sbornost'* is characteristic of our bourgeois nominally democratic political system of "majority vote" against a fractious backdrop of vengeful schemings by the "minority" of the moment. Parliamentism, and the "Rule of Laws" in all their profuse abundance, is readily subject to change in tomorrow's "majority vote". In such a nominalistic schema, on a typical Sunday morning "majority-vote", God would lose by a landslide. The Church however is not a democracy, it is something far different. And this becomes difficult for minds, societally conditioned to think in terms of "majority vote", to grasp. It would be laughable to try to imagine the MostHoly Trinity working by "majority vote", whether or not to dispatch the Holy Spirit on some mission. *Sobornost'* implies rather a coming together or gathering of the people of the Church, amidst the Christ-invoking Presence of the Holy Spirit, -- and hence it is not human only a matter, but rather in evidence of God-manhood, of Divine-human a working. Decisions rendered are rendered in a spirit of accord, not a grudging acquiescence by a minority. This accord, which at superficial a glance at the history of events surrounding the OEcumenical Councils, would seem questionable, proves actual nonetheless in the fullness of witness by the subsequent generations of all the Church, in effect validated by the Holy Spirit. At times, it is a matter of humility to acknowledge that the ways of God are beyond human kenning. Berdyaev in various of his writings mocks the psychology behind the socialist term, "tovarisch, comrade", in contrast to the archaic term, "brother". A "brother" is someone with whom we share a bond of "kinship". A "comrade" is someone with whom for a moment we share a "tactical alliance" on an issue, an utilitarian bond of convenience, and should alliances change, the comrade ceases to be "tovarisch". Political democracy too often seems a craven and hypocritical process of forming such tactical alliances, ultimately devoid of principle, to secure a "majority vote". A "brother", however, does not cease to be in "the image of God", even if he is no longer of immediate benefit to us.

Catholicity as Sobornost' signifies that the Church is not a matter of "me", but "we". The Church is a community of believers, in a spirit of mutual assent and accord, exampled upon that which obtains with the Holy Trinity. It is not some sort of a collective held together by force and blind obedience.[1] The Church is authentic a community in the sense of communality, in which the "we" (not "us" as mere objects) conversely preserves the integrity of each "I" (not "me" as mere object), comprising it. As such, this presupposes *freedom* in the cohesive bond of *love*, authentic freedom and authentic love, not narcissic egoism. Christ teaches: "...And ye shall know the truth, and the truth will set ye free" (Jn. 8: 32). But freedom proper is far different a thing than mere capricious license and arbitrary self-will, the wanton and destructive nihilism of some wild animal. Such an abuse of freedom in the name of freedom is a misnomer. Freedom implies an answerable responsibility inherent within oneself, which is why we are endowed with a conscience. Berdyaev often notes that God moreso desires man's freedom than does man. The displaced autonomy of human freedom results in man's enslavement to various forms of idolatry.

What are the dimensions of the Church in terms of its catholicity, its localised universality? The Church in its community as communality includes not only the physically alive present generation, but also all the generations past, as well as the generations yet to be. Christianity nowadays seems to have lost sight of this, which is needful if the Church be truly catholic and universal in its scope. Spiritually, if the dead be not alive in Christ for us, then we ourself be not truly alive in Christ, and in vain be our belief in His Holy Resurrection. A proper Christian response ought not to be the lacrimae of passive resignation at the grave, and then an oblivion of forgetfulness as we rush about in quest of our "daily bread". In the Orthodox Church our prayer for the dead concludes with the proclamation, "Memory Eternal", which tend to remain but formalised words of prayer, with little or no discussion of the concepts contained in the "eternalisation of memory". In this regard, the thrust of the basic motif of N. F. Fedorov is radically significant, although there was an over-emphasis on the physical means in his "Philosophy of the Common Task". Fedorov's "Common Task" involved, not a passive resignation, but rather an active participation and cooperation working together with God for the raising of the dead, all the generations of the forefathers, in the Universal Resurrection, preached to occur on the Last Day. As such, it is

---

[1] The didactic short vita on St. Akakios of Sinai (29 Nov./12 Dec.) unmasks the lie in religious "blind obedience", as regards those who would demand it.

Nicholas Berdyaev

an apocalyptic perspective, looking for an end to fallen and death-bearing time afront eternity. It is likewise a creatively pro-active view on Godmanhood, on the Church as eternal a Divine-human organism wherein man also has his answerable part to play. This potentially resusciative love is also a mark of the Church's oneness and holiness in Christ, in evidence of its true catholic and apostolic universality. *Death is the ultimate outrage, the ultimate blasphemy against the Living God.*

If any of these too lengthy and meandering thoughts have served anyone well, -- then to God be the glory!

Fr. Stephen Janos

7 April 2017

frsj Publications

1.) **N. A. BERDYAEV** "*The Philosophy of Inequality*"
   1st English Translation of Berdyaev's 1918/1923 book,
   "*Filosofia neravenstva*" (Kl. № 20).
   (ISBN-13: 9780996399203 / ISBN-10: 0996399208)
   406 pages (6/4/15)

2.) **N. A. BERDYAEV** "*The Spiritual Crisis of the Intelligentsia*"
   1st English Translation of Berdyaev's 1910 book,
   "*Dukhovnyi krizis intelligentsii*" (Kl. № 4).
   (ISBN-13: 9780996399210 / ISBN-10: 0996399216)
   346 pages (6/19/15)

3.) **FR. ALEKSANDR MEN'** "*Russian Religious Philosophy: 1989-1990 Lectures*" -- 1st English Translation
   Published in 25th Year Commemoration of Fr Men' Memory
   (ISBN-13: 9780996399227 / ISBN-10: 0996399224)
   214 pages (7/14/15)

4.) **E. SKOBTSOVA (MOTHER MARIA)**
   "*The Crucible of Doubts: Khomyakov, Dostoevsky, Solov'ev, In Search of Synthesis -- Four 1929 Works*".
   (ISBN-13: 9780996399234 / ISBN-10: 0996399232)
   166 pages (5/20/16) 1st English Translation

5.) **N. A. BERDYAEV** "*The Fate of Russia*"
   1st English Translation of Berdyaev's 1918 book,
   "*Sud'ba Rossii*". (Kl. № 15).
   (ISBN-13: 9780996399241 / ISBN-10: 0996399240)
   250 pages (10/1/16)

6.) **N. A. BERDYAEV** "*Aleksei Stepanovich Khomyakov*"
  1st English Translation of Berdyaev's 1912 book,
   "*Алексей Степанович Хомяков*" (Kl. № 6).
   (ISBN-13: 9780996399258 / ISBN-10: 0996399259)
    224 Pages (5/8/17)

*   *   *

Forthcoming Works in Preparation:

N. A. BERDYAEV "*Sub Specie Aeternitatis:*
  Essays Philosophic, Social and Literary (1900-1906)".
   1st English Translation of Berdyaev's 1907 book,
    "*Sub specie aeternitatis. Опыты философские, социальные
     и литературные (1900-1906 гг.)*". (Kl. № 3).

N. A. BERDYAEV "*The Philosophy of Freedom*"
  1st English Translation of Berdyaev's 1911 book,
   "*Filosofiia svobody*" (Kl. № 5).

www.ingramcontent.com/pod-product-compliance
Lightning Source LLC
Chambersburg PA
CBHW070423010526
44118CB00014B/1872